The Underground Railroad

A Selection of Authentic Narratives

Abridged

William Still

ARCTURUS

ARCTURUS

This edition published in 2017 by Arcturus Publishing Limited
26/27 Bickels Yard, 151–153 Bermondsey Street,
London SE1 3HA

ISBN: 978-1-78428-713-9
AD005695US

Printed in the UK

The
Underground
Railroad

Contents

Introduction

William Still's landmark *The Underground Railroad* was first published in 1872. Its emotive accounts of runaway black slaves were the product of the turbulent decade of the 1850s, as the country tumbled towards Civil War and the status of African-Americans, free and enslaved, reached its nadir. That war did not break out earlier was the result of a deal brokered between politicians from North and South that seemed to secure the future of slavery. The so-called Compromise of 1850 consisted of a clutch of new laws that sought to meet the challenges posed by the vast territories acquired by the United States at the end of the Mexican-American War of 1846–8.

At their heart lay the passing of the Fugitive Slave Act of 1850. This law strengthened the original 1793 act which had criminalized those assisting runaway slaves but had been weakly enforced. The deal benefitted the South, enraged Northerners, and undermined the security of the thousands of African-Americans living in non-slave states. The new law increased the punishment for those involved. Penalties were to be strictly enforced by federal officers across the Union committed to the recapture of fugitive slaves, even those who had been living in freedom for decades.

Unsurprisingly, the law also endangered the lives of freeborn African-Americans who, with little or no legal protection, became potential victims of ruthless Southern slave catchers supported by the might of the federal government. Reaction to the law, passed in September 1850, was immediate as anti-slavery societies across the Northern states asserted their opposition. In Philadelphia, few were more active than William Still.

Still was born in New Jersey in 1821, the son of a free black father and a fugitive slave mother who, in her escape from her owner in Maryland, had been forced to abandon two of her four children. The rescue of William's brother Peter from slavery by white abolitionist Seth Conklin more than forty years later forms the centerpiece of *The Underground Railroad*'s first gripping narrative. In 1844, Still left the family farm and moved to Philadelphia where he taught himself to read and write. By 1847, he was clerk of the city's Anti-Slavery Society, and in 1851, such were his talents that he was appointed Chairman of the society's most politicized branch, the Philadelphia Vigilance Committee. It aimed to oppose and subvert the new Fugitive Slave Law by aiding runaways in transit along the Underground Railroad to safe locations in the far North and Canada.

The rail road was, in fact, no rail road at all in the literal sense. However, whilst some historians of the mid-twentieth century argued that the term had no relevance beyond the realm of legend, it is now accepted that the concept of a rail road was very real for those involved. For William Still and others, the term "rail road" described a complex series of networks scattered across the states, North and South. This was no cohesive unified system. Instead, they operated at a local level and were linked by groups and individual agents. Together, they provided interconnected routes along which fugitives were transported via a series of safe houses to freedom. Common rail road terminology of the time was used to describe the various elements. Financial supporters were "stockholders," those who transported escapees were "conductors," the escapees themselves were "passengers," and they travelled from "station" to "station." These are all terms that resonate throughout Still's narratives. The term "underground railroad" emerged in the 1830s, though its exact origin is unclear. However, it undoubtedly reflected the transport revolution taking place across America. As rail road construction boomed, resulting in almost 30,000 miles of track by 1860, the country promoted the technological realization of its "Manifest Destiny" to span the continent. In response, African-Americans trumpeted their own aspirations for the future in the form of a railroad that led them to freedom.

Still's remit was broad. Philadelphia lay at the center of networks that extended along the east coast as far south as Georgia and as far north as Massachusetts. Throughout the 1850s, the Vigilance Committee supported the needs of hundreds of fugitives, providing medical and financial support, and assistance in securing the freedom of family members left behind. It also functioned as a communications hub for the broader African-American community, within and without the borders of the United States. Those who passed through Philadelphia were interviewed and it was Still who recorded their testimonies. Many remained in contact with him once they had reached freedom, soliciting his support and expressing their thanks.

The greatest irony, however, was that freedom for most was not to be found in the "land of liberty" itself. Some settled in the western part of New York State, but as Still's testimonies make clear, the majority opted for the neighboring province of Canada West, today's Ontario. As early as 1793, the Act Against Slavery had been passed in what was then Upper Canada, prohibiting the further importation of slaves and freeing the children of female slaves born after the passage of the act at the age of 25. In 1834, slavery was banned across the British Empire. The black population of the British colonies continued to battle prejudice and carry out most of the menial tasks, but they could run their own businesses, they had the right to vote, and, as British subjects, they received legal protection equal to whites. Many African-Americans, therefore, were more than happy to abandon the struggle for US citizenship and embrace that the protection being a British subject offered. Indeed, in the black imagination, the British provinces attained a status of mythic proportions. Crossing the Ohio River from slave to free state might have been the equivalent of crossing the Jordan. It was to the north that Canaan beckoned, and, to borrow a term coined by the African-Canadian poet Wayde Compton, the fleeing slave would arrive in an imagined "Xanada" (a combination of "Xanadu" and "Canada.")

It was not only fugitives who found succor in Canada. As early as 1829, free blacks in Cincinnati, Ohio, faced with the passing of restrictive anti-black laws, crossed the Detroit River to found the settlement of Wilberforce, named after the leading British abolitionist. Though the settlement was eventually disbanded, other communities such as Dawn and Elgin followed, ensuring that Canada West remained a Promised Land for them and their fugitive siblings. By 1860, approximately 30,000 African-Americans had fled the United States to find protection under the British flag. The letters that Still received from refugees, whose escape he had assisted, resonate with anguish over the wives, husbands, parents, and children left behind, but they also bear witness to the new-found sense of security enjoyed in British America.

Hitherto kept secret, Still's records and correspondence were published in 1872. *The Underground Railroad* was a massive work of several hundred pages, yet it immediately sold out. Such was the prestige of this archive of African-American voices that it was displayed at the Philadelphia Centennial Exhibition in 1876. Two other editions followed, in 1878 and 1883, both of which were avidly consumed by a fascinated public. What follows is a new abridged version of the 1878 edition, highlighting the most dramatic and poignant of the fugitive testimonies. Escape in a wooden crate, pursuit by bloodhounds, women disguised as men and vice versa, the terror of recapture: all are to be found in the accounts which Still entrusted to his diaries over more than a decade. The 1872 Preface was written during the high-tide of optimism that followed the passage of the Thirteenth Amendment abolishing slavery in the United States, and the Radical Reconstruction taking place in the defeated South with its promise of a bright future for the nation's newly enfranchised African-American citizens. Still made it clear that publication had been undertaken at the request of the Pennsylvania Anti-Slavery Society, which asked him to, "compile and publish his reminiscences and experiences relating to the 'Underground Rail Road.'" For him personally, the work freed the voices of those hitherto silent, raising the possibility of reunion for loved ones separated, whether by the auction block or the enforced flight to freedom, both echoing his own painful family experience. He also sought to commemorate a hard fought battle, "to show what efforts were made and what success was gained for Freedom under difficulties."

The tone of the Preface to this edition, however, is very different. By 1878, Reconstruction was on the wane leading to the emergence of a segregated society and the adoption of Jim Crow laws across the South, ghettoizing African-Americans, cheating them of the vote, relegating them to the status of second-class citizens. When Still reminds us that the antebellum South was "the prison-house," he seems to be drawing his readers' attention to both dangers overcome and those that lay ahead. Now, his aim was to reinvigorate the spirits of his fellow freedmen: "I have always cherished that this work would encourage the race in efforts for self-elevation." His testimonies have become reminders of a bitter past and aspirations only partially realized. His voices spoke of "the struggles of men and women to obtain their freedom, education and property," and for him, the future no longer seemed certain: "In the political struggles, the hopes of the race have been sadly disappointed. From this direction no great advantage is likely to arise very soon."

Throughout his life, Still continued to participate in Philadelphia's African-American community. He founded the city's first black YMCA, served as President of the Board of Managers of The Home for Aged and Infirm Colored Persons, and was known for his unstinting charitable donations. But it was for his work on the great rail road that he was remembered. Upon his death in 1902, the *New York Times* obituary of July 15th noted that Still "was known throughout the country as the 'Father of the Underground Railroad.'" This was a tribute not only to the key role he had played in assisting and supporting fellow African-Americans during their darkest hours and placing himself in great danger, but also testimony to the archival monument that he left to posterity in the form of *The Underground Railroad*.

GARETH HALLETT DAVIS
University College London
January 2017

Preface to the Revised Edition

Like millions of my race, my mother and father were born slaves, but were not contented to live and die so. My father purchased himself in early manhood by hard toil. Mother saw no way for herself and children to escape the horrors of bondage but by flight. Bravely, with her four little ones, with firm faith in God and an ardent desire to be free, she forsook the prison house, and succeeded, through the aid of my father, to reach a free State. Here life had to be begun anew. The old familiar slave names had to be changed, and others, for prudential reasons, had to be found. This was not hard work. However, hardly months had passed ere the keen scent of the slave-hunters had trailed them to where they had fancied themselves secure. In those days all power was in the hands of the oppressor, and the capture of a slave mother and her children was attended with no great difficulty other than the crushing of freedom in the breast of the victims. Without judge or jury, all were hurried back to wear the yoke again. But back this mother was resolved never to stay. She only wanted another opportunity to again strike for freedom. In a few months after being carried back, with only two of her little ones, she took her heart in her hand and her babes in her arms, and this trial was a success. Freedom was gained, although not without the sad loss of her two older children, whom she had to leave behind. Mother and father were again reunited in freedom, while two of their little boys were in slavery. What to do for them other than weep and pray, were questions unanswerable. For over forty years the mother's heart never knew what it was to be free from anxiety about her lost boys. But no tidings came in answer to her many prayers, until one of them, to the great astonishment of his relatives, turned up in Philadelphia, nearly fifty years of age, seeking his long-lost parents. Being directed to the Anti-Slavery Office for instructions as to the best plan to adopt to find out the where-abouts of his parents, fortunately he fell into the hands of his own brother, the writer, whom he had never heard of before, much less seen or known. And here began revelations connected with this marvellous coincidence, which influenced me, for years previous to Emancipation, to preserve the matter found in the pages of this humble volume.

And in looking back now over these strange and eventful Providences, in the light of the wonderful changes wrought by Emancipation, I am more and more constrained to believe that the reasons, which years ago led me to aid the bondman and preserve the records of his sufferings, are to-day quite as potent in convincing me that the necessity of the times requires this testimony.

And since the first advent of my book, wherever reviewed or read by leading friends of freedom, the press, or the race more deeply represented by it, the expressions of approval and encouragement have been hearty and unanimous, and the thousands of volumes which have been sold by me, on the subscription plan, with hardly any facilities for the work, makes it obvious that it would, in the hands of a competent publisher, have a wide circulation.

And here I may frankly state, that but for the hope I have always cherished that this work would encourage the race in

efforts for self-elevation, its publication never would have been undertaken by me.

I believe no more strongly at this moment than I have believed ever since the Proclamation of Emancipation was made by Abraham Lincoln, that as a class, in this country, no small exertion will have to be put forth before the blessings of freedom and knowledge can be fairly enjoyed by this people; and until colored men manage by dint of hard acquisition to enter the ranks of skilled industry, very little substantial respect will be shown them, even with the ballot-box and musket in their hands.

Well-conducted shops and stores; lands acquired and good farms managed in a manner to compete with any other; valuable books produced and published on interesting and important subjects – these are some of the fruits which the race are expected to exhibit from their newly gained privileges.

If it is asked "how?" I answer, "through extraordinary determination and endeavor," such as are demonstrated in hundreds of cases in the pages of this book, in the struggles of men and women to obtain their freedom, education and property.

These facts must never be lost sight of.

The race must not forget the rock from whence they were hewn, nor the pit from whence they were digged.

Like other races, this newly emancipated people will need all the knowledge of their past condition which they can get.

The bondage and deliverance of the children of Israel will never be allowed to sink into oblivion while the world stands.

Those scenes of suffering and martyrdom millions of

Christians were called upon to pass through in the days of the Inquisition are still subjects of study, and have unabated interest for all enlightened minds.

The same is true of the history of this country. The struggles of the pioneer fathers are preserved, produced and re-produced, and cherished with undying interest by all Americans, and the day will not arrive while the Republic exists, when these histories will not be found in every library.

While the grand little army of abolitionists was waging its untiring warfare for freedom, prior to the rebellion, no agency encouraged them like the heroism of fugitives. The pulse of the four millions of slaves and their desire for freedom, were better felt through "The Underground Railroad" than through any other channel.

Frederick Douglass, Henry Bibb, Wm. Wells Brown, Rev. J.W. Logan, and others, gave unmistakable evidence that the race had no more eloquent advocates than its own self-emancipated champions.

Every step they took to rid themselves of their fetters, or to gain education, or in pleading the cause of their fellow-bondmen in the lecture-room, or with their pens, met with applause on every hand, and the very argument needed was thus furnished in large measure. In those dark days previous to emancipation, such testimony was indispensable.

The free colored men are as imperatively required now to furnish the same manly testimony in support of the ability of the race to surmount the remaining obstacles growing out of oppression, ignorance, and poverty.

In the political struggles, the hopes of the race have been

sadly disappointed. From this direction no great advantage is likely to arise very soon.

Only as desert can be proved by the acquisition of knowledge and the exhibition of high moral character, in examples of economy and a disposition to encourage industrial enterprises, conducted by men of their own ranks, will it be possible to make political progress in the face of the present public sentiment.

Here, therefore, in my judgment is the best possible reason for vigorously pushing the circulation of this humble volume – that it may testify for thousands and tens of thousands, as no other work can do.

WILLIAM STILL, Author.
September, 1878. Philadelphia, Pa.

SETH CONCKLIN

In the long list of names who have suffered and died in the cause of freedom, not one, perhaps, could be found whose efforts to redeem a poor family of slaves were more Christlike than Seth Concklin's, whose noble and daring spirit has been so long completely shrouded in mystery. Except John Brown, it is a question, whether his rival could be found with respect to boldness, disinterestedness and willingness to be sacrificed for the deliverance of the oppressed.

By chance one day he came across a copy of the *Pennsylvania Freeman*, containing the story of Peter Still, "the Kidnapped and the Ransomed," – how he had been torn away from his mother, when a little boy six years old; how, for forty years and more, he had been compelled to serve under the yoke, totally destitute as to any knowledge of his parents' whereabouts; how the intense love of liberty and desire to get back to his mother had unceasingly absorbed his mind through all these years of bondage; how, amid the most appalling discouragements, prompted alone by his undying determination to be free and be reunited with those from whom he had been sold away, he contrived to buy himself; how, by extreme economy, from doing over-work, he saved up five hundred dollars, the amount of money required for his ransom, which, with his freedom, he, from necessity, placed unreservedly in the confidential keeping of a Jew, named Joseph Friedman, whom he had known for a long time and could venture to trust, – how he had further toiled to save up money to defray his expenses on an expedition in search of his mother and kindred; how, when this end was accomplished, with an earnest purpose he took his carpet-bag in his hand, and his heart throbbing for

Thursday 5th October 2017

13.30-16.00

Please drop by anytime between 13.30pm to 4pm and our local research team can tell you more

If you would like further information about these sessions please contact:

Research and Development
Trust HQ
Willerby Hill, Beverley Road
Willerby, HU10 6ED

Tel: 01482 301844

Email: HNF-TR.ResearchTeam@nhs.net

Caring, Learning and Growing

'Through research we can make a positive difference and give people a sense of hope.'

his old home and people, he turned his mind very privately towards Philadelphia, where he hoped, by having notices read in the colored churches to the effect that "forty-one or forty-two years before two little boys[1] were kidnapped and carried South" – that the memory of some of the older members might recall the circumstances, and in this way he would be aided in his ardent efforts to become restored to them.

And, furthermore, Seth Concklin had read how, on arriving in Philadelphia, after traveling sixteen hundred miles, that almost the first man whom Peter Still sought advice from was his own unknown brother (whom he had never seen or heard of), who made the discovery that he was the long-lost boy, whose history and fate had been enveloped in sadness so long, and for whom his mother had shed so many tears and offered so many prayers, during the long years of their separation; and, finally, how this self-ransomed and restored captive, notwithstanding his great success, was destined to suffer the keenest pangs of sorrow for his wife and children, whom he had left in Alabama bondage.

Seth Concklin was naturally too singularly sympathetic and humane not to feel now for Peter, and especially for his wife and children left in bonds as bound with them. Hence, as Seth was a man who seemed wholly insensible to fear, and to know no other law of humanity and right, than whenever the claims of the suffering and the wronged appealed to him, to respond unreservedly, whether those thus injured were amongst his

---

1   Sons of Levin and Sidney – the last names of his parents he was too young to remember.

nearest kin or the greatest strangers, – it mattered not to what race or clime they might belong, – he, in the spirit of the good Samaritan, owning all such as his neighbors, volunteered his services, without pay or reward, to go and rescue the wife and three children of Peter Still.

The magnitude of this offer can hardly be appreciated. It was literally laying his life on the altar of freedom for the despised and oppressed whom he had never seen, whose kins-folk even he was not acquainted with. At this juncture even Peter was not prepared to accept this proposal. He wanted to secure the freedom of his wife and children as earnestly as he had ever desired to see his mother, yet he could not, at first, hearken to the idea of having them rescued in the way suggested by Concklin, fearing a failure.

To J.M. McKim and the writer, the bold scheme for the deliverance of Peter's family was alone confided. It was never submitted to the Vigilance Committee, for the reason that it was not considered a matter belonging thereto. On first reflection, the very idea of such an undertaking seemed perfectly appalling. Frankly was he told of the great dangers and difficulties to be encountered through hundreds of miles of slave territory. Seth was told of those who, in attempting to aid slaves to escape, had fallen victims to the relentless Slave Power, and had either lost their lives, or been incarcerated for long years in penitentiaries, where no friendly aid could be afforded them; in short, he was plainly told, that without a very great chance, the undertaking would cost him his life. The occasion of this interview and conversation, the seriousness of Concklin and the utter failure in presenting the various obstacles to his plan, to create the slightest apparent misgiving in his mind, or to produce the slightest sense of fear or hesitancy, can never be effaced from the memory of the writer. The plan was, however, allowed to rest for a time.

In the meanwhile, Peter's mind was continually vacillating between Alabama, with his wife and children, and his new-found relatives in the North. Said a brother, "If you cannot get your family, what will you do? Will you come North and live with your relatives?" "I would as soon go out of the world, as not to go back and do all I can for them," was the prompt reply of Peter.

The problem of buying them was seriously considered, but here obstacles quite formidable lay in the way. Alabama laws utterly denied the right of a slave to buy himself, much less his wife and children. The right of slave masters to free their slaves, either by sale or emancipation, was positively prohibited by law. With these reflections weighing upon his mind, having stayed away from his wife as long as he could content himself to do, he took his carpet-bag in his hand, and turned his face toward Alabama, to embrace his family in the prison house of bondage.

His approach home could only be made stealthily, not daring to breathe to a living soul, save his own family, his nominal Jew master, and one other friend – a slave – where he had been, the prize he had found, or anything in relation to his travels. To his wife and children his return was unspeakably joyous. The situation of his family concerned him with tenfold more weight than ever before,

As the time drew near to make the offer to his wife's master to purchase her with his children, his heart failed him through fear of awakening the ire of slaveholders against him, as he knew that the law and public sentiment were alike deadly opposed to the spirit of freedom in the slave. Indeed, as innocent as a step in this direction might appear, in those days a man would have stood about as good a chance for his life in entering a lair of hungry hyenas, as a slave or free colored man would, in talking about freedom.

He concluded, therefore, to say nothing about buying. The plan proposed by Seth Concklin was told to Vina, his wife; also what he had heard from his brother about the Underground Rail Road, – how, that many who could not get their freedom in any other way, by being aided a little, were daily escaping to Canada. Although the wife and children had never tasted the pleasures of freedom for a single hour in their lives, they hated slavery heartily, and being about to be far separated from husband and father, they were ready to assent to any proposition that looked like deliverance.

So Peter proposed to Vina, that she should give him certain small articles, consisting of a cape, etc., which he would carry with him as memorials, and, in case Concklin or any one else should ever come for her from him, as an unmistakable sign that all was right, he would send back, by whoever was to befriend them, the cape, so that she and the children might not doubt but have faith in the man, when he gave her the sign (cape).

Again Peter returned to Philadelphia, and was now willing to accept the offer of Concklin. Ere long, the opportunity of an interview was had, and Peter gave Seth a very full description of the country and of his family, and made known to him, that he had very carefully gone over with his wife and children the matter of their freedom. This interview interested Concklin most deeply. If his own wife and children had been in bondage, scarcely could he have manifested greater sympathy for them.

For the hazardous work before him he was at once prepared to make a start. True he had two sisters in Philadelphia for whom he had always cherished the warmest affection, but he conferred not with them on this momentous mission. For full well did he know that it was not in human nature for them to acquiesce in this perilous undertaking, though one of these sisters, Mrs. Supplee, was a most faithful abolitionist.

Having once laid his hand to the plough he was not the man to look back, – not even to bid his sisters good-bye, but he actually left them as though he expected to be home to his dinner as usual. What had become of him during those many weeks of his perilous labors in Alabama to rescue this family was to none a greater mystery than to his sisters. On leaving home he simply took two or three small articles in the way of apparel with one hundred dollars to defray his expenses for a time; this sum he considered ample to start with. Of course he had very safely concealed about him Vina's cape and one or two other articles which he was to use for his identification in meeting her and the children on the plantation. His first thought was, on reaching his destination, after becoming acquainted with the family, being familiar with Southern manners, to have them all prepared at a given hour for the starting of the steamboat for Cincinnati, and to join him at the wharf, when he would boldly assume the part of a slaveholder, and the family naturally that of slaves, and in this way he hoped to reach Cincinnati direct, before their owner had fairly discovered their escape.

But alas for Southern irregularity, two or three days' delay after being advertised to start, was no uncommon circumstance with steamers; hence this plan was abandoned. What this heroic man endured from severe struggles and unyielding exertions, in traveling thousands of miles on water and on foot, hungry and fatigued, rowing his living freight for seven days and seven nights in a skiff, is hardly to be paralleled in the annals of the Underground Rail Road.

The following interesting letters penned by the hand of Concklin convey minutely his last struggles and characteristically represent the singleness of heart which impelled him to sacrifice his life for the slave –

EASTPORT, MISS.,
Feb. 3, 1851.

To Wm. Still: – Our friends in Cincinnati have failed finding anybody to assist me on my return. Searching the country opposite Paducah, I find that the whole country fifty miles round is inhabited only by Christian wolves. It is customary, when a strange negro is seen, for any white man to seize the negro and convey such negro through and out of the State of Illinois to Paducah, Ky., and lodge such stranger in Paducah jail, and there claim such reward as may be offered by the master.

There is no regularity by the steamboats on the Tennessee River. I was four days getting to Florence from Paducah. Sometimes they are four days starting, from the time appointed, which alone puts to rest the plan for returning by steamboat. The distance from the mouth of the river to Florence, is from between three hundred and five to three hundred and forty-five miles by the river; by land, two hundred and fifty, or more.

I arrived at the shoe shop on the plantation, one o'clock, Tuesday, 28th. William and two boys were making shoes. I immediately gave the first signal, anxiously waiting thirty minutes for an opportunity to give the second and main signal, during which time I was very sociable. It was rainy and muddy – my pants were rolled up to the knees. I was in the character of a man seeking employment in this country. End of thirty minutes gave the second signal.

William appeared unmoved; soon sent out the boys; instantly sociable; Peter and Levin at the Island; one of the young masters with them; not safe to undertake to see them till Saturday night, when they would be at home; appointed a place to see Vina, in an open field, that night; they to bring me something to eat; our interview only four minutes; I left; appeared by night; dark and cloudy; at ten o'clock appeared William; exchanged signals; led me a few rods to where stood Vina; gave her the signal sent by Peter; our interview ten minutes; she did not call me "master," nor did she say "sir," by which I knew she had confidence in me.

Our situation being dangerous, we decided that I meet Peter and Levin on the bank of the river early dawn of day, Sunday, to establish the laws. During our interview, William prostrated on his knees, and face to the ground; arms sprawling; head cocked back, watching for wolves, by which position a man can see better in the dark. No house to go to safely, traveled round till morning, eating hoe cake which William had given me for supper; next day going around to get employment. I thought of William, who is a Christian preacher, and of the Christian preachers in Pennsylvania. One watching for wolves by night, to rescue Vina and her three children from Christian licentiousness; the other standing erect in open day, seeking the praise of men.

During the four days waiting for the important Sunday morning, I thoroughly surveyed the rocks and shoals of the river from Florence seven miles up, where will be my place of departure. General notice was taken of me as being a stranger, lurking around. Fortunately there are several small grist mills within ten miles around. No taverns here, as in the North; any planter's house entertains travelers occasionally.

One night I stayed at a medical gentleman's, who is not a large planter; another night at an ex-magistrate's house in South Florence – a Virginian by birth – one of the late census takers; told me that many more persons cannot read and write than is reported; one fact, amongst many others, that many persons who do not know the letters of the alphabet, have learned to write their own names; such are generally reported readers and writers.

It being customary for a stranger not to leave the house early in the morning where he has lodged, I was under the necessity of staying out all night Saturday, to be able to meet Peter and Levin, which was accomplished in due time. When we approached, I gave my signal first; immediately they gave theirs. I talked freely. Levin's voice, at first, evidently trembled. No wonder, for my presence universally attracted attention by the lords of the land. Our interview was less than one hour; the laws were written. I to go to Cincinnati to get a rowing boat and provisions; a first class clipper boat to go with speed. To depart from the place where the laws were written, on Saturday night of the first of March. I to meet one of them at the same place Thursday night, previous to the fourth Saturday from the night previous to the Sunday when the laws were written. We to go down the Tennessee river to some place up the Ohio, not yet decided on, in our row boat. Peter and Levin are good oarsmen. So am I. Telegraph station at Tuscumbia, twelve miles from the plantation, also at Paducah. Came from Florence to here Sunday night by steamboat. Eastport is in Mississippi. Waiting here for a steamboat to go down; paying one dollar a day for board. Like other taverns here, the wretchedness is indescribable; no pen, ink, paper or newspaper to be had; only one room for everybody, except the gambling rooms. It is difficult for me to write. Vina intends to get a pass for Catharine and herself for the first Sunday in March.

The bank of the river where I met Peter and Levin is two miles from the plantation. I have avoided saying I am from Philadelphia. Also avoided talking about negroes. I never talked so much about milling before. I consider most of the trouble over, till I arrive in a free State with my crew, the first week in March; then will I have to be wiser than Christian serpents, and more cautious than doves. I do not consider it safe to keep this letter in my possession, yet I dare not put it in the post-office here; there is so little business in these post-offices that notice might be taken.

I am evidently watched; everybody knows me to be a miller. I may write again when I get to Cincinnati, if I should have time. The ex-magistrate, with whom I stayed in South Florence, held three hours' talk with me, exclusive of our morning talk. Is a man of good general information; he was exceedingly inquisitive. "I am from Cincinnati, formerly from the *State of New York*." I had no opportunity to get anything to eat from seven o'clock Tuesday morning till six o'clock Wednesday evening, except the hoe cake, and no sleep.

Florence is the head of navigation for small steamboats. Seven miles, all the way up to my place of departure, is swift water, and rocky. Eight hundred miles to Cincinnati. I found all things here as Peter told me, except the distance of the river. South Florence contains twenty white families, three warehouses of considerable business, a post-office, but no school. McKiernon is here waiting for a steamboat to go to New Orleans, so we are in company.

PRINCETON, GIBSON COUNTY, INDIANA,
Feb. 18, 1851.

To Wm. Still: – The plan is to go to Canada, on the Wabash, opposite Detroit. There are four routes to Canada. One through Illinois, commencing above and below Alton; one through to North Indiana, and the Cincinnati route, being the largest route in the United States.

I intended to have gone through Pennsylvania, but the risk going up the Ohio river has caused me to go to Canada.

Steamboat traveling is universally condemned, though many go in boats, consequently many get lost. Going in a skiff is new, and is approved of in my case. After I arrive at the mouth of the Tennessee river, I will go up the Ohio seventy-five miles, to the mouth of the Wabash, then up the Wabash, forty-four miles to New Harmony, where I shall go ashore by night, and go thirteen miles east, to Charles Grier, a farmer, (colored man), who will entertain us, and next night convey us sixteen miles to David Stormon, near Princeton, who will take the command, and I be released.

David Stormon estimates the expenses from his house to Canada, at forty dollars, without which, no sure protection will be given. They might be instructed concerning the course, and beg their way through without money. If you wish to do what should be done, you will send me fifty dollars, in a letter, to Princeton, Gibson county, Inda., so as to arrive there by the 8th of March. Eight days should be estimated for a letter to arrive from Philadelphia.

The money to be State Bank of Ohio, or State Bank, or Northern Bank of Kentucky, or any other Eastern bank. Send no notes larger than twenty dollars.

Levi Coffin had no money for me. I paid twenty dollars for the skiff. No money to get back to Philadelphia. It was not understood that I would have to be at any expense seeking aid.

One half of my time has been used in trying to find persons to assist, when I may arrive on the Ohio river, in which I have failed, except Stormon.

Having no letter of introduction to Stormon from any source, on which I could fully rely, I traveled two hundred miles around, to find out his stability. I have found many

Abolitionists, nearly all who have made propositions, which themselves would not comply with, and nobody else would. Already I have traveled over three thousand miles. Two thousand and four hundred by steamboat, two hundred by railroad, one hundred by stage, four hundred on foot, forty-eight in a skiff.

I have yet five hundred miles to go to the plantation, to commence operations. I have been two weeks on the decks of steamboats, three nights out, two of which I got perfectly wet. If I had had paper money, as McKim desired, it would have been destroyed. I have not been entertained gratis at any place except Stormon's. I had one hundred and twenty-six dollars when I left Philadelphia, one hundred from you, twenty-six mine.

Telegraphed to station at Evansville, thirty-three miles from Stormon's, and at Vinclure's, twenty-five miles from Stormon's. The Wabash route is considered the safest route. No one has ever been lost from Stormon's to Canada. Some have been lost between Stormon's and the Ohio. The wolves have never suspected Stormon. Your asking aid in money for a case properly belonging east of Ohio, is detested. If you have sent money to Cincinnati, you should recall it. I will have no opportunity to use it.

Seth Concklin, Princeton, Gibson county, Ind.

P.S. First of April, will be about the time Peter's family will arrive opposite Detroit. You should inform yourself how to find them there. I may have no opportunity.

I will look promptly for your letter at Princeton, till the 10th of March, and longer if there should have been any delay by the mails.

In March, as contemplated, Concklin arrived in Indiana, at the place designated, with Peter's wife and three children, and sent a thrilling letter to the writer, portraying in the most vivid light his adventurous flight from the hour they left Alabama until their arrival in Indiana. In this report he stated, that instead of starting early in the morning, owing to some unforeseen delay on the part of the family, they did not reach the designated place till towards day, which greatly exposed them in passing a certain town which he had hoped to avoid.

But as his brave heart was bent on prosecuting his journey without further delay, he concluded to start at all hazards, notwithstanding the dangers he apprehended from passing said town by daylight. For safety he endeavored to hide his freight by having them all lie flat down on the bottom of the skiff; covered them with blankets, concealing them from the effulgent beams of the early morning sun, or rather from the "Christian Wolves" who might perchance espy him from the shore in passing the town.

The wind blew fearfully. Concklin was rowing heroically when loud voices from the shore hailed him, but he was utterly deaf to the sound. Immediately one or two guns were fired in the direction of the skiff, but he heeded not this significant call; consequently here ended this difficulty. He supposed, as the wind was blowing so hard, those on shore who hailed him must have concluded that he did not hear them and that he meant no disrespect in treating them with seeming indifference. Whilst many straits and great dangers had to be passed, this was the greatest before reaching their destination.

But suffice it to say that the glad tidings which this letter contained filled the breast of Peter with unutterable delight and his friends and relations with wonder beyond degree.[2] No fond wife had ever waited with more longing desire for the return of her husband than Peter had for this blessed news. All doubts had disappeared, and a well grounded hope was cherished that within a few short days Peter and his fond wife and children would be reunited in Freedom on the Canada side, and that Concklin and the friends would be rejoicing with joy unspeakable over this great triumph. But alas, before the few days had expired the subjoined brief paragraph of news was discovered in the morning *Ledger*.

RUNAWAY NEGROES CAUGHT. – At Vincennes, Indiana, on Saturday last, a white man and four negroes were arrested. The negroes belong to B. McKiernon, of South Florence, Alabama, and the man who was running them off calls himself John H. Miller. The prisoners were taken charge of by the Marshall of Evansville. – *April 9th*.

How suddenly these sad tidings turned into mourning and gloom the hope and joy of Peter and his relatives no pen could possibly describe; at least the writer will not attempt it here, but will at once introduce a witness who met the noble Concklin and the panting fugitives in Indiana and proffered them sympathy and advice. And it may safely be said from a

---

2 In some unaccountable manner this, the last letter Concklin ever penned, perhaps, has been unfortunately lost.

truer and more devoted friend of the slave they could not have
received counsel.

EVANSVILLE, INDIANA,
March 31st, 1851.

WM. STILL: *Dear Sir*, – On last Tuesday I mailed a letter
to you, written by Seth Concklin. I presume you have received
that letter. It gave an account of his rescue of the family of
your brother. If that is the last news you have had from them,
I have very painful intelligence for you. They passed on from
near Princeton, where I saw them and had a lengthy interview
with them, up north, I think twenty-three miles above
Vincennes, Ind., where they were seized by a party of men,
and lodged in jail. Telegraphic dispatches were sent all
through the South. I have since learned that the Marshall of
Evansville received a dispatch from Tuscumbia, to look out
for them. By some means, he and the master, so says report,
went to Vincennes and claimed the fugitives, chained Mr.
Concklin and hurried all off. Mr. Concklin wrote to Mr. David
Stormon, Princeton, as soon as he was cast into prison, to
find bail. So soon as we got the letter and could get off, two
of us were about setting off to render all possible aid, when
we were told they all had passed, a few hours before, through
Princeton, Mr. Concklin in chains. What kind of process was
had, if any, I know not. I immediately came down to this
place, and learned that they had been put on a boat at 3 P.M.
I did not arrive until 6. Now all hopes of their recovery are
gone. No case ever so enlisted my sympathies. I had seen
Mr. Concklin in Cincinnati. I had given him aid and counsel.

I happened to see them after they landed in Indiana. I heard Peter and Levin tell their tale of suffering, shed tears of sorrow for them all; but now, since they have fallen a prey to the unmerciful blood-hounds of this state, and have again been dragged back to unrelenting bondage, I am entirely unmanned. And poor Concklin! I fear for him. When he is dragged back to Alabama, I fear they will go far beyond the utmost rigor of the law, and vent their savage cruelty upon him. It is with pain I have to communicate these things. But you may not hear them from him. I could not get to see him or them, as Vincennes is about thirty miles from Princeton, where I was when I heard of the capture.

I take pleasure in stating that, according to the letter he (Concklin) wrote to Mr. D. Stewart, Mr. Concklin did not abandon them, but risked his own liberty to save them. He was not with them when they were taken; but went afterwards to take them out of jail upon a writ of Habeas Corpus, when they seized him too and lodged him in prison.

I write in much haste. If I can learn any more facts of importance, I may write you. If you desire to hear from me again, or if you should learn any thing specific from Mr. Concklin, be pleased to write me at Cincinnati, where I expect to be in a short time. If curious to know your correspondent, I may say I was formerly Editor of the *New Concord Free Press*, Ohio. I only add that every case of this kind only tends to make me abhor my (no!) *this* country more and more. It is the Devil's Government, and God will destroy it.

Yours for the slave, N.R. JOHNSTON.

P.S. I broke open this letter to write you some more. The foregoing pages were written at night. I expected to mail it next morning before leaving Evansville; but the boat for which I was waiting came down about three in the morning; so I had to hurry on board, bringing the letter along. As it now is I am not sorry, for coming down, on my way to St. Louis, as far as Paducah, there I learned from a colored man at the wharf that, that same day, in the morning, the master and the family of fugitives arrived off the boat, and had then gone on their journey to Tuscumbia, but that the "white man" (Mr. Concklin) had "got away from them," about twelve miles up the river. It seems he got off the boat some way, near or at Smithland, Ky., a town at the mouth of the Cumberland River. I presume the report is true, and hope he will finally escape, though I was also told that they were in pursuit of him. Would that the others had also escaped. Peter and Levin could have done so, I think, if they had had resolution. One of them rode a horse, he not tied either, behind the coach in which the others were. He followed apparently "contented and happy." From report, they told their master, and even their pursuers, before the master came, that Concklin had decoyed them away, they coming unwillingly. I write on a very unsteady boat.

Yours, N.R. JOHNSTON.

A report found its way into the papers to the effect that "Miller," the white man arrested in connection with the capture of the family, was found drowned, with his hands and feet in chains and his skull fractured. It proved, as his friends feared, to be Seth Concklin. And in irons, upon the river bank, there is no doubt he was buried.

In this dreadful hour one sad duty still remained to be performed. Up to this moment the two sisters were totally ignorant of their brother's whereabouts. Not the first whisper of his death had reached them. But they must now be made acquainted with all the facts in the case. Accordingly an interview was arranged for a meeting, and the duty of conveying this painful intelligence to one of the sisters, Mrs. Supplee, devolved upon Mr. McKim. And most tenderly and considerately did he perform his mournful task.

Although a woman of nerve, and a true friend to the slave, an earnest worker and a liberal giver in the Female Anti-Slavery Society, for a time she was overwhelmed by the intelligence of her brother's death. As soon as possible, however, through very great effort, she controlled her emotions, and calmly expressed herself as being fully resigned to the awful event. Not a word of complaint had she to make because she had not been apprised of his move-ments; but said repeatedly, that, had she known ever so much of his intentions, she would have been totally powerless in opposing him if she had felt so disposed, and as an illustra-tion of the true character of the man, from his boyhood up to the day he died for his fellow-man, she related his eventful career, and recalled a number of instances of his heroic and daring deeds for others, sacrificing his time and often periling his life in the cause of those who he considered were suffering gross wrongs and oppression. Hence, she concluded, that it was only natural for him in this case to have taken the steps he did. Now and then overflowing tears would obstruct this deeply thrilling and most remarkable story she was telling of her brother, but her memory seemed quickened by the sadness of the occasion, and she was enabled to recall vividly the chief events connected with his past history. Thus his agency in this movement, which cost him his life, could readily enough be accounted for, and the individuals who listened attentively to the story were prepared to fully appreciate his character, for, prior to offering his services in this mission, he had been a stranger to them.

The following extract, taken from a letter of a subsequent date, in addition to the above letter, throws still further light upon the heart-rending affair, and shows Mr. Johnston's deep sympathy with the sufferers and the oppressed generally –

EXTRACT OF A LETTER FROM REV. N.R. JOHNSTON.

My heart bleeds when I think of those poor, hunted and heart-broken fugitives, though a most interesting family, taken back to bondage ten-fold worse than Egyptian. And then poor Concklin! How my heart expanded in love to him, as he told me his adventures, his trials, his toils, his fears and his hopes! After hearing all, and then seeing and communing with the family, now joyful in hopes of soon seeing their husband and father in the land of freedom; now in terror lest the human blood-hounds should be at their heels, I felt as though I could lay down my life in the cause of the oppressed. In that hour or two of intercourse with Peter's family, my heart warmed with love to them. I never saw more interesting young men. They would make Remonds or Douglasses, if they had the same opportunities.

While I was with them, I was elated with joy at their escape, and yet, when I heard their tale of woe, especially that of the mother, I could not suppress tears of deepest emotion.

My joy was short-lived. Soon I heard of their capture. The telegraph had been the means of their being claimed. I could have torn down all the telegraph wires in the land. It was a strange dispensation of Providence.

On Saturday the sad news of their capture came to my ears. We had resolved to go to their aid on Monday, as the trial was set for Thursday. On Sabbath, I spoke from Psalm xii. 5. "For the oppression of the poor, for the sighing of the needy, now will I arise," saith the Lord: "I will set him in safety from him that puffeth at (from them that would enslave) him." When on Monday morning I learned that the fugitives had passed through the place on Sabbath, and Concklin in chains, probably at the very time I was speaking on the subject referred to, my heart sank within me. And even yet, I cannot but exclaim, when I think of it – O, Father! how long ere Thou wilt arise to avenge the wrongs of the poor slave! Indeed, my dear brother, His ways are very mysterious. We have the consolation, however, to know that all is for the best. Our Redeemer does all things well. When He hung upon the cross, His poor broken hearted disciples could not understand the providence; it was a dark time to them; and yet that was an event that was fraught with more joy to the world than any that has occurred or could occur. Let us stand at our post and wait God's time. Let us have on the whole armor of God, and fight for the right, knowing, that though we may fall in battle, the victory will be ours, sooner or later.

May God lead you into all truth, and sustain you in your labors, and fulfill your prayers and hopes. Adieu.

N.R. JOHNSTON.

LETTERS FROM LEVI COFFIN.

The following letters on the subject were received from the untiring and devoted friend of the slave, Levi Coffin, who for many years had occupied in Cincinnati a similar position to that of Thomas Garrett in Delaware, a sentinel and watchman commissioned of God to succor the fleeing bondman –

CINCINNATI, 4TH MO.,
10th, 1851.

FRIEND WM. STILL: – We have sorrowful news from our friend Concklin, through the papers and otherwise. I received a letter a few days ago from a friend near Princeton, Ind., stating that Concklin and the four slaves are in prison in Vincennes, and that their trial would come on in a few days. He states that they rowed seven days and nights in the skiff, and got safe to Harmony, Ind., on the Wabash river, thence to Princeton, and were conveyed to Vincennes by friends, where they were taken. The papers state, that they were all given up to the Marshal of Evansville, Indiana.

We have telegraphed to different points, to try to get some information concerning them, but failed. The last information is published in the *Times* of yesterday, though quite incorrect in the particulars of the case. Inclosed is the slip containing it. I fear all is over in regard to the freedom of the slaves. If the last account be true, we have some hope that Concklin will escape from those bloody tyrants. I cannot describe my feelings on hearing this sad intelligence. I feel ashamed to own my country. Oh! what shall I say. Surely a God of justice will avenge the wrongs of the oppressed.

Thine for the poor slave,
LEVI COFFIN.

N.B. – If thou hast any information, please write me forthwith.

CINCINNATI, 5TH MO.,
11th, 1851.

WM. STILL: – *Dear Friend –* Thy letter of 1st inst., came duly to hand, but not being able to give any further information concerning our friend, Concklin, I thought best to wait a little before I wrote, still hoping to learn something more definite concerning him.

We that became acquainted with Seth Concklin and his hazardous enterprises (here at Cincinnati), who were very few, have felt intense and inexpressible anxiety about them. And particularly about poor Seth, since we heard of his falling into the hands of the tyrants. I fear that he has fallen a victim to their inhuman thirst for blood.

I seriously doubt the rumor, that he had made his escape. I fear that he was sacrificed.

Language would fail to express my feelings; the intense and deep anxiety I felt about them for weeks before I heard of their capture in Indiana, and then it seemed too much to bear. O! my heart almost bleeds when I think of it. The hopes of the dear family all blasted by the wretched blood-hounds in human shape. And poor Seth, after all his toil, and dangerous, shrewd and wise management, and almost unheard of adventures, the many narrow and almost miraculous escapes. Then to be given up to Indianians, to these fiendish tyrants, to be sacrificed. O! Shame, Shame!!

My heart aches, my eyes fill with tears, I cannot write more. I cannot dwell longer on this painful subject now. If you get any intelligence, please inform me. Friend N.R. Johnston, who took so much interest in them, and saw them just before they were taken, has just returned to the city. He is a minister of the Covenanter order. He is truly a lovely man, and his heart is full of the milk of humanity; one of our best Anti-Slavery spirits. I spent last evening with him. He related the whole story to me as he had it from friend Concklin and the mother and children, and then the story of their capture. We wept together. He found thy letter when he got here.

He said he would write the whole history to thee in a few days, as far as he could. He can tell it much better than I can.

Concklin left his carpet sack and clothes here with me, except a shirt or two he took with him. What shall I do with them? For if we do not hear from him soon, we must conclude that he is lost, and the report of his escape all a hoax.

Truly thy friend,
LEVI COFFIN.

Stunning and discouraging as this horrible ending was to all concerned, and serious as the matter looked in the eyes of Peter's friends with regard to Peter's family, he could not for a moment abandon the idea of rescuing them from the jaws of the destroyer. But most formidable difficulties stood in the way of opening correspondence with reliable persons in Alabama. Indeed it seemed impossible to find a merchant, lawyer, doctor, planter or minister, who was not too completely interlinked with slavery to be relied upon to manage a negotiation of this nature. Whilst waiting and hoping for something favorable to turn up, the subjoined letter from the owner of Peter's family was received and is here inserted precisely as it was written, spelled and punctuated –

McKIERNON'S LETTER

SOUTH FLORENCE ALA
6 Augest 1851

Mr WILLIAM STILL
No 31 North Fifth street Philadelphia
    Sir a few days sinc mr Lewis Tharenton of Tuscumbia Ala shewed me a letter dated 6 June 51 from Cincinnati signd samuel Lewis in behalf of a Negro man by the name of peter Gist who informed the writer of the Letter that you ware his brother and wished an answer to be directed to you as he peter would be in philadelphi. the object of the letter was to purchis from me 4 Negros that is peters wife & 3 children 2 sons & 1

Girl the Name of said Negres are the woman Viney the (mother) Eldest son peter 21 or 2 years old second son Leven 19 or 20 years 1 Girl about 13 or 14 years old. the Husband & Father of these people once Belonged to a relation of mine by the name of Gist now Decest & some few years since he peter was sold to a man by the Name of Freedman who removed to cincinnati ohio & Tuck peter with him of course peter became free by the volentary act of the master some time last march a white man by the name of Miller apperd in the nabourhood & abducted the bove negroes was caut at vincanes Indi with said negroes & was thare convicted of steling & remanded back to Ala to Abide the penalty of the law & on his return met his Just reward by Getting drownded at the mouth of cumberland River on the ohio in attempting to make his escape I recovered & Braught Back said 4 negroes or as You would say coulard people under the Belief that peter the Husband was accessory to the offence thareby putting me to much Expense & Truble to the amt $1000 which if he gets them he or his Friends must refund these 4 negroes are worth in the market about 4000 for thea are Extraordinary fine & likely & but for the fact of Elopement I would not take 8000 Dollars for them but as the thing now stands you can say to peter & his new discovered Relations in Philadelphia I will take 5000 for the 4 culerd people & if this will suite him & he can raise the money I will delever to him or his agent at paduca at mouth of Tennessee river said negroes but the money must be Deposeted in the Hands of some respectabl person at paduca before I remove the property it wold not be safe for peter to come to this countery write me a line on recpt of this & let me Know peters views on the above

I am Yours &c B. McKIERNON.

N B say to peter to write & let me Know his viewes amediately as I am determined to act in a way if he don't take this offer he will never have an other opportunity

B McKIERNON.

WM. STILL'S ANSWER

PHILADELPHIA,
Aug. 16th, 1851.

To B. McKIERNON, ESQ.: *Sir* – I have received your letter from South Florence, Ala., under date of the 6th inst. To say that it took me by surprise, as well as afforded me pleasure, for which I feel to be very much indebted to you, is no more than true. In regard to your informants of myself – Mr. Thornton, of Ala., and Mr. Samuel Lewis, of Cincinnati – to them both I am a stranger. However, I am the brother of Peter, referred to, and with the fact of his having a wife and three children in your service I am also familiar. This brother, Peter, I have only had the pleasure of knowing for the brief space of one year and thirteen days, although he is now past forty and I twenty-nine years of age. Time will not allow me at present, or I should give you a detailed account of how Peter became a slave, the forty long years which intervened between the time he was kidnapped, when a boy, being only six years of age, and his arrival in this city, from Alabama, one year and fourteen days ago, when he was re-united to his mother, five brothers and three sisters.

None but a father's heart can fathom the anguish and sorrows felt by Peter during the many vicissitudes through which he has passed. He looked back to his boyhood and saw himself snatched from the tender embraces of his parents and home to be made a slave for life. During all his prime days he was in the faithful and constant service of those who had no just claim upon him. In the meanwhile he married a wife, who bore him eleven children, the greater part of whom were emancipated from the troubles of life by death, and three only survived. To them and his wife he was devoted. Indeed I have never seen attachment between parents and children, or husband and wife, more entire than was manifested in the case of Peter.

Through these many years of servitude, Peter was sold and resold, from one State to another, from one owner to another, till he reached the forty-ninth year of his age, when, in a good Providence, through the kindness of a friend and the sweat of his brow, he regained the God-given blessings of liberty. He eagerly sought his parents and home with all possible speed and pains, when, to his heart's joy, he found his relatives.

Your present humble correspondent is the youngest of Peter's brothers, and the first one of the family he saw after arriving in this part of the country. I think you could not fail to be interested in hearing how we became known to each other, and the proof of our being brothers, etc., all of which I should be most glad to relate, but time will not permit me to do so. The news of this wonderful occurrence, of Peter finding his kindred, was published quite extensively, shortly afterwards, in various newspapers, in this quarter, which may account for the fact of "Miller's" knowledge of the whereabouts of the "fugitives." Let me say, it is my firm conviction that no one had any hand in persuading "Miller" to go down from Cincinnati, or any other place, after the family. As glad as I should be, and as much as I would do for the liberation of Peter's family (now no longer young), and his three "likely" children, in whom he prides himself – how much, if you are a father, you can imagine; yet I would not, and could not, think of persuading any friend to peril his life, as would be the case, in an errand of that kind.

As regards the price fixed upon by you for the family, I must say I do not think it possible to raise half that amount, though Peter authorized me to say he would give you twenty-five hundred for them. Probably he is not as well aware as I am, how difficult it is to raise so large a sum of money from the public. The applications for such objects are so frequent among us in the North, and have always been so liberally met, that it is no wonder if many get tired of being called upon. To be sure some of us brothers own some property, but no great amount; certainly not enough to enable us to bear so great a burden. Mother owns a small farm in New Jersey, on which she has lived for nearly forty years, from which she derives her support in her old age. This small farm contains between forty and fifty acres, and is the fruit of my father's toil. Two of my brothers own small places also, but they have young families, and consequently consume nearly as much as they make, with the exception of adding some improvements to their places.

For my own part, I am employed as a clerk for a living, but my salary is quite too limited to enable me to contribute any great amount towards so large a sum as is demanded. Thus you see how we are situated financially. We have plenty of friends, but little money. Now, sir, allow me to make an appeal to your humanity, although we are aware of your power to hold as property those poor slaves, mother, daughter and two sons, – that in no part of the United States could they escape and be secure from your claim – nevertheless, would your understanding, your heart, or your conscience reprove you, should you restore to them, without price, that dear freedom, which is theirs by right of nature, or would you not feel a satisfaction in so doing which all the wealth of the world could not equal? At all events, could you not so reduce the price as to place it in the power of Peter's relatives and friends to raise the means for their purchase? At first, I doubt not, but that you will think my appeal very unreasonable; but, sir, serious reflection will decide, whether the money demanded by you, after all, will be of as great a benefit to you, as the satisfaction you would find in bestowing so great a favor upon those whose entire happiness in this life depends mainly upon your decision in the matter. If the entire family cannot be purchased or freed, what can Vina and her daughter be purchased for? Hoping, sir, to hear from you, at your earliest convenience, I subscribe myself,

Your obedient servant, WM. STILL.

To B. McKiernon, Esq.

No reply to this letter was ever received from McKiernon. The cause of his reticence can be as well conjectured by the reader as the writer.

Time will not admit of further details kindred to this narrative. The life, struggles, and success of Peter and his family were ably brought before the public in the *Kidnapped and the Ransomed*, being the personal recollections of Peter Still and his wife "Vina," after forty years of slavery, by Mrs. Kate E.R. Pickard; with an introduction by Rev. Samuel J. May, and an appendix by William H. Furness, D.D., in 1856. But, of course it was not prudent or safe, in the days of Slavery, to publish such facts as are now brought to light; all such had to be kept concealed in the breasts of the fugitives and their friends.

The following brief sketch, touching the separation of Peter and his mother, will fitly illustrate this point, and at the same time explain certain mysteries which have been hitherto kept hidden –

THE SEPARATION

With regard to Peter's separation from his mother, when a little boy, in few words, the facts were these: His parents, Levin and Sidney, were both slaves on the Eastern Shore of Maryland. "I will die before I submit to the yoke," was the declaration of his father to his young master before either was twenty-one years of age. Consequently he was allowed to buy himself at a very low figure, and he paid the required sum and obtained his "free papers" when quite a young man – the young wife and mother remaining in slavery under Saunders Griffin, as also her children, the latter having increased to the number of four, two little boys and two little girls. But to escape from chains, stripes, and bondage, she took her four little children and fled to a place near Greenwich, New Jersey. Not a great while, however, did she remain there in a state of freedom before the slave-hunters pursued her, and one night they pounced upon the whole family, and, without judge or jury, hurried them all back to slavery. Whether this was kidnapping or not is for the reader to decide for himself.

Safe back in the hands of her owner, to prevent her from escaping a second time, every night for about three months she was cautiously "kept locked up in the garret," until, as they supposed, she was fully "cured of the desire to do so again." But she was incurable. She had been a witness to the fact that her own father's brains had been blown out by the discharge of a heavily loaded gun, deliberately aimed at his head by his drunken master. She only needed half a chance to make still greater struggles than ever for freedom.

She had great faith in God, and found much solace in singing some of the good old Methodist tunes, by day and night. Her owner, observing this apparently tranquil state of mind, indicating that she "seemed better contented than ever," concluded that it was safe to let the garret door remain unlocked at night. Not many weeks were allowed to pass before she resolved to again make a bold strike for freedom. This time she had to leave the two little boys, Levin and Peter, behind.

On the night she started she went to the bed where they were sleeping, kissed them, and, consigning them into the hands of God, bade her mother good-bye, and with her two little girls wended her way again to Burlington County, New

Jersey, but to a different neighborhood from that where she had been seized. She changed her name to Charity, and succeeded in again joining her husband, but, alas, with the heart-breaking thought that she had been compelled to leave her two little boys in slavery and one of the little girls on the road for the father to go back after. Thus she began life in freedom anew.

Levin and Peter, eight and six years of age respectively, were now left at the mercy of the enraged owner, and were soon hurried off to a Southern market and sold, while their mother, for whom they were daily weeping, was they knew not where. They were too young to know that they were slaves, or to understand the nature of the afflicting separation. Sixteen years before Peter's return, his older brother (Levin) died a slave in the State of Alabama, and was buried by his surviving brother, Peter.

No idea other than that they had been "kidnapped" from their mother ever entered their minds; nor had they any knowledge of the State from whence they supposed they had been taken, the last names of their mother and father, or where they were born. On the other hand, the mother was aware that the safety of herself and her rescued children depended on keeping the whole transaction a strict family secret. During the forty years of separation, except two or three Quaker friends, including the devoted friend of the slave, Benjamin Lundy, it is doubtful whether any other individuals were let into the secret of her slave life. And when the account given of Peter's return, etc., was published in 1850, it led some of the family to apprehend serious danger from the partial revelation of the early condition of the mother, especially as it was about the time that the Fugitive Slave law was passed.

Hence, the author of *The Kidnapped and the Ransomed* was compelled to omit these dangerous facts, and had to confine herself strictly to the "personal recollections of Peter Still" with regard to his being "kidnapped." Likewise, in the sketch of Seth Concklin's eventful life, written by Dr. W.H. Furness, for similar reasons he felt obliged to make but bare reference to his wonderful agency in relation to Peter's family, although he was fully aware of all the facts in the case.

WILLIAM PEEL

ALIAS WILLIAM
BOX PEEL JONES

ARRIVED PER ERRICSON LINE
OF STEAMERS, WRAPPED IN STRAW
AND BOXED UP.

APRIL, 1859.

William is twenty-five years of age, unmistakably colored, good-looking, rather under the medium size, and of pleasing manners. William had himself boxed up by a near relative and forwarded by the Erricson line of steamers. He gave the slip to Robert H. Carr, his owner (a grocer and commission merchant), after this wise, and for the following reasons: For some time previous his master had been selling off his slaves every now and then, the same as other groceries, and this admonished William that he was liable to be in the market any day; consequently, he preferred the box to the auction-block.

He did not complain of having been treated very badly by Carr, but felt that no man was safe while owned by another. In fact, he "hated the very name of slaveholder." The limit of the box not admitting of straightening himself out he was taken with the cramp on the road, suffered indescribable misery, and had his faith taxed to the utmost, – indeed was brought to the very verge of "screaming aloud" ere relief came. However, he controlled himself, though only for a short season, for before a great while an excessive faintness came over him. Here nature became quite exhausted. He thought he must "die;" but his time had not yet come. After a severe struggle he revived, but only to encounter a third ordeal no less painful than the one through which he had just passed. Next a very "cold chill" came over him, which seemed almost to freeze the very blood in his veins and gave him intense agony, from which he only found relief on awaking, having actually fallen asleep in that condition.

Finally, however, he arrived at Philadelphia, on a steamer, Sabbath morning. A devoted friend of his, expecting him, engaged a carriage and repaired to the wharf for the box. The bill of lading and the receipt he had with him, and likewise knew where the box was located on the boat. Although he well knew freight was not usually delivered on Sunday, yet his deep solicitude for the safety of his friend determined him to do all that lay in his power to rescue him from his perilous situation. Handing his bill of lading to the proper officer of the boat, he asked if he could get the freight that it called for. The officer looked at the bill and said, "No, we do not deliver freight on Sunday;" but, noticing the anxiety of the man, he asked him if he would know it if he were to see it. Slowly – fearing that too much interest mani-fested might excite suspicion – he replied: "I think I should." Deliberately looking around amongst all the "freight," he discovered the box, and said, "I think that is it there." Said officer stepped to it, looked at the directions on it, then at the bill of lading, and said, "That is right, take it along." Here the interest in these two bosoms was thrilling in the highest degree. But the size of the box was too large for the carriage, and the driver refused to take it. Nearly an hour and a half was spent in looking for a furniture car. Finally one was procured, and again the box was laid hold of by the occupant's particular friend, when, to his dread alarm, the poor fellow within gave a sudden cough. At this startling circumstance he dropped the box; equally as quick, although dreadfully frightened, and, as if helped by some invisible agency, he commenced singing, "Hush, my babe, lie still and slumber," with the most apparent indifference, at the same time slowly making his way from the box. Soon his fears subsided, and it was presumed that no one was any the wiser on account of the accident, or coughing. Thus, after summoning courage, he laid hold of the box a third time, and the Rubicon was passed. The car driver, totally ignorant of the contents of the box, drove to the number to which he was directed to take it – left it and went about his business. Now is a moment of intense interest – now of inexpressible delight. The box is opened, the straw removed, and the poor fellow is loosed; and is rejoicing, I will venture to say, as mortal never did rejoice, who had not been in similar peril. This particular friend was scarcely less overjoyed, however, and their joy did not abate for several hours; nor was it confined to themselves, for two invited members of the Vigilance Committee also partook of a full share. This box man was named Wm. Jones. He was boxed up in Baltimore by the friend who received him at the wharf, who did not come in the boat with him, but came in the cars and met him at the wharf.

The trial in the box lasted just seventeen hours before victory was achieved. Jones was well cared for by the Vigilance Committee and sent on his way rejoicing, feeling that Resolution, Underground Rail Road, and Liberty were invaluable.

On his way to Canada, he stopped at Albany, and the subjoined letter gives his view of things from that stand-point –

MR. STILL: – I take this opportunity of writing a few lines to you hoping that tha may find you in good health and femaly. i am well at present and doing well at present i am now in a store and getting sixteen dollars a month at the present. i feel very much o blige to you and your family for your kindnes to me while i was with you i have got a long without any trub le a tal. i am now in albany City. give my lov to mrs and mr miller and tel them i am very much a blige to them for there kind ns. give my lov to my Brother nore Jones tel him i should like to here from him very much and he must write. tel him to give my love to all of my perticnlar frends and tel them i should like to see them very much. tel him that he must come to see me for i want to see him for sum thing very perticler. please ansure this letter as soon as posabul and excuse me for not writting sooner as i don't write myself. no more at the present.

WILLIAM JONES.

derect to one hundred 125 lydus. Stt

His good friend returned to Baltimore the same day the box man started for the North, and immediately dispatched through the post the following brief letter, worded in Underground Rail Road parables:

BALTIMO
April 16, 1859.

W. STILL: – Dear brother i have taken the opportunity of writing you these few lines to inform you that i am well an hoping these few lines may find you enjoying the same good blessing please to write me word at what time was it when isreal went to Jerico i am very anxious to hear for thare is a mighty host will pass over and you and i my brother will sing hally luja i shall notify you when the great catastrophe shal take place No more at the present but remain your brother

N.L.J.

WESLEY HARRIS

ALIAS ROBERT JACKSON,
AND THE MATTERSON BROTHERS

In setting out for freedom, Wesley was the leader of this party. After two nights of fatiguing travel at a distance of about sixty miles from home, the young aspirants for liberty were betrayed, and in an attempt made to capture them a most bloody conflict ensued. Both fugitives and pursuers were the recipients of severe wounds from gun shots, and other weapons used in the contest.

Wesley bravely used his firearms until almost fatally wounded by one of the pursuers, who with a heavily loaded gun discharged the contents with deadly aim in his left arm, which raked the flesh from the bone for a space of about six inches in length. One of Wesley's companions also fought heroically and only yielded when badly wounded and quite overpowered. The two younger (brothers of C. Matterson) it seemed made no resistance.

In order to recall the adventures of this struggle, and the success of Wesley Harris, it is only necessary to copy the report as then penned from the lips of this young hero, while on the Underground Rail Road, even then in a very critical state. Most fearful indeed was his condition when he was brought to the Vigilance Committee in this City.

UNDERGROUND RAIL ROAD RECORD

November 2d, 1853. – Arrived: Robert Jackson (shot man), alias Wesley Harris; age twenty-two years; dark color; medium height, and of slender stature.

Robert was born in Martinsburg, Va., and was owned by Philip Pendleton. From a boy he had always been hired out. At the first of this year he commenced services with Mrs. Carroll, proprietress of the United States Hotel at Harper's Ferry. Of Mrs. Carroll he speaks in very grateful terms, saying that she was kind to him and all the servants, and promised them their freedom at her death. She excused herself for not giving them their freedom on the ground that her husband died insolvent, leaving her the responsibility of settling his debts. But while Mrs. Carroll was very kind to her servants, her manager was equally as cruel. About a month before Wesley left, the overseer, for some trifling cause, attempted to flog him, but was resisted, and himself flogged. This resistance of the slave was regarded by the overseer as an unpardonable offence; consequently he communicated the intelligence to his owner, which had the desired effect on his mind as appeared from his answer to the overseer, which was nothing less than instructions that if he should again attempt to correct Wesley and he should repel the wholesome treatment, the overseer was to put him in prison and sell him. Whether he offended again or not, the following Christmas he was to be sold without fail.

Wesley's mistress was kind enough to apprise him of the intention of his owner and the overseer, and told him that if he could help himself he had better do so. So from that time Wesley began to contemplate how he should escape the doom which had been planned for him.

A friend [says he] by the name of C. Matterson, told me that he was going off. Then I told him of my master's writing to Mrs. Carroll concerning selling, etc., and that I was going off too. We then concluded to go together. There were two others

– brothers of Matterson – who were told of our plan to escape, and readily joined with us in the undertaking. So one Saturday night, at twelve o'clock, we set out for the North. After traveling upwards of two days and over sixty miles, we found ourselves unexpectedly in Terrytown, Md. There we were informed by a friendly colored man of the danger we were in and of the bad character of the place towards colored people, especially those who were escaping to freedom; and he advised us to hide as quickly as we could. We at once went to the woods and hid. Soon after we had secreted ourselves a man came near by and commenced splitting wood, or rails, which alarmed us. We then moved to another hiding-place in a thicket near a farmer's barn, where we were soon startled again by a dog approaching and barking at us. The attention of the owner of the dog was drawn to his barking and to where we were. The owner of the dog was a farmer. He asked us where we were going. We replied to Gettysburg – to visit some relatives, etc. He told us that we were running off. He then offered friendly advice, talked like a Quaker, and urged us to go with him to his barn for protection. After much persuasion, we consented to go with him.

Soon after putting us in his barn, himself and daughter prepared us a nice breakfast, which cheered our spirits, as we were hungry. For this kindness we paid him one dollar. He next told us to hide on the mow till eve, when he would safely direct us on our road to Gettysburg. All, very much fatigued from traveling, fell asleep, excepting myself; I could not sleep; I felt as if all was not right.

About noon men were heard talking around the barn. I woke my companions up and told them that that man had betrayed us. At first they did not believe me. In a moment afterwards the barn door was opened, and in came the men, eight in number. One of the men asked the owner of the barn if he had any long straw. "Yes," was the answer. So up on the mow came three of the men, when, to their great surprise, as they pretended, we were discovered. The question was then asked the owner of the barn by one of the men, if he harbored runaway negroes in his barn? He answered, "No," and pretended to be entirely ignorant of their being in his barn. One of the men replied that four negroes were on the mow, and he knew of it. The men then asked us where we were, going. We told them to Gettysburg, that we had aunts and a mother there. Also we spoke of a Mr. Houghman, a gentleman we happened to have some knowledge of, having seen him in Virginia. We were next asked for our passes. We told them that we hadn't any, that we had not been required to carry them where we came from. They then said that we would have to go before a magistrate, and if he allowed us to go on, well and good. The men all being armed and furnished with ropes, we were ordered to be tied. I told them if they took me they would have to take me dead or crippled. At that instant one of my friends cried out – "Where is the man that betrayed us?" Spying him at the same moment, he shot him (badly wounding him). Then the conflict fairly began. The constable seized me by the collar, or rather behind my shoulder. I at once shot him with my pistol, but in consequence of his throwing up his arm, which hit mine as I fired, the effect of the load of my pistol was much turned aside; his face, however, was badly burned, besides his shoulder being wounded. I again fired on the pursuers, but do not know whether I hit anybody or not. I then drew a sword, I had brought with me, and was about cutting my way to the door, when I was shot by one of the men, receiving the entire contents of one load of a double barreled gun in my left arm, that being the arm with which I was defending myself. The load brought me to the ground, and I was unable to make further struggle for myself. I was then badly beaten with guns, &c. In the meantime, my friend Craven, who was defending himself, was shot badly in the face, and most violently beaten until he was conquered and tied. The two young brothers of Craven stood still, without making the least resistance. After we were fairly captured, we were taken to Terrytown, which was in sight of where we were betrayed. By this time I had lost so much blood from my wounds, that they concluded my situation was too dangerous to admit of being taken further; so I was made a prisoner at a tavern, kept by a man named Fisher. There my wounds were dressed, and thirty-two shot were taken from my arm. For three days I was crazy, and they thought I would die. During the first two weeks, while I was a prisoner at the tavern, I raised a great deal of blood, and was considered in a very dangerous condition – so much so that persons desiring to see me were not permitted. Afterwards I began to get better, and was then kept privately – was strictly watched day and night. Occasionally, however, the cook, a colored woman (Mrs. Smith), would manage to get to see me. Also James Matthews succeeded in getting to see me; consequently, as my wounds healed, and my senses came to me, I began to plan how to make another effort to escape. I asked one of the friends, alluded to above, to get me a rope. He got it. I kept it about me four days in my pocket; in the meantime I procured three nails. On Friday night, October 14th, I fastened my nails in under the window sill; tied my rope to the nails, threw my shoes out of the window, put the rope in my mouth, then took hold of it with my well hand, clambered into the window, very weak, but I managed to let myself down to the ground. I was so weak, that I could scarcely walk, but I managed to hobble off to a place three quarters of a mile from the tavern, where a friend had fixed upon for me to go, if I succeeded in making my escape. There I was found by my friend, who kept me secure till Saturday eve, when a swift horse was furnished by James Rogers, and a colored man found to conduct me to Gettysburg. Instead of going direct to Gettysburg, we took a different road, in order to shun our pursuers, as the news of my escape had created general excitement. My three other companions, who were captured, were sent to Westminster jail, where they were kept three weeks, and afterwards sent to Baltimore and sold for twelve hundred dollars a piece, as I was informed while at the tavern in Terrytown.

The Vigilance Committee procured good medical attention and afforded the fugitive time for recuperation, furnished him with clothing and a free ticket, and sent him on his way greatly improved in health, and strong in the faith that, "He who would be free, himself must strike the blow." His safe arrival in Canada, with his thanks, were duly announced. And some time after becoming naturalized, in one of his letters, he wrote that he was a brakesman on the Great Western R.R., (in Canada – promoted from the U.G.R.R.,) the result of being under the protection of the British Lion.

JAMES MERCER

WM. H. GILLIAM,
AND JOHN CLAYTON

STOWED AWAY IN A HOT BERTH.

This arrival came by Steamer. But they neither came in State-room nor as Cabin, Steerage, or Deck passengers.

A certain space, not far from the boiler, where the heat and coal dust were almost intolerable, – the colored steward on the boat in answer to an appeal from these unhappy bondmen, could point to no other place for concealment but this. Nor was he at all certain that they could endure the intense heat of that place. It admitted of no other posture than lying flat down, wholly shut out from the light, and nearly in the same predicament in regard to the air. Here, however, was a chance of throwing off the yoke, even if it cost them their lives. They considered and resolved to try it at all hazards.

Henry Box Brown's sufferings were nothing, compared to what these men submitted to during the entire journey.

They reached the house of one of the Committee about three o'clock, A.M.

All the way from the wharf the cold rain poured down in torrents and they got completely drenched, but their hearts were swelling with joy and gladness unutterable. From the thick coating of coal dust, and the effect of the rain added thereto, all traces of natural appearance were entirely oblite-rated, and they looked frightful in the extreme. But they had placed their lives in mortal peril for freedom.

Every step of their critical journey was reviewed and commented on, with matchless natural eloquence, – how, when almost on the eve of suffocating in their warm berths, in order to catch a breath of air, they were compelled to crawl, one at a time, to a small aperture; but scarcely would one poor fellow pass three minutes being thus refreshed, ere the others would insist that he should "go back to his hole." Air was precious, but for the time being they valued their liberty at still greater price.

After they had talked to their hearts' content, and after they had been thoroughly cleansed and changed in apparel, their physical appearance could be easily discerned, which made it less a wonder whence such outbursts of eloquence had emanated. They bore every mark of determined manhood.

The date of this arrival was February 26, 1854, and the following description was then recorded –

> Arrived, by Steamer *Pennsylvania*, James Mercer, William H. Gilliam and John Clayton, from Richmond.

James was owned by the widow, Mrs. T.E. White. He is thirty-two years of age, of dark complexion, well made, good-looking, reads and writes, is very fluent in speech, and remarkably intelligent. From a boy, he had been hired out. The last place he had the honor to fill before escaping, was with Messrs. Williams and Brother, wholesale commission merchants. For his services in this store the widow had been drawing one hundred and twenty-five dollars per annum, clear of all expenses.

He did not complain of bad treatment from his mistress, indeed, he spoke rather favorably of her. But he could not close his eyes to the fact, that at one time Mrs. White had been in possession of thirty head of slaves, although at the time he was counting the cost of escaping, two only remained – himself and William, (save a little boy) and on himself a mortgage for seven hundred and fifty dollars was then resting.

He could, therefore, with his remarkably quick intellect, calculate about how long it would be before he reached the auction block.

He had a wife but no child. She was owned by Mr. Henry W. Quarles. So out of that Sodom he felt he would have to escape, even at the cost of leaving his wife behind. Of course he felt hopeful that the way would open by which she could escape at a future time, and so it did, as will appear by and by. His aged mother he had to leave also.

Wm. Henry Gilliam likewise belonged to the Widow White, and he had been hired to Messrs. White and Brother to drive their bread wagon. William was a baker by trade. For his services his mistress had received one hundred and thirty-five dollars per year. He thought his mistress quite as good, if not a little better than most slave-holders. But he had never felt persuaded to believe that she was good enough for him to remain a slave for her support.

Indeed, he had made several unsuccessful attempts before this time to escape from slavery and its horrors. He was fully posted from A to Z, but in his own person he had been smart enough to escape most of the more brutal outrages. He knew how to read and write, and in readiness of speech and general natural ability was far above the average of slaves.

He was twenty-five years of age, well made, of light complexion, and might be put down as a valuable piece of property.

This loss fell with crushing weight upon the kind-hearted mistress, as will be seen in a letter subjoined which she wrote to the unfaithful William, some time after he had fled.

LETTER FROM MRS. L.E. WHITE

RICHMOND,
16th, 1854.

DEAR HENRY: – Your mother and myself received your letter; she is much distressed at your conduct; she is remaining just as you left her, she says, and she will never be reconciled to your conduct.

I think Henry, you have acted most dishonorably; had you have made a confidant of me I would have been better off; and you as you are. I am badly situated, living with Mrs. Palmer, and having to put up with everything – your mother is also dissatisfied – I am miserably poor, do not get a cent of your hire or James', besides losing you both, but if you can *reconcile* so do. By renting a cheap house, I might have lived, now it seems starvation is before me. Martha and the Doctor are living in Portsmouth, it is not in her power to do much for me. I know you will repent it. I heard six weeks before you went, that you were trying to persuade him off – but we all liked you, and I was unwilling to believe it – however, I leave it in God's hands He will know what to do. Your mother says that I must tell you servant Jones is *dead* and old *Mrs. Galt.* Kit is well, but we are very uneasy, losing your and *James' hire*, I fear poor little fellow, that he will be obliged to go, as I am compelled to live, and it will be your fault. I am quite unwell, but of course, you don't care.

Yours,
L.E. WHITE.

If you choose to come back you could. I would do a very good part by you, Toler and Cooke has none.

This touching epistle was given by the disobedient William to a member of the Vigilant Committee, when on a visit to Canada, in 1855, and it was thought to be of too much value to be lost. It was put away with other valuable U.G.R.R. documents for future reference. Touching the "rascality" of William and James and the unfortunate predicament in which it placed the kind-hearted widow, Mrs. Louisa White, the following editorial clipped from the wide-awake *Richmond Despatch*, was also highly appreciated, and preserved as conclusive testimony to the successful working of the U.G.R.R. in the Old Dominion. It reads thus –

RASCALITY SOMEWHERE. – We called attention yesterday to the advertisement of two negroes belonging to Mrs. Louisa White, by Toler & Cook, and in the call we expressed the opinion that they were still lurking about the city, preparatory to going off. Mr. Toler, we find, is of a different opinion. He believes that they have already cleared themselves – have escaped to a Free State, and we think it extremely probable that he is in the right. They were both of them uncommonly intelligent negroes. One of them, the one hired to Mr. White, was a tip-top baker. He had been all about the country, and had been in the habit of supplying the U.S. *Pennsylvania* with bread; Mr. W. having the contract. In his visits for this purpose, of course, he formed acquaintances with all sorts of sea-faring characters; and there is every reason to believe that he has been assisted to get off in that way, along with the other boy, hired to the Messrs. Williams. That the two acted in concert, can admit of no doubt. The question is now to find out how they got off. They must undoubtedly have had white men in the secret. Have we then a nest of Abolition scoundrels among us? There ought to be a law to put a police officer on board every vessel as soon as she lands at the wharf. There is one, we believe for inspecting vessels before they leave. If there is not there ought to be one.

These negroes belong to a widow lady and constitute all the property she has on earth. They have both been raised with the greatest indulgence. Had it been otherwise, they would never have had an opportunity to escape, as they have done. Their flight has left her penniless. Either of them would readily have sold for $1,200; and Mr. Toler advised their owner to sell them at the commencement of the year, probably anticipating the very thing that has happened. She refused to do so, because she felt too much attachment to them. They have made a fine return, truly.

No comment is necessary on the above editorial except simply to express the hope that the editor and his friends who seemed to be utterly befogged as to how these "uncommonly intelligent negroes" made their escape, will find the problem satisfactorily solved in this book.

However, in order to do even-handed justice to all concerned, it seems but proper that William and James should be heard from, and hence a letter from each is here appended for what they are worth. True they were intended only for private use, but since the "True light" (Freedom) has come, all things may be made manifest.

LETTER FROM WILLIAM HENRY GILLIAM

ST. CATHARINES, C.W.,
May 15th, 1854.

My Dear Friend: – I receaved yours, Dated the 10th and the papers on the 13th, I also saw the pice that was in Miss Shadd's paper About me. I think Tolar is right About my being in A free State, I am and think A great del of it. Also I have no compassion on the penniless widow lady, I have Served her 25 yers 2 months, I think that is long Enough for me to live A Slave. Dear Sir, I am very sorry to hear of the Accadent that happened to our Friend Mr. Meakins, I have read the letter to all that lives in St. Catharines, that came from old Virginia, and then I Sented to Toronto to Mercer & Clayton to see, and to Farman to read fur themselves. Sir, you must write to me soon and let me know how Meakins gets on with his tryal, and you must pray for him, I have told all here to do the same for him. May God bless and protect him from prison, I have heard A great del of old Richmond and Norfolk. Dear Sir, if you see Mr. or Mrs. Gilbert Give my love to them and tell them to write to me, also give my respect to your Family and A part for yourself, love from the friends to you Soloman Brown, H. Atkins, Was. Johnson, Mrs. Brooks, Mr. Dykes. Mr. Smith is better at presant. And do not forget to write the News of Meakin's tryal. I cannot say any more at this time; but remain yours and A true Friend ontell Death.

W.H. GILLIAM, the widow's Mite.

"Our friend Minkins," in whose behalf William asks the united prayers of his friends, was one of the "scoundrels" who assisted him and his two companions to escape on the steamer. Being suspected of "rascality" in this direction, he was arrested and put in jail, but as no evidence could be found against him he was soon released.

JAMES MERCER'S LETTER

TORONTO,
March 17th, 1854.

My dear friend Still: – I take this method of informing you that I am well, and when this comes to hand it may find you and your family enjoying good health. Sir, my particular for writing is that I wish to hear from you, and to hear all the news from down South. I wish to know if all things are working Right for the Rest of my Brotheran whom in bondage. I will also Say that I am very much please with Toronto, So also the friends that came over with. It is true that we have not been Employed as yet; but we are in hopes of be'en so in a few days. We happen here in good time jest about time the people in this country are going work. I am in good health and good Spirits, and feeles Rejoiced in the Lord for my liberty. I Received cople of paper from you to-day. I wish you see James Morris whom or Abram George the first and second on the Ship *Penn.*, give my respects to them, and ask James if he will call at Henry W. Quarles on May street oppisit the Jews synagogue and call for Marena Mercer, give my love to her ask her of all the times about

Richmond, tell her to Send me all the news. Tell Mr. Morris that there will be no danger in going to that place. You will also tell M. to make himself known to her as she may know who sent him. And I wish to get a letter from you.

JAMES M. MERCER.

JOHN H. HILL'S LETTER

My friend, I would like to hear from you, I have been looking for a letter from you for Several days as the last was very interesting to me, please to write Right away.

Yours most Respectfully,
JOHN H. HILL.

Instead of weeping over the sad situation of his "penniless" mistress and showing any signs of contrition for having wronged the man who held the mortgage of seven hundred and fifty dollars on him, James actually "feels rejoiced in the Lord for his liberty," and is "very much pleased with Toronto;" but is not satisfied yet, he is even concocting a plan by which his wife might be run off from Richmond, which would be the cause of her owner (Henry W. Quarles, Esq.) losing at least one thousand dollars,

ST. CATHARINE, CANADA,
June 8th, 1854.

MR. STILL, DEAR FRIEND: – I received a letter from the poor old widow, Mrs. L.E. White, and she says I may come back if I choose and she will do a good part by me. Yes, yes I am choosing the western side of the South for my home. She is smart, but cannot bung my eye, so she shall have to die in the poor house at last, so she says, and Mercer and myself will be the cause of it. That is all right. I am getting even with her now for I was in the poor house for twenty-five years and have just got out. And she said she knew I was coming away six weeks before I started, so you may know my chance was slim. But Mr. John Wright said I came off like a gentleman and he did not blame me for coming for I was a great boy. Yes I here him enough he is all gas. I am in Canada, and they cannot help themselves.

About that subject I will not say anything more. You must write to me as soon as you can and let me here the news and how the Family is and yourself. Let me know how the times is with the U.G.R.R. Co. Is it doing good business? Mr. Dykes sends his respects to you. Give mine to your family.

Your true friend,
W.H. GILLIAM.

John Clayton, the companion in tribulation of William and James, must not be lost sight of any longer. He was owned by the Widow Clayton, and was white enough to have been nearly related to her, being a mulatto. He was about thirty-five years of age, a man of fine appearance, and quite intelligent. Several years previous he had made an attempt to escape, but failed. Prior to escaping in this instance, he had been laboring in a tobacco factory at $150 a year. It is needless to say that he did not approve of the "peculiar institution." He left a wife and one child behind to mourn after him. Of his views of Canada and Freedom, the following frank and sensible letter, penned shortly after his arrival, speaks for itself –

TORONTO,
March 6th, 1854.

DEAR MR. STILL: – I take this method of informing you that I am well both in health and mind. You may rest assured that I fells myself a free man and do not fell as I did when I was in Virginia thanks be to God I have no master into Canada but I am my own man. I arrived safe into Canada on friday last. I must request of you to write a few lines to my wife and jest state to her that her friend arrived safe into this glorious land of liberty and I am well and she will make very short her time in Virginia. tell her that I likes here very well and hopes to like it better when I gets to work I don't meane for you to write the same words that are written above but I wish you give her a clear understanding where I am and Shall Remain here untel She comes or I hears from her.

Nothing more at present but remain yours most respectfully, JOHN CLAYTON.

You will please to direct the to Petersburg Luenena Johns or Clayton John is best.

CLARISSA DAVIS

*ARRIVED DRESSED IN
MALE ATTIRE.*

Clarissa fled from Portsmouth, Va., in May, 1854, with two of her brothers. Two months and a half before she succeeded in getting off, Clarissa had made a desperate effort, but failed. The brothers succeeded, but she was left. She had not given up all hope of escape, however, and therefore sought "a safe hiding-place until an opportunity might offer," by which she could follow her brothers on the U.G.R.R. Clarissa was owned by Mrs. Brown and Mrs. Burkley, of Portsmouth, under whom she had always served.

Of them she spoke favorably, saying that she "had not been used as hard as many others were." At this period, Clarissa was about twenty-two years of age, of a bright brown complexion, with handsome features, exceedingly respectful and modest, and possessed all the characteristics of a well-bred young lady. For one so little acquainted with books as she was, the correctness of her speech was perfectly astonishing.

For Clarissa and her two brothers a "reward of one thousand dollars" was kept standing in the papers for a length of time, as these (articles) were considered very rare and valuable; the best that could be produced in Virginia.

In the meanwhile the brothers had passed safely on to New Bedford, but Clarissa remained secluded, "waiting for the storm to subside." Keeping up courage day by day, for seventy-five days, with the fear of being detected and severely punished, and then sold, after all her hopes and struggles, required the faith of a martyr. Time after time, when she hoped to succeed in making her escape, ill luck seemed to disappoint her, and nothing but intense suffering appeared to be in store. Like many others, under the crushing weight of oppression, she thought she "should have to die" ere she tasted liberty. In this state of mind, one day, word was conveyed to her that the steamship, *City of Richmond*, had arrived from Philadelphia, and that the steward on board (with whom she was acquainted) had consented to secrete her this trip, if she could manage to reach the ship safely, which was to start the next day. This news to Clarissa was both cheering and painful. She had been "praying all the time while waiting," but now she felt "that if it would only rain right hard the next morning about three o'clock, to drive the police officers off the street, then she could safely make her way to the boat." Therefore she prayed anxiously all that day that it would rain, "but no sign of rain appeared till towards midnight." The prospect looked horribly discouraging; but she prayed on, and at the appointed hour (three o'clock – before day), the rain descended in torrents. Dressed in male attire, Clarissa left the miserable coop where she had been almost without light or air for two and a half months, and unmolested, reached the boat safely, and was secreted in a box by Wm. Bagnal, a clever young man who sincerely sympathized with the slave, having a wife in slavery himself; and by him she was safely delivered into the hands of the Vigilance Committee.

Clarissa Davis here, by advice of the Committee, dropped her old name, and was straightway christened "Mary D. Armstead." Desiring to join her brothers and sister in New Bedford, she was duly furnished with her U.G.R.R. passport and directed thitherward. Her father, who was left behind when she got off, soon after made his way on North, and joined his children. He was too old and infirm probably to be worth anything, and had been allowed to go free, or to purchase himself for a mere nominal sum. Slaveholders would, on some such occasions, show wonderful liberality in letting their old slaves go free, when they could work no more. After reaching New Bedford, Clarissa manifested her gratitude in writing to her friends in Philadelphia repeatedly, and evinced a very lively interest in the U.G.R.R. The appended letter indicates her sincere feelings of gratitude and deep interest in the cause –

NEW BEDFORD,
August 26, 1855.

MR. STILL: – I avail my self to write you thes few lines hopeing they may find you and your family well as they leaves me very well and all the family well except my father he seams to be improveing with his shoulder he has been able to work a little I received the papers I was highly delighted to receive them I was very glad to hear from you in the wheler case I was very glad to hear that the persons ware safe I was very sory to hear that mr Williamson was put in prison but I know if the praying part of the people will pray for him and if he will put his trust in the lord he will bring him out more than conquer please remember my Dear old farther and sisters and brothers to your family kiss the children for me I hear that the yellow fever is very bad down south now if the underground railroad could have free course the emergrant would cross the river of gordan rapidly I hope it may continue to run and I hope the wheels of the car may be greesed with more substantial greese so they may run over swiftly I would have wrote before but circumstances would not permit me Miss Sanders and all the friends desired to be remembered to you and your family I shall be pleased to hear from the underground rail road often.

Yours respectfully,

MARY D. ARMSTEAD.

ANTHONY BLOW

ALIAS HENRY LEVISON

SECRETED TEN MONTHS BEFORE STARTING – EIGHT DAYS STOWED AWAY ON A STEAMER BOUND FOR PHILADELPHIA.

Arrived from Norfolk, about the 1st of November, 1854. Ten months before starting, Anthony had been closely concealed. He belonged to the estate of Mrs. Peters, a widow, who had been dead about one year before his concealment.

On the settlement of his old mistress' estate, which was to take place one year after her death, Anthony was to be transferred to Mrs. Lewis, a daughter of Mrs. Peters (the wife of James Lewis, Esq.). Anthony felt well satisfied that he was not the slave to please the "tyrannical whims" of his anticipated master, young Lewis, and of course he hated the idea of having to come under his yoke. And what made it still more unpleasant for Anthony was that Mr. Lewis would frequently remind him that it was his intention to "sell him as soon as he got possession – the first day of January." "I can get fifteen hundred dollars for you easily, and I will do it." This contemptuous threat had caused Anthony's blood to boil time and again. But Anthony had to take the matter as calmly as possible, which, however, he was not always able to do.

At any rate, Anthony concluded that his "young master had counted the chickens before they were hatched." Indeed here Anthony began to be a deep thinker. He thought, for instance, that he had already been shot three times, at the instance of slave-holders. The first time he was shot was for refusing a flogging when only eighteen years of age. The second time, he was shot in the head with squirrel shot by the sheriff, who was attempting to arrest him for having resisted three "young white ruffians," who wished to have the pleasure of beating him, but got beaten themselves. And in addition to being shot this time, Anthony was still further "broke in" by a terrible

flogging from the Sheriff. The third time Anthony was shot
he was about twenty-one years of age. In this instance he was
punished for his old offence – he "would not be whipped."

This time his injury from being shot was light, compared
with the two preceding attacks. Also in connection with these
murderous conflicts, he could not forget that he had been sold
on the auction block. But he had still deeper thinking to do
yet. He determined that his young master should never get
"fifteen hundred dollars for him on the 1st of January," unless
he got them while he (Anthony) was running. For Anthony
had fully made up his mind that when the last day of December
ended, his bondage should end also, even if he should have
to accept death as a substitute. He then began to think of the
Underground Rail Road and of Canada; but who the agents
were, or how to find the depot, was a serious puzzle to him.
But his time was getting so short he was convinced that whatever he did would have to be done quickly. In this frame of
mind he found a man who professed to know something about
the Underground Rail Road, and for "thirty dollars" promised
to aid him in the matter.

The thirty dollars were raised by the hardest effort and
passed over to the pretended friend, with the expectation that
it would avail greatly in the emergency. But Anthony found
himself sold for thirty dollars, as nothing was done for him.
However, the 1st day of January arrived, but Anthony was not
to be found to answer to his name at roll call. He had "took
out" very early in the morning. Daily he prayed in his place
of concealment how to find the U.G.R.R. Ten months passed
away, during which time he suffered almost death, but

persuaded himself to believe that even that was better than slavery. With Anthony, as it has been with thousands of others similarly situated, just as everything was looking the most hopeless, word came to him in his place of concealment that a friend named Minkins, employed on the steamship *City of Richmond*, would undertake to conceal him on the boat, if he could be crowded in a certain place, which was about the only spot that would be perfectly safe. This was glorious news to Anthony; but it was well for him that he was ignorant of the situation that awaited him on the boat, or his heart might have failed him. He was willing, however, to risk his life for freedom, and, therefore, went joyfully.

The hiding-place was small and he was large. A sitting attitude was the only way he could possibly occupy it. He was contented. This place was "near the range, directly over the boiler," and of course, was very warm. Nevertheless, Anthony felt that he would not murmur, as he knew what suffering was pretty well, and especially as he took it for granted that he would be free in about a day and a half – the usual time it took the steamer to make her trip. At the appointed hour the steamer left Norfolk for Philadelphia, with Anthony sitting flat down in his U.G.R.R. berth, thoughtful and hopeful. But before the steamer had made half her distance the storm was tossing the ship hither and thither fearfully. Head winds blew terribly, and for a number of days the elements seemed perfectly mad. In addition to the extraordinary state of the weather, when the storm subsided the fog took its place and held the mastery of the ship with equal despotism until the end of over seven days, when finally the storm, wind, and fog all disappeared, and on the eighth day of her boisterous passage the steamship *City of Richmond* landed at the wharf of Philadelphia, with this giant and hero on board who had suffered for ten months in his concealment on land and for eight days on the ship.

Anthony was of very powerful physical proportions, being six feet three inches in height, quite black, very intelligent, and of a temperament that would not submit to slavery. For some years his master, Col. Cunnagan, had hired him out in Washington, where he was accused of being in the schooner *Pearl*, with Capt. Drayton's memorable "seventy fugitives on board, bound for Canada." At this time he was stoker in a machine shop, and was at work on an anchor weighing "ten thousand pounds." In the excitement over the attempt to escape in the *Pearl*, many were arrested, and the officers with irons visited Anthony at the machine shop to arrest him, but he declined to let them put the hand-cuffs on him, but consented to go with them, if permitted to do so without being ironed. The officers yielded, and Anthony went willingly to the jail. Passing unnoticed other interesting conflicts in his hard life, suffice it to say, he left his wife, Ann, and three children, Benjamin, John and Alfred, all owned by Col. Cunnagan. In this brave-hearted man, the Committee felt a deep interest, and accorded him their usual hospitalities.

SHERIDAN FORD

SECRETED IN THE WOODS –
ESCAPES IN A STEAMER.

About the twenty-ninth of January, 1855, Sheridan arrived from the Old Dominion and a life of bondage, and was welcomed cordially by the Vigilance Committee. Miss Elizabeth Brown of Portsmouth, Va. claimed Sheridan as her property. He spoke rather kindly of her, and felt that he "had not been used very hard" as a general thing, although, he wisely added, "the best usage was bad enough." Sheridan had nearly reached his twenty-eighth year, was tall and well made, and possessed of a considerable share of intelligence.

Not a great while before making up his mind to escape, for some trifling offence he had been "stretched up with a rope by his hands," and "whipped unmercifully." In addition to this he had "got wind of the fact," that he was to be auctioneered off; soon these things brought serious reflections to Sheridan's mind, and among other questions, he began to ponder how he could get a ticket on the U.G.R.R., and get out of this "place of torment," to where he might have the benefit of his own labor. In this state of mind, about the fourteenth day of November, he took his first and daring step. He went not, however, to learned lawyers or able ministers of the Gospel in his distress and trouble, but wended his way "directly to the woods," where he felt that he would be safer with the wild animals and reptiles, in solitude, than with the barbarous civilization that existed in Portsmouth.

The first day in the woods he passed in prayer incessantly, all alone. In this particular place of seclusion he remained "four days and nights," "two days suffered severely from hunger, cold and thirst." However, one who was a "friend" to him, and knew of his whereabouts, managed to get some food to him and consoling words; but at the end of the four days this friend got into some difficulty and thus Sheridan was left to "wade through deep waters and head winds" in an almost hopeless state. There he could not consent to stay and starve to death. Accordingly he left and found another place of seclusion – with a friend in the town – for a pecuniary consideration. A secret passage was procured for him on one of the steamers running between Philadelphia and Richmond, Va. When he left his poor wife, Julia, she was then "lying in prison to be sold," on the simple charge of having been suspected of conniving at her husband's escape. As a woman she had known something of the "barbarism of slavery", from every-day experience, which the large scars about her head indicated – according to Sheridan's testimony. She was the mother of two children, but had never been allowed to have the care of either of them. The husband, utterly powerless to offer her the least sympathy in word or deed, left this dark habitation of cruelty, as above referred to, with no hope of ever seeing wife or child again in this world.

The Committee afforded him the usual aid and comfort, and passed him on to the next station, with his face set towards Boston. He had heard the slaveholders "curse" Boston so much, that he concluded it must be a pretty safe place for the fugitive.

HENRY PREDO

BROKE JAIL, JUMPED OUT OF THE
WINDOW AND MADE HIS ESCAPE.

Henry fled from Buckstown, Dorchester Co., Md., March, 1857. Physically he is a giant. About 27 years of age, stout and well-made, quite black, and no fool, as will appear presently. Only a short time before he escaped, his master threatened to sell him south. To avoid that fate, therefore, he concluded to try his luck on the Underground Rail Road, and, in company with seven others – two of them females – he started for Canada. For two or three days and nights they managed to outgeneral all their adversaries, and succeeded bravely in making the best of their way to a Free State.

In the meantime, however, a reward of $3,000 was offered for their arrest. This temptation was too great to be resisted, even by the man who had been intrusted with the care of them, and who had faithfully promised to pilot them to a safe place. One night, through the treachery of their pretended conductor, they were all taken into Dover Jail, where the Sheriff and several others, who had been notified beforehand by the betrayer, were in readiness to receive them. Up stairs they were taken, the betrayer remarking as they were going up, that they were "cold, but would soon have a good warming." On a light being lit they discovered the iron bars and the fact that they had been betrayed. Their liberty-loving spirits and purposes, however, did not quail. Though resisted brutally by the Sheriff with revolver in hand, they made their way down one flight of stairs, and in the moment of excitement, as good luck would have it, plunged into the Sheriff's private apartment, where his wife and children were sleeping. The wife cried murder lustily. A shovel full of fire, to the great danger of burning the premises, was scattered over the room; out of the window jumped two of the female fugitives. Our hero Henry, seizing a heavy andiron, smashed out the window entire, through which the others leaped a distance of twelve feet. The railing or wall around the jail, though at first it looked forbidding, was soon surmounted by a desperate effort.

At this stage of the proceedings, Henry found himself without the walls, and also lost sight of his comrades at the same time. The last enemy he spied was the sheriff in his stockings without his shoes. He snapped his pistol at him, but it did not go off. Six of the others, however, marvellously got off safely together; where the eighth went, or how he got off, was not known.

MARY EPPS

ALIAS EMMA BROWN –
JOSEPH AND
ROBERT ROBINSON

A SLAVE MOTHER LOSES HER SPEECH AT THE SALE OF HER CHILD – BOB ESCAPES FROM HIS MASTER, A TRADER, WITH $1,500 IN NORTH CAROLINA MONEY.

Mary fled from Petersburg and the Robinsons from Richmond. A fugitive slave law-breaking captain by the name of B., who owned a schooner, and would bring any kind of freight that would pay the most, was the conductor in this instance. Quite a number of passengers at different times availed themselves of his accommodations and thus succeeded in reaching Canada.

His risk was very great. On this account he claimed, as did certain others, that it was no more than fair to charge for his services – indeed he did not profess to bring persons for nothing, except in rare instances. In this matter the Committee did not feel disposed to interfere directly in any way, further than to suggest that whatever understanding was agreed upon by the parties themselves should be faithfully adhered to.

Many slaves in cities could raise, "by hook or by crook," fifty or one hundred dollars to pay for a passage, providing they could find one who was willing to risk aiding them. Thus, while the Vigilance Committee of Philadelphia especially neither charged nor accepted anything for their services, it was not to be expected that any of the Southern agents could afford to do likewise.

The husband of Mary had for a long time wanted his own freedom, but did not feel that he could go without his wife; in fact, he resolved to get her off first, then to try and escape himself, if possible. The first essential step towards success, he considered, was to save his money and make it an object to the captain to help him. So when he had managed to lay by one hundred dollars, he willingly offered this sum to Captain B., if he would engage to deliver his wife into the hands of the Vigilance Committee of Philadelphia. The captain agreed to the terms and fulfilled his engagement to the letter. About the 1st of March, 1855, Mary was presented to the Vigilance Committee. She was of agreeable manners, about forty-five years of age, dark complexion, round built, and intelligent. She had been the mother of fifteen children, four of whom had been sold away from her; one was still held in slavery in Petersburg; the others were all dead.

At the sale of one of her children she was so affected with grief that she was thrown into violent convulsions, which caused the loss of her speech for one entire month. But this little episode was not a matter to excite sympathy in the breasts of the highly refined and tender-hearted Christian mothers of Petersburg. In the mercy of Providence, however, her reason and strength returned.

She had formerly belonged to the late Littleton Reeves, whom she represented as having been "kind" to her, much more so than her mistress (Mrs. Reeves). Said Mary, "She being of a jealous disposition, caused me to be hired out with a hard family, where I was much abused, frequently flogged, and stinted for food," etc.

But the sweets of freedom in the care of the Vigilance Committee now delighted her mind, and the hope that her husband would soon follow her to Canada, inspired her with expectations that she would one day "sit under her own vine and fig tree where none dared to molest or make her afraid."

The Committee rendered her the usual assistance, and in due time, forwarded her on to Queen Victoria's free land in Canada. On her arrival she wrote back as follows –

TORONTO,
March 14th, 1855.

DEAR MR. STILL: – I take this opportunity of addressing you with these few lines to inform you that I arrived here to-day, and hope that this may find yourself and Mrs. Still well, as this leaves me at the present. I will also say to you, that I had no difficulty in getting along. the two young men that was with me left me at Suspension Bridge. they went another way.

I cannot say much about the place as I have ben here but a short time but so far as I have seen I like very well. you will give my Respect to your lady, & Mr & Mrs Brown. If you have not written to Petersburg you will please to write as soon as can I have nothing More to Write at present but yours Respectfully

EMMA BROWN (old name MARY EPPS).

Now, Joseph and Robert (Mary's associate passengers from Richmond) must here be noticed. Joseph was of a dark orange color, medium size, very active and intelligent, and doubtless, well understood the art of behaving himself. He was well acquainted with the auction block – having been sold three times, and had had the misfortune to fall into the hands of a cruel master each time. Under these circumstances he had had but few privileges. Sundays and week days alike he was kept pretty severely bent down to duty. He had been beaten and knocked around shamefully. He had a wife, and spoke of her in most endearing language, although, on leaving, he did not feel at liberty to apprise her of his movements, "fearing that it would not be safe so to do." His four little children, to whom he appeared warmly attached, he left as he did his wife – in Slavery. He declared that he "stuck to them as long as he could." George E. Sadler, the keeper of an oyster house, held the deed for "Joe," and a most heartless wretch he was in Joe's estimation. The truth was, Joe could not stand the burdens and abuses which Sadler was inclined to heap upon him. So he concluded to join his brother and go off on the U.G.R.R.

Robert, his younger brother, was owned by Robert Slater, Esq., a regular negro trader. Eight years this slave's duties had been at the slave prison, and among other daily offices he had to attend to, was to lock up the prison, prepare the slaves for sale, etc. Robert was a very intelligent young man, and from long and daily experience with the customs and usages of the slave prison, he was as familiar with the business as a Pennsylvania farmer with his barn-yard stock. His account of things was too harrowing for detail here, except in the briefest manner, and that only with reference to a few particulars. In order to prepare slaves for the market, it was usual to have them greased and rubbed to make them look bright and shining. And he went on further to state, that "females as well as males were not uncommonly stripped naked, lashed flat to a bench, and then held by two men, sometimes four, while the brutal trader would strap them with a broad leather strap." The strap being preferred to the cow-hide, as it would not break the skin, and damage the sale. "One hundred lashes would only be a common flogging." The separation of families was thought nothing of. "Often I have been flogged for refusing to flog others." While not yet twenty-three years of age, Robert expressed himself as having become so daily sick of the brutality and suffering he could not help witnessing, that he felt he could not possibly stand it any longer, let the cost be what it might. In this state of mind he met with Captain B. Only one obstacle stood in his way – material aid. It occurred to Robert that he had frequent access to the money drawer, and often it contained the proceeds of fresh sales of flesh and blood; and he reasoned that if some of that would help him and his brother to freedom, there could be no harm in helping himself the first opportunity.

The captain was all ready, and provided he could get three passengers at $100 each he would set sail without much other freight. Of course he was too shrewd to get out papers for Philadelphia. That would betray him at once. Washington or Baltimore, or even Wilmington, Del., were names which stood fair in the eyes of Virginia. Consequently, being able to pack the fugitives away in a very private hole of his boat, and being only bound for a Southern port, the captain was willing to risk his share of the danger. "Very well," said Robert, "to-day I will please my master so well, that I will catch him at an unguarded moment, and will ask him for a pass to go to a ball to-night (slave-holders love to see their slaves fiddling and dancing of nights), and as I shall be leaving in a hurry, I will take a grab from the day's sale, and when Slater hears of me again, I will be in Canada." So after having attended to all his disagreeable duties, he made his "grab," and got a hand full. He did not know, however, how it would hold out. That evening, instead of participating with the gay dancers, he was just one degree lower down than the regular bottom of Captain B's. deck, with several hundred dollars in his pocket, after paying the worthy captain one hundred each for himself and his brother, besides making the captain an additional present of nearly one hundred. Wind and tide were now what they prayed for to speed on the U.G.R.R. schooner, until they might reach the depot at Philadelphia.

The Richmond *Dispatch*, an enterprising paper in the interest of slaveholders, which came daily to the Committee, was received in advance of the passengers, when lo! and behold, in turning to the interesting column containing the elegant illustrations of "runaway negroes," it was seen that the unfortunate Slater had "lost $1,500 in North Carolina money, and also his dark orange-colored, intelligent, and good-looking turnkey, Bob." "Served him right, it is no stealing for one piece of property to go off with another piece," reasoned a member of the Committee.

In a couple of days after the *Dispatch* brought the news, the three U.G.R.R. passengers were safely landed at the usual place, and so accurate were the descriptions in the paper, that, on first seeing them, the Committee recognized them instantly, and, without any previous ceremonies, read to them the advertisement relative to the "$1,500 in N.C. money, &c.," and put the question to them direct: "Are you the ones?" "We are," they owned up without hesitation. The Committee did not see a dollar of their money, but understood they had about $900, after paying the captain; while Bob considered he made a "very good grab," he did not admit that the amount advertised was correct. After a reasonable time for recruiting, having been so long in the hole of the vessel, they took their departure for Canada.

From Joseph, the elder brother, is appended a short letter, announcing their arrival and condition under the British Lion –

SAINT CATHARINE,
April 16, 1855.

MR. WILLIAM STILL, DEAR SIR: – Your letter of date April 7th I have just got, it had been opened before it came to me. I have not received any other letter from you and can get no account of them in the Post Office in this place. I am well and have got a good situation in this city and intend staying here. I should be very glad to hear from you as soon as convenient and also from all of my friends near you. My Brother is also at work with me and doing well.

There is nothing here that would interest you in the way of news. There is a Masonic Lodge of our people and two churches and societys here and some other institutions for our benefit. Be kind enough to send a few lines to the Lady spoken of for that mocking bird and much oblige me. Write me soon and believe me your obedient Serv't

Love & respects to Lady and daughter

JOSEPH ROBINSON.

As well as writing to a member of the Committee, Joe and Bob had the assurance to write back to the trader and oyster-house keeper. In their letter they stated that they had arrived safely in Canada, and were having good times, – in the eating line had an abundance of the best, – also had very choice wines and brandies, which they supposed that they (trader and oyster-house keeper) would give a great deal to have a "smack at." And then they gave them a very cordial invitation to make them a visit, and suggested that the quickest way they could come would be by telegraph, which they admitted was slightly dangerous, and without first greasing themselves, and then hanging on very fast, the journey might not prove altogether advantageous to them. This was wormwood and gall to the trader and oyster-house man. A most remarkable coincidence was that, about the time this letter was received in Richmond, the captain who brought away the three passengers, made it his business for some reason or other, to call at the oyster-house kept by the owner of Joe, and while there, this letter was read and commented on in torrents of Billingsgate phrases; and the trader told the captain that he would give him "two thousand dollars if he would get them;" finally he told him he would "give every cent they would bring, which would be much over $2,000," as they were "so very likely." How far the captain talked approvingly, he did not exactly tell the Committee, but they guessed he talked strong Democratic doctrine to them under the frightful circumstances. But he was good at concealing his feelings, and obviously managed to avoid suspicion.

HENRY BOX BROWN

ARRIVED BY ADAMS' EXPRESS.

Although the name of Henry Box Brown has been echoed over the land for a number of years, and the simple facts connected with his marvelous escape from slavery in a box published widely through the medium of anti-slavery papers, nevertheless it is not unreasonable to suppose that very little is generally known in relation to this case.

Briefly, the facts are these, which doubtless have never before been fully published –

Brown was a man of invention as well as a hero. In point of interest, however, his case is no more remarkable than many others. Indeed, neither before nor after escaping did he suffer one-half what many others have experienced.

He was decidedly an unhappy piece of property in the city of Richmond, Va. In the condition of a slave he felt that it would be impossible for him to remain. Full well did he know, however, that it was no holiday task to escape the vigilance of Virginia slave-hunters, or the wrath of an enraged master for committing the unpardonable sin of attempting to escape to a land of liberty. So Brown counted well the cost before venturing upon this hazardous undertaking. Ordinary modes of travel he concluded might prove disastrous to his hopes; he, therefore, hit upon a new invention altogether, which was to have himself boxed up and forwarded to Philadelphia direct by express. The size of the box and how it was to be made to fit him most comfortably, was of his own ordering. Two feet eight inches deep, two feet wide, and three feet long were the exact dimensions of the box, lined with baize. His resources with regard to food and water consisted of the following: One bladder of water and a few small biscuits. His mechanical implement to meet the death-struggle for fresh air, all told, was one large gimlet. Satisfied that it would be far better to peril his life for freedom in this way than to remain under the galling yoke of Slavery, he entered his box, which was safely nailed up and hooped with five hickory hoops, and was then addressed by his next friend, James A. Smith, a shoe dealer, to Wm. H. Johnson, Arch street, Philadelphia, marked, "This side up with care." In this condition he was sent to Adams' Express office in a dray, and thence by overland express to Philadelphia. It was twenty-six hours from the time he left Richmond until his arrival in the City of Brotherly Love. The notice, "This side up, &c.," did not avail with the different expressmen, who hesitated not to handle the box in the usual rough manner common to this class of men. For a while they actually had the box upside down, and had him on his head for miles. A few days before he was expected, certain intimation was conveyed to a member of the Vigilance Committee that a box might be expected by the three o'clock morning train from the South, which might contain a man. One of the most serious walks he ever took – and they had not been a few – to meet and accompany passengers, he took at half past two o'clock that morning to the depot. Not once, but for more than a score of times, he fancied the slave would be dead. He anxiously looked while the freight was being unloaded from the cars, to see if he could recognize a box that might contain a man; one alone had that appearance, and he confessed it really seemed as if there was the scent of death about it. But on inquiry, he soon learned that it was not the one he was looking after, and he was free to say he experienced a marked sense of relief. That same afternoon, however, he received from Richmond a telegram, which read thus, "Your case of goods is shipped and will arrive to-morrow morning."

At this exciting juncture of affairs, Mr. McKim, who had been engineering this important undertaking, deemed it expedient to change the programme slightly in one particular at least to insure greater safety. Instead of having a member of the Committee go again to the depot for the box, which might excite suspicion, it was decided that it would be safest to have the express bring it direct to the Anti-Slavery Office.

But all apprehension of danger did not now disappear, for there was no room to suppose that Adams' Express office had any sympathy with the Abolitionist or the fugitive, consequently for Mr. McKim to appear personally at the express office to give directions with reference to the coming of a box from Richmond which would be directed to Arch street, and yet not intended for that street, but for the Anti-Slavery office at 107 North Fifth street, it needed of course no great discernment to foresee that a step of this kind was wholly impracticable and that a more indirect and covert method would have to be adopted. In this dreadful crisis Mr. McKim, with his usual good judgment and remarkably quick, strategical mind, especially in matters pertaining to the U.G.R.R., hit upon the following plan, namely, to go to his friend, E.M. Davis,[3] who was then extensively engaged in mercantile business, and relate

---

3   E.M. Davis was a member of the Executive Committee of the Pennsylvania Anti-Slavery Society and a long-tried Abolitionist, son-in-law of James and Lucretia Mott.

the circumstances. Having daily intercourse with said Adams' Express office, and being well acquainted with the firm and some of the drivers, Mr. Davis could, as Mr. McKim thought, talk about "boxes, freight, etc.," from any part of the country without risk. Mr. Davis heard Mr. McKim's plan and instantly approved of it, and was heartily at his service.

RESURRECTION OF HENRY BOX BROWN

"Dan, an Irishman, one of Adams' Express drivers, is just the fellow to go to the depot after the box," said Davis. "He drinks a little too much whiskey sometimes, but he will do anything I ask him to do, promptly and obligingly. I'll trust Dan, for I believe he is the very man." The difficulty which Mr. McKim had been so anxious to overcome was thus pretty well settled. It was agreed that Dan should go after the box next morning before daylight and bring it to the Anti-Slavery office direct, and to make it all the more agreeable for Dan to get up out of his warm bed and go on this errand before day, it was decided that he should have a five dollar gold piece for himself. Thus these preliminaries having been satisfactorily arranged, it only remained for Mr. Davis to see Dan and give him instructions accordingly, etc.

Next morning, according to arrangement, the box was at the Anti-Slavery office in due time. The witnesses present to behold the resurrection were J.M. McKim, Professor C.D. Cleveland, Lewis Thompson, and the writer.

Mr. McKim was deeply interested; but having been long identified with the Anti-Slavery cause as one of its oldest and ablest advocates in the darkest days of slavery and mobs, and always found by the side of the fugitive to counsel and succor, he was on this occasion perfectly composed.

Professor Cleveland, however, was greatly moved. His zeal and earnestness in the cause of freedom, especially in rendering aid to passengers, knew no limit. Ordinarily he could not too often visit these travelers, shake them too warmly by the hand, or impart to them too freely of his substance to aid them on their journey. But now his emotion was overpowering.

Mr. Thompson, of the firm of Merrihew & Thompson – about the only printers in the city who for many years dared to print such incendiary documents as anti-slavery papers and pamphlets – one of the truest friends of the slave, was composed and prepared to witness the scene.

All was quiet. The door had been safely locked. The proceedings commenced. Mr. McKim rapped quietly on the lid of the box and called out, "All right!" Instantly came the answer from within, "All right, sir!"

The witnesses will never forget that moment. Saw and hatchet quickly had the five hickory hoops cut and the lid off, and the marvellous resurrection of Brown ensued. Rising up in his box, he reached out his hand, saying, "How do you do, gentlemen?" The little assemblage hardly knew what to think or do at the moment. He was about as wet as if he had come up out of the Delaware. Very soon he remarked that, before leaving Richmond he had selected for his arrival-hymn (if he lived) the Psalm beginning with these words: "I waited patiently for the Lord, and He heard my prayer." And most touchingly did he sing the psalm, much to his own relief, as well as to the delight of his small audience.

He was then christened Henry Box Brown, and soon afterwards was sent to the hospitable residence of James Mott and E.M. Davis, on Ninth street, where, it is needless to say, he met a most cordial reception from Mrs. Lucretia Mott and her household. Clothing and creature comforts were furnished in abundance, and delight and joy filled all hearts in that stronghold of philanthropy.

As he had been so long doubled up in the box he needed to promenade considerably in the fresh air, so James Mott put one of his broad-brim hats on his head and tendered him the hospitalities of his yard as well as his house, and while Brown promenaded the yard flushed with victory, great was the joy of his friends.

After his visit at Mr. Mott's, he spent two days with the writer, and then took his departure for Boston, evidently feeling quite conscious of the wonderful feat he had performed, and at the same time it may be safely said that those who witnessed this strange resurrection were not only elated at his success, but were made to sympathize more deeply than ever before with the slave. Also the noble-hearted Smith who boxed him up was made to rejoice over Brown's victory, and was thereby encouraged to render similar service to two other young bondmen, who appealed to him for deliverance. But, unfortunately, in this attempt the undertaking proved a failure. Two boxes containing the young men alluded to above, after having been duly expressed and some distance on the road, were, through the agency of the telegraph, betrayed, and the heroic young fugitives were captured in their boxes and dragged back to hopeless bondage. Consequently, through this deplorable failure, Samuel A. Smith was arrested, imprisoned, and was called upon to suffer severely, as may be seen from the subjoined correspondence, taken from the *New York Tribune* soon after his release from the penitentiary.

THE DELIVERER OF BOX BROWN – MEETING OF THE COLORED CITIZENS OF PHILADELPHIA
[Correspondence of the *N.Y. Tribune*.]

PHILADELPHIA,
Saturday, July 5, 1856.

Samuel A. Smith, who boxed up Henry Box Brown in Richmond, Va., and forwarded him by overland express to Philadelphia, and who was arrested and convicted, eight years ago, for boxing up two other slaves, also directed to Philadelphia, having served out his imprisonment in the Penitentiary, was released on the 18th ultimo, and arrived in this city on the 21st.

Though he lost all his property; though he was refused witnesses on his trial (no officer could be found, who would serve a summons on a witness); though for five long months, in hot weather, he was kept heavily chained in a cell four by eight feet in dimensions; though he received five dreadful stabs, aimed at his heart, by a bribed assassin, nevertheless he still rejoices in the motives which prompted him to "undo the heavy burdens, and let the oppressed go free." Having resided nearly all his life in the South, where he had traveled and seen much of the "peculiar institution," and had witnessed the most horrid enormities inflicted upon the slave, whose cries were ever ringing in his ears, and for whom he had the warmest sympathy, Mr. Smith could not refrain from believing that the black man, as well as the white, had God-given rights. Consequently, he was not accustomed to shed tears when a poor creature escaped ftom his "kind master;" nor was he willing to turn a deaf ear to his appeals and groans, when he knew he was thirsting for freedom. From 1828 up to the day he was incarcerated, many had sought his aid and counsel, nor had they sought in vain. In various places he operated with success. In Richmond, however, it seemed expedient to invent a new plan for certain emergencies, hence the Box and Express plan was devised, at the instance of a few heroic slaves, who had manifested their willingness to die in a box, on the road to liberty, rather than continue longer under the yoke. But these heroes fell into the power of their enemies. Mr. Smith had not been long in the Penitentiary before he had fully gained the esteem and confidence of the Superintendent and other officers. Finding him to be humane and generous-hearted – showing kindness toward all, especially in buying bread, &c., for the starving prisoners, and by a timely note of warning, which had saved the life of one of the keepers, for whose destruction a bold plot had been arranged – the officers felt disposed to show him such favors as the law would allow. But their good intentions were soon frustrated. The Inquisition (commonly called the Legislature), being in session in Richmond, hearing that the Superintendent had been speaking well of Smith, and circulating a petition for his pardon, indignantly demanded to know if the rumor was well founded. Two weeks were spent by the Inquisition, and many witnesses were placed upon oath, to solemnly testify in the matter. One of the keepers swore that his life had been saved by Smith. Col. Morgan, the Superintendent, frequently testified in writing and verbally to Smith's good deportment; acknowledging that he had circulated petitions, &c.; and took the position, that he sincerely believed, that it would be to the interest of the institution to pardon him; calling the attention of the Inquisition, at the same time, to the fact, that not unfrequently pardons had been granted to criminals, under sentence of death, for the most cold-blooded murder, to say nothing of other gross crimes. The effort for pardon was soon abandoned, for the following reason given by the Governor: "I can't, and I won't pardon him!"

In view of the unparalleled injustice which Mr. S. had suffered, as well as on account of the aid he had rendered to the slaves, on his arrival in this city the colored citizens of Philadelphia felt that he was entitled to sympathy and aid, and straightway invited him to remain a few days, until arrangements could be made for a mass meeting to receive him. Accordingly, on last Monday evening, a mass meeting convened in the Israel church, and the Rev. Wm. T. Catto was called to the chair, and Wm. Still was appointed secretary. The chairman briefly stated the object of the meeting. Having lived in the South, he claimed to know something of the workings of the oppressive system of slavery generally, and declared that, notwithstanding the many exposures of the evil which came under his own observation, the most vivid descriptions fell far short of the realities his own eyes had witnessed. He then introduced Mr. Smith, who arose and in a plain manner briefly told his story, assuring the audience that he had always hated slavery, and had taken great pleasure in helping many out of it, and though he had suffered much physically and pecuniarily for the cause' sake, yet he murmured not, but rejoiced in what he had done. After taking his seat, addresses were made by the Rev. S. Smith, Messrs. Kinnard, Brunner, Bradway, and others. The following preamble and resolutions were adopted –

WHEREAS, We, the colored citizens of Philadelphia, have among us Samuel A. Smith, who was incarcerated over seven years in the Richmond Penitentiary, for doing an act that was honorable to his feelings and his sense of justice and humanity, therefore,

Resolved, That we welcome him to this city as a martyr to the cause of Freedom.

Resolved, That we heartily tender him our gratitude for the good he has done to our suffering race.

Resolved, That we sympathize with him in his losses and sufferings in the cause of the poor, down-trodden slave.

W.S.

During his stay in Philadelphia, on this occasion, he stopped for about a fortnight with the writer, and it was most gratifying to learn from him that he was no new worker on the U.G.R.R. But that he had long hated slavery thoroughly, and although surrounded with perils on every side, he had not failed to help a poor slave whenever the opportunity was presented.

Pecuniary aid, to some extent, was rendered him in this city, for which he was grateful, and after being united in marriage, by Wm. H. Furness, D.D., to a lady who had remained faithful to him through all his sore trials and sufferings, he took his departure for Western New York, with a good conscience and an unshaken faith in the belief that in aiding his fellow-man to freedom he had but simply obeyed the word of Him who taught man to do unto others as he would be done by.

A SLAVE GIRL'S NARRATIVE

CORDELIA LONEY, SLAVE OF MRS. JOSEPH CAHELL (WIDOW OF THE LATE HON. JOSEPH CAHELL, OF VA.), OF FREDERICKSBURG, VA. – CORDELIA'S ESCAPE FROM HER MISTRESS IN PHILADELPHIA.

Rarely did the peculiar institution present the relations of mistress and maid-servant in a light so apparently favorable as in the case of Mrs. Joseph Cahell (widow of the late Hon. Jos. Cahell, of Va.), and her slave, Cordelia. The Vigilance Committee's first knowledge of either of these memorable personages was brought about in the following manner.

About the 30th of March, in the year 1859, a member of the Vigilance Committee was notified by a colored servant, living at a fashionable boarding-house on Chestnut street that a lady with a slave woman from Fredericksburg, Va., was boarding at said house, and, that said slave woman desired to receive counsel and aid from the Committee, as she was anxious to secure her freedom, before her mistress returned to the South. On further consultation about the matter, a suitable hour was named for the meeting of the Committee and the Slave at the above named boarding-house. Finding that the woman was thoroughly reliable, the Committee told her "that two modes of deliverance were open before her. One was to take her trunk and all her clothing and quietly retire." The other was to "sue out a writ of habeas corpus; and bring the mistress before the Court, where she would be required, under the laws of Pennsylvania, to show cause why she restrained this woman of her freedom." Cordelia concluded to adopt the former expedient, provided the Committee would protect her. Without hesitation the Committee answered her, that to the extent of their ability, she should have their aid with pleasure, without delay. Consequently a member of the Committee was directed to be on hand at a given hour that evening, as Cordelia would certainly be ready to leave her mistress to take care of herself. Thus, at the appointed hour, Cordelia, very deliberately, accompanied the Committee away from her "kind hearted old mistress."

In the quiet and security of the Vigilance Committee Room, Cordelia related substantially the following brief story touching her relationship as a slave to Mrs. Joseph Cahell. In this case, as with thousands and tens of thousands of others, as the old adage fitly expresses it, "All is not gold that glitters." Under this apparently pious and noble-minded lady, it will be seen, that Cordelia had known naught but misery and sorrow.

Mrs. Cahell, having engaged board for a month at a fashionable private boarding-house on Chestnut street, took an early opportunity to caution Cordelia against going into the streets, and against having anything to say or do with "free niggers in particular"; withal, she appeared unusually kind, so much so, that before retiring to bed in the evening, she would call Cordelia to her chamber, and by her side would take her Prayer-book and Bible, and go through the forms of devotional service. She stood very high both as a church communicant and a lady in society.

For a fortnight it seemed as though her prayers were to be answered, for Cordelia apparently bore herself as submissively as ever, and Madame received calls and accepted invitations from some of the *elite* of the city, without suspecting any intention on the part of Cordelia to escape. But Cordelia could not forget how her children had all been sold by her mistress!

Cordelia was about fifty-seven years of age, with about an equal proportion of colored and white blood in her veins; very neat, respectful and prepossessing in manner.

From her birth to the hour of her escape she had worn the yoke under Mrs. C., as her most efficient and reliable maid-servant. She had been at her mistress' beck and call as seamstress, dressing-maid, nurse in the sickroom, etc., etc., under circumstances that might appear to the casual observer uncommonly favorable for a slave. Indeed, on his first interview with her, the Committee man was so forcibly impressed with the belief, that her condition in Virginia had been favorable, that he hesitated to ask her if she did not desire her liberty. A few moments' conversation with her, however, convinced him of her good sense and decision of purpose with regard to this matter. For, in answer to the first question he put to her, she answered, that, "As many creature comforts and religious privileges as she had been the recipient of under her 'kind mistress,' still she 'wanted to be free,' and 'was bound to leave,' that she had been 'treated very cruelly,' that her children had 'all been sold away' from her; that she had been threatened with sale herself 'on the first insult,'" etc.

She was willing to take the entire responsibility of taking care of herself. On the suggestion of a friend, before leaving her mistress, she was disposed to sue for her freedom, but, upon a reconsideration of the matter, she chose rather to accept the hospitality of the Underground Rail Road, and leave in a quiet way and go to Canada, where she would be free indeed. Accordingly she left her mistress and was soon a free woman.

The following sad experience she related calmly, in the presence of several friends, an evening or two after she left her mistress:

Two sons and two daughters had been sold from her by her mistress, within the last three years, since the death of her master. Three of her children had been sold to the Richmond market and the other in Nelson county.

Paulina was the first sold, two years ago last May. Nat was the next; he was sold to Abram Warrick, of Richmond. Paulina was sold before it was named to her mother that it had entered her mistress's mind to dispose of her. Nancy, from infancy, had been in poor health. Nevertheless, she had been obliged to take her place in the field with the rest of the slaves, of more rugged constitution, until she had passed her twentieth year, and had become a mother. Under these circumstances, the overseer and his wife complained to the mistress that her health was really too bad for a field hand and begged that she might be taken where her duties would be less oppressive. Accordingly, she was withdrawn from the field, and was set to spinning and weaving. When too sick to work her mistress invariably took the ground, that "nothing was the matter," notwithstanding the fact, that her family physician, Dr. Ellsom, had pronounced her "quite weakly and sick."

In an angry mood one day, Mrs. Cahell declared she would cure her; and again sent her to the field, "with orders to the overseer, to whip her every day, and make her work or kill her." Again the overseer said it was "no use to try, for her health would not stand it," and she was forthwith returned. The mistress then concluded to sell her.

One Sabbath evening a nephew of hers, who resided in New Orleans, happened to be on a visit to his aunt, when it occurred to her, that she had "better get Nancy off if possible."

Accordingly, Nancy was called in for examination. Being dressed in her "Sunday best" and "before a poor candle-light," she appeared to good advantage; and the nephew concluded to start with her on the following Tuesday morning. However, the next morning, he happened to see her by the light of the sun, and in her working garments, which satisfied him that he had been grossly deceived; that she would barely live to reach New Orleans; he positively refused to carry out the previous evening's contract, thus leaving her in the hands of her mistress, with the advice, that she should "doctor her up."

The mistress, not disposed to be defeated, obviated the difficulty by selecting a little boy, made a lot of the two, and thus made it an inducement to a purchaser to buy the sick woman; the boy and the woman brought $700.

In the sale of her children, Cordelia was as little regarded as if she had been a cow.

"I felt wretched," she said, with emphasis, "when I heard that Nancy had been sold," which was not until after she had been removed. "But," she continued, "I was not at liberty to make my grief known to a single white soul. I wept and couldn't help it." But remembering that she was liable, "on the first insult," to be sold herself, she sought no sympathy from her mistress, whom she describes as "a woman who shows as little kindness towards her servants as any woman in the States of America. She neither likes to feed nor clothe well."

With regard to flogging, however, in days past, she had been up to the mark. "A many a slap and blow" had Cordelia received since she arrived at womanhood, directly from the madam's own hand.

One day smarting under cruel treatment, she appealed to her mistress in the following strain: "I stood by your mother in all her sickness and nursed her till she died!" "I waited on your niece, night and day for months, till she died." "I waited upon your husband all my life – in his sickness especially, and shrouded him in death, etc., yet I am treated cruelly." It was of no avail.

Her mistress, at one time, was the owner of about five hundred slaves, but within the last few years she had greatly lessened the number by sales.

She stood very high as a lady, and was a member of the Episcopal Church.

To punish Cordelia, on several occasions, she had been sent to one of the plantations to work as a field hand. Fortunately, however, she found the overseers more compassionate than her mistress, though she received no particular favors from any of them.

Asking her to name the overseers, etc., she did so. The first was "Marks, a thin-visaged, poor-looking man, great for swearing." The second was "Gilbert Brower, a very rash, portly man." The third was "Buck Young, a stout man, and very sharp." The fourth was "Lynn Powell, a tall man with red whiskers, very contrary and spiteful." There was also a fifth one, but his name was lost.

Thus Cordelia's experience, though chiefly confined to the "great house," extended occasionally over the corn and tobacco fields, among the overseers and field hands generally. But under no circumstances could she find it in her heart to be thankful for the privileges of Slavery.

After leaving her mistress she learned, with no little degree of pleasure, that a perplexed state of things existed at the boarding-house; that her mistress was seriously puzzled to imagine how she would get her shoes and stockings on and off; how she would get her head combed, get dressed, be attended to in sickness, etc., as she (Cordelia), had been compelled to discharge these offices all her life.

Most of the boarders, being slave-holders, naturally sympathized in her affliction; and some of them went so far as to offer a reward to some of the colored servants to gain a knowledge of her whereabouts. Some charged the servants with having a hand in her leaving, but all agreed that "she had left a very kind and indulgent mistress," and had acted very foolishly in running out of Slavery into Freedom.

A certain Doctor of Divinity, the pastor of an Episcopal church in this city and a friend of the mistress, hearing of her distress, by request or voluntarily, undertook to find out Cordelia's place of seclusion. Hailing on the street a certain colored man with a familiar face, who he thought knew nearly all the colored people about town, he related to him the predicament of his lady friend from the South, remarked how kindly she had always treated her servants, signified that Cordelia would rue the change, and be left to suffer among the "miserable blacks down town," that she would not be able to take care of herself; quoted Scripture justifying Slavery, and finally suggested that he (the colored man) would be doing a duty and a kindness to the fugitive by using his influence to "find her and prevail upon her to return."

It so happened that the colored man thus addressed, was Thomas Dorsey, the well-known fashionable caterer of Philadelphia, who had had the experience of quite a number of years as a slave at the South, – had himself once been pursued as a fugitive, and having, by his industry in the condition of Freedom, acquired a handsome estate, he felt entirely qualified to reply to the reverend gentleman, which he did, though in not very respectful phrases, telling him that Cordelia had as good a right to her liberty as he had, or her mistress either; that God had never intended one man to be the slave of another; that it was all false about the slaves being better off than the free colored people; that he would find as many "poor, miserably degraded," of his own color "down-town," as among the "degraded blacks"; and concluded by telling him that he would "rather give her a hundred dollars to help her off, than to do aught to make known her whereabouts, if he knew ever so much about her."

What further steps were taken by the discomfited divine, the mistress, or her boarding-house sympathizers, the Committee was not informed.

But with regard to Cordelia: she took her departure for Canada, in the midst of the Daniel Webster (fugitive) trial, with the hope of being permitted to enjoy the remainder of her life in Freedom and peace. Being a member of the Baptist Church, and professing to be a Christian, she was persuaded that, by industry and assistance of the Lord, a way would be opened to the seeker of Freedom even in a strange land and among strangers.

This story appeared in part in the *N.Y. Evening Post*, having been furnished by the writer, without his name to it. It is certainly none the less interesting now, as it may be read in the light of Universal Emancipation.

ARRIVAL OF
JACKSON, ISAAC, AND
EDMONDSON TURNER
FROM PETERSBURG

*TOUCHING SCENE ON MEETING
THEIR OLD BLIND FATHER AT THE
U.G.R.R. DEPOT.*

LETTERS AND WARNING TO SLAVEHOLDERS.

About the latter part of December, 1857, Isaac and Edmondson, brothers, succeeded in making their escape together from Petersburg, Va. They barely escaped the auction block, as their mistress, Mrs. Ann Colley, a widow, had just completed arrangements for their sale on the coming first day of January. In this kind of property, however, Mrs. Colley had not largely invested. In the days of her prosperity, while all was happy and contented, she could only boast of "four head:" these brothers, Jackson, Isaac and Edmondson and one other. In May, 1857, Jackson had fled and was received by the Vigilance Committee, who placed upon their books briefly in the following light:

RUNAWAY – *Fifty Dollars Reward,* – Ran away some time in May last, my *Servantman*, who calls himself *Jackson Turner*. He is about 27 years of age, and has one of his front teeth out. He is quite black, with thick lips, a little bow-legged, and looks down when spoken to. I will give a reward of Fifty dollars if taken out of the city, and, twenty five Dollars if taken within the city. I forewarn all masters of vessels from harboring or employing the said slave; all persons who disregard this Notice will be punished as the law directs.

Petersburg, June 8th, 1857

ANN COLLEY.

JACKSON is quite dark, medium size, and well informed for one in his condition. In Slavery, he had been "pressed hard." His hire, "ten dollars per month" he was obliged to produce at the end of each month, no matter how much he had been called upon to expend for "doctor bills, &c." The woman he called mistress went by the name of Ann Colley, a widow, living near Petersburg. "She was very quarrelsome," although a "member of the Methodist Church." Jackson seeing that his mistress was yearly growing "harder and harder," concluded to try and better his condition "if possible." Having a free wife in the North, who was in the habit of communicating with him, he was kept fully awake to the love of Freedom. The Underground Rail Road expense the Committee gladly bore. No further record of Jackson was made. Jackson found his poor old father here, where he had resided for a number of years in a state of almost total blindness, and of course in much parental anxiety about his boys in chains. On the arrival of Jackson, his heart overflowed with joy and gratitude not easily described, as the old man had hardly been able to muster faith enough to believe that he should ever look with his dim eyes upon one of his sons in Freedom. After a day or two's tarrying, Jackson took his departure for safer and more healthful localities, – her "British Majesty's possessions." The old man remained only to feel more keenly than ever, the pang of having sons still toiling in hopeless servitude.

In less than seven months after Jackson had shaken off the yoke, to the unspeakable joy of the father, Isaac and Edmondson succeeded in following their brother's example, and were made happy partakers of the benefits and blessings of the Vigilance Committee of Philadelphia. On first meeting his two boys, at the Underground Rail Road Depot, the old man took each one in his arms, and as looking through a glass darkly, straining every nerve of his almost lost sight, exclaiming, whilst hugging them closer and closer to his bosom for some minutes, in tears of joy and wonder, "My son Isaac, is this you? my son Isaac, is this you, &c.?" The scene was calculated to awaken the deepest emotion and to bring tears to eyes not accustomed to weep. Little had the old man dreamed in his days of sadness, that he should share such a feast of joy over the deliverance of his sons. But it is in vain to attempt to picture the affecting scene at this reunion, for that would be impossible. Of their slave life, the records contain but a short notice, simply as follows:

"Isaac is twenty-eight years of age, hearty-looking, well made, dark color and intelligent. He was owned by Mrs. Ann Colley, a widow, residing near Petersburg, Va. Isaac and Edmondson were to have been sold, on New Year's day; a few days hence. How sad her disappointment must have been on finding them gone, may be more easily imagined than described."

Edmondson is about twenty-five, a brother of Isaac, and a smart, good-looking young man, was owned by Mrs. Colley also. "This is just the class of fugitives to make good subjects for John Bull," thought the Committee, feeling pretty well assured that they would make good reports after having enjoyed free air in Canada for a short time. Of course, the Committee enjoined upon them very earnestly "not to forget their brethren left behind groaning in fetters; but to prove by their industry, uprightness, economy, sobriety and thrift, by the remembrance of their former days of oppression and their obligations to their God, that they were worthy of the country to which they were going, and so to help break the bands of the oppressors, and undo the heavy burdens of the oppressed." Similar advice was impressed upon the minds of all travelers passing over this branch of the Underground Rail Road. From hundreds thus admonished, letters came affording the most gratifying evidence that the counsel of the Committee was not in vain. The appended letter from the youngest brother, written with his own hand, will indicate his feelings and views in Canada:

HAMILTON, CANADA WEST
Mar. 1, 1858.

MR. STILL, DEAR SIR: – I have taken the oppertunity to enform you yur letter came to hand 27th I ware glad to hear from you and yer famly i hope this letter May fine you and the famly Well i am Well my self My Brother join me in Love to you and all the frend. I ware sorry to hear of the death of Mrs freaman. We all must die sune or Late this a date we all must pay we must Perpar for the time she ware a nise lady dear sir the all is well and san thar love to you Emerline have Ben sick But is better at this time. I saw the hills the war well and san thar Love to you. I war sory to hear that My brother war sol i am glad that i did come away when i did god works all the things for the Best he is young he may get a long in the wole May god Bless hem ef you have any News from Petersburg Va Plas Rite me a word when you anser this Letter and ef any person came form home Letter Me know. Please sen me one of your Paper that had the under grands R wrod give My Love to Mr Careter and his family I am Seving with a barber at this time he have promust to give me the trad ef i can lane it he is much of a gentman. Mr Still sir i have writing a letter to Mr Brown of Petersburg Va Pleas reed it and ef you think it right Plas sen it by the Mail or by hand you wall see how i have writen it the will know how sent it by the way this writing ef the ancer it you can sen it to Me i have tol them direc to yor care for Ed. t. Smith Philadelphia i hope it may be right i promorst to rite to hear Please rite to me sune and let me know ef you do sen it on write wit you did with that ma a bught the cappet Bage do not fergit to rite tal John he mite rite to Me. I am doing as well is i can at this time but i get no wagges But my Bord but is satfid at that thes hard time and glad that i am Hear and in good helth. Northing More at this time

yor truly

EDMUND TURNER.

ROBERT BROWN
ALIAS THOMAS JONES

CROSSING THE RIVER ON
HORSEBACK IN THE NIGHT.

In very desperate straits many new inventions were sought after by deep-thinking and resolute slaves, determined to be free at any cost. But it must here be admitted, that, in looking carefully over the more perilous methods resorted to, Robert Brown, alias Thomas Jones, stands second to none, with regard to deeds of bold daring. This hero escaped from Martinsburg, Va., in 1856. He was a man of medium size, mulatto, about thirty-eight years of age, could read and write, and was naturally sharp-witted. He had formerly been owned by Col. John F. Franie, whom Robert charged with various offences of a serious domestic character.

Furthermore, he also alleged, that his "mistress was cruel to all the slaves," declaring that "they (the slaves), could not live with her," that "she had to hire servants," etc.

In order to effect his escape, Robert was obliged to swim the Potomac river on horseback, on Christmas night, while the cold, wind, storm, and darkness were indescribably dismal. This daring bondman, rather than submit to his oppressor any longer, perilled his life as above stated. Where he crossed the river was about a half a mile wide. Where could be found in history a more noble and daring struggle for Freedom?

The wife of his bosom and his four children, only five days before he fled, were sold to a trader in Richmond, Va., for no other offence than simply "because she had resisted" the lustful designs of her master, being "true to her own companion." After this poor slave mother and her children were cast into prison for sale, the husband and some of his friends tried hard to find a purchaser in the neighborhood; but the malicious and brutal master refused to sell her – wishing to gratify his malice to the utmost, and to punish his victims all that lay in his power, he sent them to the place above named.

In this trying hour, the severed and bleeding heart of the husband resolved to escape at all hazards, taking with him a daguerreotype likeness of his wife which he happened to have on hand, and a lock of hair from her head, and from each of the children, as mementoes of his unbounded (though sundered) affection for them.

After crossing the river, his wet clothing freezing to him, he rode all night, a distance of about forty miles. In the morning he left his faithful horse tied to a fence, quite broken down. He then commenced his dreary journey on foot – cold and hungry – in a strange place, where it was quite unsafe to make known his condition and wants. Thus for a day or two, without food or shelter, he traveled until his feet were literally worn out, and in this condition he arrived at Harrisburg, where he found friends. Passing over many of the interesting incidents on the road, suffice it to say, he arrived safely in this city, on New Year's night, 1857, about two hours before day break (the telegraph having announced his coming from Harrisburg), having been a week on the way. The night he arrived was very cold; besides, the Underground train, that morning, was about three hours behind time; in waiting for it, entirely out in the cold, a member of the Vigilance Committee thought he was frosted. But when he came to listen to the story of the Fugitive's sufferings, his mind changed.

Scarcely had Robert entered the house of one of the Committee, where he was kindly received, when he took from his pocket his wife's likeness, speaking very touchingly while gazing upon it and showing it. Subsequently, in speaking of his family, he showed the locks of hair referred to, which he had carefully rolled up in paper separately. Unrolling them, he said, "this is my wife's;" "this is from my oldest daughter, eleven years old;" "and this is from my next oldest;" "and this from the next," "and this from my infant, only eight weeks old." These mementoes he cherished with the utmost care as the last remains of his affectionate family. At the sight of these locks of hair so tenderly preserved, the member of the Committee could fully appreciate the resolution of the fugitive in plunging into the Potomac, on the back of a dumb beast, in order to flee from a place and people who had made such barbarous havoc in his household.

His wife, as represented by the likeness, was of fair complexion, prepossessing, and good looking – perhaps not over thirty-three years of age.

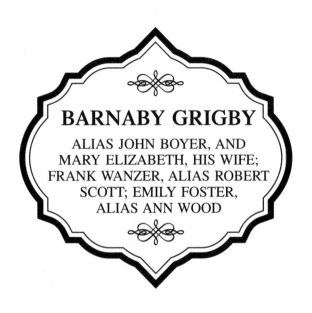

BARNABY GRIGBY

ALIAS JOHN BOYER, AND
MARY ELIZABETH, HIS WIFE;
FRANK WANZER, ALIAS ROBERT
SCOTT; EMILY FOSTER,
ALIAS ANN WOOD

*(TWO OTHERS WHO STARTED WITH
THEM WERE CAPTURED.)*

All these persons journeyed together from Loudon Co., Va. on horseback and in a carriage for more than one hundred miles. Availing themselves of a holiday and their master's horses and carriage, they as deliberately started for Canada, as though they had never been taught that it was their duty, as servants, to "obey their masters." In this particular showing a most utter disregard of the interest of their "kind-hearted and indulgent owners." They left home on Monday, Christmas Eve, 1855, under the leadership of Frank Wanzer, and arrived in Columbia the following Wednesday at one o'clock. As willfully as they had thus made their way along, they had not found it smooth sailing by any means. The biting frost and snow rendered their travel anything but agreeable. Nor did they escape the gnawings of hunger, traveling day and night. And whilst these "articles" were in the very act of running away with themselves and their kind master's best horses and carriage – when about one hundred miles from home, in the neighborhood of Cheat river, Maryland, they were attacked by "six white men, and a boy," who, doubtless, supposing that their intentions were of a "wicked and unlawful character" felt it to be their duty in kindness to their masters, if not to the travelers to demand of them an account of themselves. In other words, the assailants positively commanded the fugitives to "show what right" they possessed, to be found in a condition apparently so unwarranted.

The *spokesman* amongst the fugitives, affecting no ordinary amount of dignity, told their assailants plainly, that "no gentleman would interfere with persons riding along civilly" – not allowing it to be supposed that they were slaves, of course. These "gentlemen," however, were not willing to accept this account of the travelers, as their very decided steps indicated. Having the law on their side, they were for compelling the fugitives to surrender without further parley.

At this juncture, the fugitives verily believing that the time had arrived for the practical use of their pistols and dirks, pulled them out of their concealment – the young women as well as the young men – and declared they would not be "taken!" One of the white men raised his gun, pointing the muzzle directly towards one of the young women, with the threat that he would "shoot," etc. "Shoot! Shoot!! Shoot!!!" she exclaimed, with a double barrelled pistol in one hand and a long dirk knife in the other, utterly unterrified and fully ready for a death struggle. The male *leader* of the fugitives by this time had "pulled back the hammers" of his "pistols," and was about to fire! Their adversaries seeing the weapons, and the unflinching determination on the part of the *runaways* to stand their ground, "spill blood, kill, or die," rather than be "taken," very prudently "sidled over to the other side of the road," leaving at least four of the victors to travel on their way.

At this moment the four in the carriage lost sight of the two on horseback. Soon after the separation they heard firing, but what the result was, they knew not. They were fearful, however, that their companions had been captured.

The following paragraph, which was shortly afterwards taken from a Southern paper, leaves no room to doubt, as to the fate of the two.

Six fugitive slaves from Virginia were arrested at the Maryland line, near Hood's Mill, on Christmas day, but, after a severe fight, four of them escaped and have not since been heard of. They came from Loudoun and Fauquier counties.

Though the four who were successful, saw no "severe fight," it is not unreasonable to suppose, that there was a fight, nevertheless; but not till after the number of the fugitives had been reduced to two, instead of six. As chivalrous as slave-holders and slave-catchers were, they knew the value of their precious lives and the fearful risk of attempting a capture, when the numbers were equal.

The party in the carriage, after the conflict, went on their way rejoicing.

The young men, one cold night, when they were compelled to take rest in the woods and snow, in vain strove to keep the feet of their female companions from freezing by lying on them; but the frost was merciless and bit them severely, as their feet very plainly showed. The following disjointed report was cut from the *Frederick (Md.) Examiner*, soon after the occurrence took place:

Six slaves, four men and two women, fugitives from Virginia, having with them two spring wagons and four horses, came to Hood's Mill, on the Baltimore and Ohio Railroad, near the dividing line between Frederick and Carroll counties, on Christmas day. After feeding their animals, one of them told a Mr. Dixon whence they came; believing them to be fugitives, he spread the alarm, and some eight or ten persons

gathered round to arrest them; but the negroes drawing
revolvers and bowie-knives, kept their assailants at bay, until
five of the party succeeded in escaping in one of the wagons,
and as the last one jumped on a horse to flee, he was fired
at, the load taking effect in the small of the back. The prisoner says he belongs to Charles W. Simpson, Esq., of
Fauquier county, Va., and ran away with the others on the
preceding evening.

This report from the *Examiner*, while it is not wholly correct,
evidently relates to the fugitives above described. Why the
reporter made such glaring mistakes, may be accounted for
on the ground that the bold stand made by the fugitives was
so bewildering and alarming, that the "assailants" were not in
a proper condition to make correct statements. Nevertheless
the *Examiner's* report was preserved with other records, and
is here given for what it is worth.

These victors were individually noted on the Record thus:
Barnaby was owned by William Rogers, a farmer, who was
considered a "moderate slaveholder," although of late "addicted
to intemperance." He was the owner of about one "dozen head
of slaves," and had besides a wife and two children.

Barnaby's chances for making extra "change" for himself
were never favorable; sometimes of "nights" he would manage
to earn a "trifle." He was prompted to escape because he
"wanted to live by the sweat of his own brow," believing that
all men ought so to live. This was the only reason he gave
for fleeing.

Mary Elizabeth had been owned by Townsend McVee (likewise a farmer), and in Mary's judgment, he was "severe," but

she added, "his wife made him so." McVee owned about twenty-five slaves; "he hardly allowed them to talk – would not allow them to raise chickens," and "only allowed Mary three dresses a year;" the rest she had to get as she could. Sometimes McVee would sell slaves – last year he sold two. Mary said that she could not say anything good of her mistress. On the contrary, she declared that her mistress "knew no mercy nor showed any favor."

It was on account of this "domineering spirit," that Mary was induced to escape.

Frank was owned by Luther Sullivan, "the meanest man in Virginia," he said; he treated his people just as bad as he could in every respect. "Sullivan," added Frank, "would 'lowance the slaves and stint them to save food and get rich," and "would sell and whip," etc. To Frank's knowledge, he had sold some twenty-five head. "He sold my mother and her two children to Georgia some four years previous." But the motive which hurried Frank to make his flight was his laboring under the apprehension that his master had some "pretty heavy creditors who might come on him at any time." Frank, therefore, wanted to be from home in Canada when these gentry should make their visit. "My poor mother has been often flogged by master," said Frank. As to his mistress, he said she was "tolerably good."

Ann Wood was owned by McVee also, and was own sister to Elizabeth. Ann very fully sustained her sister Elizabeth's statement respecting the character of her master.

The above-mentioned four were all young and likely. Barnaby was twenty-six years of age, mulatto, medium size, and intelligent – his wife was about twenty-four years of age, quite dark, good-looking, and of pleasant appearance. Frank was twenty-five years of age, mulatto, and very smart; Ann was twenty-two, good-looking, and smart. After their pressing wants had been met by the Vigilance Committee, and after partial recuperation from their hard travel, etc., they were forwarded on to the Vigilance Committee in New York. In Syracuse, Frank (the leader), who was engaged to Emily, concluded that the knot might as well be tied on the U.G.R.R., although penniless, as to delay the matter a single day longer. Doubtless, the bravery, struggles, and trials of Emily throughout the journey, had, in his estimation, added not a little to her charms. Thus after consulting with her on the matter, her approval was soon obtained, she being too prudent and wise to refuse the hand of one who had proved himself so true a friend to Freedom, as well as so devoted to her. The twain were accordingly made one at the U.G.R.R. Station, in Syracuse, by Superintendent-Rev. J.W. Loguen. After this joyful event, they proceeded to Toronto, and were there gladly received by the Ladies' Society for aiding colored refugees.

The following letter from Mrs. Agnes Willis, wife of the distinguished Rev. Dr. Willis, brought the gratifying intelligence that these brave young adventurers fell into the hands of distinguished characters and warm friends of Freedom:

TORONTO,
28th January, Monday evening, 1856.

MR. STILL, DEAR SIR: – I have very great pleasure in making you aware that the following respectable persons have arrived here in safety without being annoyed in any way after you saw them. The women, two of them, viz: Mrs. Greegsby and Mrs. Graham, have been rather ailing, but we hope they will very soon be well. They have been attended to by the Ladies' Society, and are most grateful for any attention they have received. The solitary person, Mrs. Graves, has also been attended to; also her box will be looked after. She is pretty well, but rather dull; however, she will get friends and feel more at home by and bye. Mrs. Wanzer is quite well; and also young William Henry Sanderson. They are all of them in pretty good spirits, and I have no doubt they will succeed in whatever business they take up. In the mean time the men are chopping wood, and the ladies are getting plenty sewing. We are always glad to see our colored refugees safe here. I remain, dear sir,

yours respectfully,
AGNES WILLIS,

Treasurer to the Ladies' Society to aid colored refugees.

For a time Frank enjoyed his newly won freedom and happy bride with bright prospects all around; but the thought of having left sisters and other relatives in bondage was a source of sadness in the midst of his joy. He was not long, however, in making up his mind that he would deliver them or "die in the attempt." Deliberately forming his plans to go South, he resolved to take upon himself the entire responsibility of all the risks to be encountered. Not a word did he reveal to a living soul of what he was about to undertake. With "twenty-two dollars" in cash and "three pistols" in his pockets, he started in the lightning train from Toronto for Virginia. On reaching Columbia in this State, he deemed it not safe to go any further by public conveyance, consequently he commenced his long journey on foot, and as he neared the slave territory he traveled by night altogether. For two weeks, night and day, he avoided trusting himself in any house, consequently was compelled to lodge in the woods. Nevertheless, during that space of time he succeeded in delivering one of his sisters and her husband, and another friend in the bargain. You can scarcely imagine the Committee's amazement on his return, as they looked upon him and listened to his "noble deeds of daring" and his triumph. A more brave and self-possessed man they had never seen.

He knew what Slavery was and the dangers surrounding him on his mission, but possessing true courage unlike most men, he pictured no alarming difficulties in a distance of nearly one thousand miles by the mail route, through the enemy's country, where he might have in truth said, "I could not pass without running the gauntlet of mobs and assassins, prisons and penitentiaries, bailiffs and constables, &c." If this hero had dwelt upon and magnified the obstacles in his way he would most assuredly have kept off the enemy's country, and his sister and friends would have remained in chains.

The following were the persons delivered by Frank Wanzer. They were his trophies, and this noble act of Frank's should ever be held as a memorial and honor. The Committee's brief record made on their arrival runs thus:

"August 18, 1856. Frank Wanzer, Robert Stewart, alias Gasberry Robison, Vincent Smith, alias John Jackson, Betsey

Smith, wife of Vincent Smith, alias Fanny Jackson. They all came from Alder, Loudon county, Virginia."

Robert is about thirty years of age, medium size, dark chestnut color, intelligent and resolute. He was held by the widow Hutchinson, who was also the owner of about one hundred others. Robert regarded her as a "very hard mistress" until the death of her husband, which took place the Fall previous to his escape. That sad affliction, he thought, was the cause of a considerable change in her treatment of her slaves. But yet "nothing was said about freedom," on her part. This reticence Robert understood to mean, that she was still unconverted on this great cardinal principle at least. As he could see no prospect of freedom through her agency, when Frank approached him with a good report from Canada and his friends there, he could scarcely wait to listen to the glorious news; he was so willing and anxious to get out of slavery. His dear old mother, Sarah Davis, and four brothers and two sisters, William, Thomas, Frederick and Samuel, Violet and Ellen, were all owned by Mrs. Hutchinson. Dear as they were to him, he saw no way to take them with him, nor was he prepared to remain a day longer under the yoke; so he decided to accompany Frank, let the cost be what it might.

Vincent is about twenty-three years of age, very "likely-looking," dark color, and more than ordinarily intelligent for one having only the common chances of slaves.

He was owned by the estate of Nathan Skinner, who was "looked upon," by those who knew him, "as a good slave-holder." In slave property, however, he was only interested to the number of twelve head. Skinner "neither sold nor emancipated." A year and a half before Vincent escaped, his master was called to give an account of his stewardship, and there in the spirit land Vincent was willing to let him remain, without much more to add about him.

Vincent left his mother, Judah Smith, and brothers and sisters, Edwin, Angeline, Sina Ann, Adaline Susan, George, John and Lewis, all belonging to the estate of Skinner.

Vincent was fortunate enough to bring his wife along with him. She was about twenty-seven years of age, of a brown color, and smart, and was owned by the daughter of the widow Hutchinson. This mistress was said to be a "clever woman."

WILLIAM JORDAN

ALIAS WILLIAM PRICE

Under Governor Badger, of North Carolina, William had experienced Slavery in its most hateful form. True, he had only been twelve months under the yoke of this high functionary. But William's experience in this short space of time, was of a nature very painful.

Previous to coming into the governor's hands, William was held as the property of Mrs. Mary Jordon, who owned large numbers of slaves. Whether the governor was moved by this consideration, or by the fascinating charms of Mrs. Jordon, or both, William was not able to decide. But the governor offered her his hand, and they became united in wedlock. By this circumstance, William was brought into his unhappy relations with the Chief Magistrate of the State of North Carolina. This was the third time the governor had been married. Thus it may be seen, that the governor was a firm believer in wives as well as slaves. Commonly he was regarded as a man of wealth. William being an intelligent piece of property, his knowledge of the governor's rules and customs was quite complete, as he readily answered such questions as were propounded to him. In this way a great amount of interesting information was learned from William respecting the governor, slaves, on the plantation, in the swamps, etc. The governor owned large plantations, and was interested in raising cotton, corn, and peas, and was also a practical planter. He was willing to trust neither overseers nor slaves any further than he could help.

The governor and his wife were both equally severe towards them; would stint them shamefully in clothing and food, though they did not get flogged quite as often as some others on neighboring plantations. Frequently, the governor would be out on the plantation from early in the morning till noon, inspecting the operations of the overseers and slaves.

In order to serve the governor, William had been separated from his wife by sale, which was the cause of his escape. He parted not with his companion willingly. At the time, however, he was promised that he should have some favors shown him; – could make over-work, and earn a little money, and once or twice in the year, have the opportunity of making visits to her. Two hundred miles was the distance between them.

He had not been long on the governor's plantation before his honor gave him distinctly to understand that the idea of his going two hundred miles to see his wife was all nonsense, and entirely out of the question. "If I said so, I did not mean it," said his honor, when the slave, on a certain occasion, alluded to the conditions on which he consented to leave home, etc.

Against this cruel decision of the governor, William's heart revolted, for he was warmly attached to his wife, and so he made up his mind, if he could not see her "once or twice a year even," as he had been promised, he had rather "die," or live in a "cave in the wood," than to remain all his life under the governor's yoke. Obeying the dictates of his feelings, he went to the woods. For ten months before he was successful in finding the Underground Road, this brave-hearted young fugitive abode in the swamps – three months in a cave – surrounded with bears, wild cats, rattle-snakes and the like.

While in the swamps and cave, he was not troubled, however, about ferocious animals and venomous reptiles. He feared only man!

From his own story there was no escaping the conclusion, that if the choice had been left to him, he would have preferred at any time to have encountered at the mouth of his cave a ferocious bear than his master, the governor of North Carolina. How he managed to subsist, and ultimately effected his escape, was listened to with the deepest interest, though the recital of these incidents must here be very brief.

After night he would come out of his cave, and, in some instances, would succeed in making his way to a plantation, and if he could get nothing else, he would help himself to a "pig," or anything else he could conveniently convert into food. Also, as opportunity would offer, a friend of his would favor him with some meal, etc. With this mode of living he labored to content himself until he could do better. During these ten months he suffered indescribable hardships, but he felt that his condition in the cave was far preferable to that on the plantation, under the control of his Excellency, the Governor. All this time, however, William had a true friend, with whom he could communicate; one who was wide awake, and was on the alert to find a reliable captain from the North, who would consent to take this "property," or "freight," for a consideration. He heard at last of a certain Captain, who was then doing quite a successful business in an Underground way. This good news was conveyed to William, and afforded him a ray of hope in the wilderness. As Providence would have it, his hope did not meet with disappointment; nor did his ten months' trial, warring against the barbarism of Slavery, seem too great to endure for Freedom. He was about to leave his cave and his animal and reptile neighbors, – his heart swelling with gladness, – but the thought of soon being beyond the reach of his mistress and master thrilled him with inexpressible delight. He was brought away by Captain F., and turned over to the Committee, who were made to rejoice with him over the signal victory he had gained in his martyr-like endeavors to throw off the yoke, and of course they took much pleasure in aiding him. William was of a dark color, stout made physically, and well knew the value of Freedom, and how to hate and combat Slavery. It will be seen by the appended letter of Thomas Garrett, that William had the good luck to fall into the hands of this tried friend, by whom he was aided to Philadelphia:

WILMINGTON,
12th mo., 19th, 1855.

DEAR FRIEND, WILLIAM STILL: – The bearer of this is one of the twenty-one that I thought had all gone North; he left home on Christmas day, one year since, wandered about the forests of North Carolina for about ten months, and then came here with those forwarded to New Bedford, where he is anxious to go. I have furnished him with a pretty good pair of boots, and gave him money to pay his passage to Philadelphia. He has been at work in the country near here for some three weeks, till taken sick; he is, by no means, well, but thinks he had better try to get farther North, which I hope his friends in Philadelphia will aid him to do. I handed this morning Captain Lambson's[4] wife twenty dollars to help

4   Captain Lambson had been suspected of having aided in the escape of slaves from the neighborhood of Norfolk, and was in prison awaiting his trial.

fee a lawyer to defend him. She leaves this morning, with her child, for Norfolk, to be at the trial before the Commissioner on the 24th instant. Passmore Williamson agreed to raise fifty dollars for him. As none came to hand, and a good chance to send it by his wife, I thought best to advance that much.

Thy friend,
THOS. GARRETT.

JOSEPH GRANT
AND
JOHN SPEAKS

*TWO PASSENGERS ON THE
UNDERGROUND RAIL ROAD,
VIA LIVERPOOL.*

It is to be regretted that, owing to circumstances, the account of these persons has not been fully preserved. Could justice be done them, probably their narratives would not be surpassed in interest by any other in the history of fugitives. In 1857, when these remarkable travelers came under the notice of the Vigilance Committee, as Slavery seemed likely to last for generations, and there was but little expectation that these records would ever have the historical value which they now possess, care was not always taken to prepare and preserve them. Besides, the cases coming under the notice of the Committee were so numerous and so interesting, that it seemed almost impossible to do them anything like justice. In many instances the rapt attention paid by friends, when listening to the sad recitals of such passengers, would unavoidably consume so much time that but little opportunity was afforded to make any record of them. Particularly was this the case with regard to the above-mentioned individuals. The story of each was so long and sad, that a member of the Committee in attempting to write it out, found that the two narratives would take volumes. That all traces of these heroes might not be lost, a mere fragment is all that was preserved.

The original names of these adventurers were Joseph Grant and John Speaks. Between two and three years before escaping, they were sold from Maryland to John B. Campbell, a negro trader, living in Baltimore, and thence to Campbell's brother, another trader in New Orleans, and subsequently to Daniel McBeans and Mr. Henry, of Harrison county, Mississippi.

Though both had to pass through nearly the same trial, and belonged to the same masters, this recital must be confined chiefly to the incidents in the career of Joseph. He was about twenty-seven years of age, well made, quite black, intelligent and self-possessed in his manner.

He was owned in Maryland by Mrs. Mary Gibson, who resided at St. Michael's on the Eastern Shore. She was a *nice woman* he said, but her property was under mortgage and had to be sold, and he was in danger of sharing the same fate.

Joseph was a married man, and spoke tenderly of his wife. She "promised" him when he was sold that she would "never marry," and earnestly entreated him, if he "ever met with the luck, to come and see her." She was unaware perhaps at that time of the great distance that was to divide them; his feelings on being thus sundered need not be stated. However, he had scarcely been in Mississippi three weeks, ere his desire to return to his wife, and the place of his nativity, constrained him to attempt to return; accordingly he set off, crossing a lake eighty miles wide in a small boat, he reached Kent Island. There he was captured by the watchman on the Island, who with *pistols, dirk and cutlass* in hand, threatened if he resisted that death would be his instant doom. Of course he was returned to his master.

He remained there a few months, but could content himself no longer to endure the ills of his condition. So he again started for home, walked to Mobile, and thence he succeeded in stowing himself away in a steamboat and was thus conveyed to Montgomery, a distance of five hundred and fifty miles through solid slave territory. Again he was captured and returned to his owners; one of whom always went for immediate punishment, the other being mild thought persuasion the better plan in such cases. On the whole, Joseph thus far had been pretty fortunate, considering the magnitude of his offence.

A third time he summoned courage and steered his course homewards towards Maryland, but as in the preceding attempts, he was again unsuccessful.

In this instance Mr. Henry, the harsh owner, was exasperated, and the mild one's patience so exhausted that they concluded that nothing short of stern measures would cause Joe to reform. Said Mr. Henry: "I had rather lose my right arm than for him to get off without being punished, after having put us to so much trouble."

Joseph will now speak for himself.

He (master) sent the overseer to tie me. I told him I would not be tied. I ran and stayed away four days, which made Mr. Henry very anxious. Mr. Beans told the servants if they saw me, to tell me to come back and I should not be hurt. Thinking that Mr. Beans had always stood to his word, I was over persuaded and came back. He sent for me in his parlor, talked the matter over, sent me to the steamboat (perhaps the one he tried to escape on). After getting cleverly on board the captain told me, I am sorry to tell you, you have to be tied. I was tied and Mr. Henry was sent for. He came: "Well, I have got you at last, beg my pardon and promise you will never run away again and I will not be so hard on you." I could not do it. He then gave me three hundred lashes well laid on. I was stripped entirely naked, and my flesh was as raw as a piece of beef. He made John (the companion who escaped with him) hold one of my feet which I broke loose while being whipped, and when done made him bathe me in salt and water.

Then I resolved to 'go or die' in the attempt. Before starting, one week, I could not work. On getting better we went to Ship Island; the sailors, who were Englishmen, were very sorry to hear of the treatment we had received, and counselled us how we might get free.

The counsel was heeded, and in due time they found themselves in Liverpool. There their stay was brief. Utterly destitute of money, education, and in a strange land, they very naturally turned their eyes again in the direction of their native land. Accordingly their host, the keeper of a sailor's boarding house, shipped them to Philadelphia.

But to go back, Joseph saw many things in New Orleans and Mississippi of a nature too horrible to relate, among which were the following:

> I have seen Mr. Beans whip one of his slaves to death, at the tree to which he was tied.
>
> Mr. Henry would make them lie down across a log, stripped naked, and with every stroke would lay the flesh open. Being used to it, some would lie on the log without being tied.
>
> In New Orleans, I have seen women stretched out just as naked as my hand, on boxes, and given one hundred and fifty lashes, four men holding them. I have helped hold them myself: when released they could hardly sit or walk. This whipping was at the *Fancy House*.

The "chain-gangs" he also saw in constant operation. Four and five slaves chained together and at work on the streets, cleaning, &c., was a common sight. He could hardly tell Sunday from Monday in New Orleans, the slaves were kept so constantly going.

ARRIVAL FROM BALTIMORE

JEFFERSON PIPKINS, ALIAS DAVID JONES; LOUISA PIPKINS; ELIZABETH BRIT; HARRIET BROWN, ALIAS JANE WOOTON; GRACY MURRY, ALIAS SOPHIA SIMS; EDWARD WILLIAMS, ALIAS HENRY JOHNSON; CHAS. LEE, ALIAS THOMAS BUSHIER.

Six very clever-looking passengers, all in one party from Baltimore, Md., the first Sunday in April, 1853. Baltimore used to be in the days of Slavery one of the most difficult places in the South for even free colored people to get away from, much more for slaves. The rule forbade any colored person leaving there by rail road or steamboat, without such applicant had been weighed, measured, and then given a bond signed by unquestionable signatures, well known. Baltimore was rigid in the extreme, and was a never-failing source of annoyance, trouble and expense to colored people generally, and not unfrequently to slave-holders too, when they were traveling North with "colored servants." Just as they were ready to start, the "Rules" would forbid colored servants until the law was complied with. Parties hurrying on would on account of this obstruction "have to wait until their hurry was over." As this was all done in the interest of Slavery, the matter was not very loudly condemned. But, notwithstanding all this weighing, measuring and requiring of bonds, many travelers by the Underground Rail Road took passage from Baltimore.

The enterprising individual, whose name stands at the head of this narrative, came directly from this stronghold of Slavery. The widow Pipkins held the title deed for Jefferson. She was unfortunate in losing him, as she was living in ease and luxury off of Jefferson's sweat and labor. Louisa, Harriet, and Grace owed service to Geo. Stewart of Baltimore; Edward was owned by Chas. Moondo, and Chas. Lee by the above Stewart.

Those who would have taken this party for stupid, or for know-nothings, would have found themselves very much mistaken. Indeed they were far from being dull or sleepy on the subject of Slavery at any rate. They had considered pretty thoroughly how wrongfully they, with all others in similar circumstances, had been year in and year out subjected to unrequited toil so resolved to leave masters and mistresses to shift for themselves, while they would try their fortunes in Canada.

Four of the party ranged in age from twenty to twenty-eight years of age, and the other two from thirty-seven to forty. The Committee on whom they called, rendered them due aid and advice, and forwarded them to the Committee in New York.

The following letter from Jefferson, appealing for assistance on behalf of his children in Slavery, was peculiarly touching, as were all similar letters. But the mournful thought that these appeals, sighs, tears and prayers would continue in most cases to be made till death, that nothing could be done directly for the deliverance of such sufferers was often as painful as the escape from the auction block was gratifying.

LETTER FROM JEFFERSON PIPKINS.

Sept. 28, 1856.

To WM. STILL. SIR: – I take the liberty of writing to you a few lines concerning my children, for I am very anxious to get them and I wish you to please try what you can do for me. Their names are Charles and Patrick and are living with Mrs. Joseph G. Wray Murphysborough Hartford county, North Carolina; Emma lives with a Lawyer Baker in Gatesville North Carolina and Susan lives in Portsmouth

Virginia and is stopping with Dr. Collins sister a Mrs. Nash you can find her out by enquiring for Dr. Collins at the ferry boat at Portsmouth, and Rose a coloured woman at the Crawford House can tell where she is. And I trust you will try what you think will be the best way. And you will do me a great favour.

Yours Respectfully,
JEFFERSON PIPKINS.

P.S. I am living at Yorkville near Toronto Canada West. My wife sends her best respects to Mrs. Still.

BLOOD FLOWED FREELY

ABRAM GALLOWAY AND RICHARD EDEN, TWO PASSENGERS SECRETED IN A VESSEL LOADED WITH SPIRITS OF TURPENTINE. SHROUDS PREPARED TO PREVENT BEING SMOKED TO DEATH.

The Philadelphia branch of the Underground Rail Road was not fortunate in having very frequent arrivals from North Carolina. Of course such of her slave population as managed to become initiated in the mysteries of traveling North by the Underground Rail Road were sensible enough to find out nearer and safer routes than through Pennsylvania.

Nevertheless the Vigilance Committee of Philadelphia occasionally had the pleasure of receiving some heroes who were worthy to be classed among the bravest of the brave, no matter who they may be who have claims to this distinction.

In proof of this bold assertion the two individuals whose names stand at the beginning of this chapter are presented. Abram was only twenty-one years of age, mulatto, five feet six inches high, intelligent and the picture of good health. "What was your master's name?" inquired a member of the Committee. "Milton Hawkins," answered Abram. "What business did Milton Hawkins follow?" again queried said member. "He was chief engineer on the Wilmington and Manchester Rail Road" (not a branch of the Underground Rail Road), responded Richard. "Describe him," said the member. "He was a slim built, tall man with whiskers. He was a man of very good disposition. I always belonged to him; he owned three. He always said he would sell before he would use a whip. His wife was a very mean woman; she would whip contrary to his orders." "Who was your father?" was further inquired. "John Wesley Galloway," was the prompt response. "Describe your father?" "He was captain of a government vessel; he recognized me as his son, and protected me as far as he was allowed so to do; he lived at Smithfield, North

Carolina. Abram's master, Milton Hawkins, lived at Wilmington, N.C." "What prompted you to escape?" was next asked. "Because times were hard and I could not come up with my wages as I was required to do, so I thought I would try and do better." At this juncture Abram explained substantially in what sense times were hard, &c. In the first place he was not allowed to own himself; he, however, preferred hiring his time to serving in the usual way. This favor was granted Abram; but he was compelled to pay $15 per month for his time, besides finding himself in clothing, food, paying doctor bills, and a head tax of $15 a year.

Even under this master, who was a man of very good disposition, Abram was not contented. In the second place, he "always thought Slavery was wrong," although he had "never suffered any personal abuse." Toiling month after month the year round to support his master and not himself, was the one intolerable thought. Abram and Richard were intimate friends, and lived near each other. Being similarly situated, they could venture to communicate the secret feelings of their hearts to each other. Richard was four years older than Abram, with not quite so much Anglo-Saxon blood in his veins, but was equally as intelligent, and was by trade, a "fashionable barber," well-known to the ladies and gentlemen of Wilmington. Richard owed service to Mrs. Mary Loren, a widow. "She was very kind and tender to all her slaves." "If I was sick," said Richard, "she would treat me the same as a mother would." She was the owner of twenty, men, women and children, who were all hired out, except the children too young for hire. Besides having his food, clothing and doctor's expenses to meet, he had to pay the "very kind and tender-hearted widow" $12.50 per month, and head tax to the State, amounting to twenty-five cents per month. It so happened, that Richard at this time, was involved in a matrimonial difficulty. Contrary to the laws of North Carolina, he had lately married a free girl, which was an indictable offence, and for which the penalty was then in soak for him – said penalty to consist of thirty-nine lashes, and imprisonment at the discretion of the judge.

So Abram and Richard put their heads together, and resolved to try the Underground Rail Road. They concluded that liberty was worth dying for, and that it was their duty to strike for Freedom even if it should cost them their lives. The next thing needed was information about the Underground Rail Road. Before a great while the captain of a schooner turned up, from Wilmington, Delaware. Learning that his voyage extended to Philadelphia, they sought to find out whether this captain was true to Freedom. To ascertain this fact required no little address. It had to be done in such a way, that even the captain would not really understand what they were up to, should he be found untrue. In this instance, however, he was the right man in the right place, and very well understood his business.

Abram and Richard made arrangements with him to bring them away; they learned when the vessel would start, and that she was loaded with tar, rosin, and spirits of turpentine, amongst which the captain was to secrete them. But here came the difficulty. In order that slaves might not be secreted in vessels, the slave-holders of North Carolina had procured the enactment of a law requiring all vessels coming North to be smoked.

To escape this dilemma, the inventive genius of Abram and Richard soon devised a safe-guard against the smoke. This safe-guard consisted in silk oil cloth shrouds, made large, with drawing strings, which, when pulled over their heads, might be drawn very tightly around their waists, whilst the process of smoking might be in operation. A bladder of water and towels were provided, the latter to be wet and held to their nostrils, should there be need. In this manner they had determined to struggle against death for liberty. The hour approached for being at the wharf. At the appointed time they were on hand ready to go on the boat; the captain secreted them, according to agreement. They were ready to run the risk of being smoked to death; but as good luck would have it, the law was not carried into effect in this instance, so that the "smell of smoke was not upon them." The effect of the turpentine, however, of the nature of which they were totally ignorant, was worse, if possible, than the smoke would have been. The blood was literally drawn from them at every pore in frightful quantities. But as heroes of the bravest type they resolved to continue steadfast as long as a pulse continued to beat, and thus they finally conquered.

The invigorating northern air and the kind treatment of the Vigilance Committee acted like a charm upon them, and they improved very rapidly from their exhaustive and heavy loss of blood. Desiring to retain some memorial of them, a member of the Committee begged one of their silk shrouds, and likewise procured an artist to take the photograph of one of them; which keepsakes have been valued very highly. In the regular order of arrangements the wants of Abram and Richard were duly met by the Committee, financially and otherwise, and they were forwarded to Canada. After their safe arrival in Canada, Richard addressed a member of the Committee thus:

KINGSTON,
July 20, 1857.

MR. WILLIAM STILL – *Dear Friend*: – I take the opertunity of wrighting a few lines to let you no that we air all in good health hoping thos few lines may find you and your family engoying the same blessing. We arived in King all saft Canada West Abram Galway gos to work this morning at $1.75 per day and John pediford is at work for mr george mink and i will opne a shop for my self in a few days My wif will send a daugretipe to your cair whitch you will pleas to send on to me Richard Edons to the cair of George Mink

Kingston C W
Yours with Respect,

RICHARD EDONS.

Abram, his comrade, allied himself faithfully to John Bull until Uncle Sam became involved in the contest with the rebels. In this hour of need Abram hastened back to North Carolina to help fight the battles of Freedom. How well he acted his part, we are not informed. We only know that, after the war was over, in the reconstruction of North Carolina, Abram was promoted to a seat in its Senate. He died in office only a few months since. The portrait is almost a "fac-simile."

THE ESCAPE
OF A CHILD
FOURTEEN
MONTHS OLD

There is found the following brief memorandum on the Records of the Underground Rail Road Book, dated July, 1857:

"A little child of fourteen months old was conveyed to its mother, who had been compelled to flee without it nearly nine months ago."

While the circumstances connected with the coming of this slave child were deeply interesting, no further particulars than the simple notice above were at that time recorded. Fortunately, however, letters from the good friends, who plucked this infant from the jaws of Slavery, have been preserved to throw light on this little one, and to show how true-hearted sympathizers with the Slave labored amid dangers and difficulties to save the helpless bondman from oppression. It will be observed, that both these friends wrote from Washington, D.C., the seat of Government, where, if Slavery was not seen in its worst aspects, the Government in its support of Slavery appeared in a most revolting light.

LETTER FROM "J.B."

WASHINGTON, D.C.,
July 12, 1857.

DEAR SIR: – Some of our citizens, I am told, lately left here for Philadelphia, three of whom were arrested and brought back.

I beg you will inform me whether two others – (I., whose wife is in Philadelphia, was one of them), ever reached your city.

To-morrow morning Mrs. Weems, *with her baby*, will start for Philadelphia and see you probably over night.

Yours Truly,
J.B.

"J.B." was not only a trusty and capable conductor of the Underground Rail Road in Washington, but was also a practical lawyer, at the same time. His lawyer-like letter, in view of the critical nature of the case, contained but few words, and those few naturally enough were susceptible of more than one construction.

Doubtless those styled "our citizens," – three of whom were arrested and brought back," – were causing great anxiety to this correspondent, not knowing how soon he might find himself implicated in the "running off," etc. So, while he felt it to be his duty, to still aid the child, he was determined, if the enemy intercepted his letter, he should not find much comfort or information. The cause was safe in such careful hands. The following letters, bearing on the same case, are also from another good conductor, who was then living in Washington.

LETTERS FROM E.L. STEVENS

WASHINGTON, D.C.,
July 8,1857.

MY DEAR SIR: – I write you now to let you know that the children of E. are yet well, and that Mrs. Arrah Weems will start with one of them for Philadelphia to-morrow or next day. She will be with you probably in the day train. She goes for the purpose of making an effort to redeem her last child, now in Slavery. The whole amount necessary is raised, except about $300. She will take her credentials with her, and you can place the most implicit reliance on her statements. The story in regard to the Weems' family was published in Frederick Douglass' paper two years ago. Since then the two middle boys have been redeemed and there is only one left in Slavery, and he is in Alabama. The master has agreed to take for him just what he gave, $1,100. Mr. Lewis Tappan has his letter and the money, except the amount specified. There were about $5,000 raised in England to redeem this family, and they are now all free except this one. And there never was a more excellent and worthy family than the Weems' family. I do hope, that Mrs. W. will find friends who can advance the amount required.

Truly Yours,

E.L. STEVENS.

WASHINGTON, D.C.,
July 13th, 1857.

MY FRIEND: – Your kind letter in reply to mine about Arrah was duly received. As she is doubtless with you before this, she will explain all. I propose that a second journey be made by her or some one else, in order to take the other. They have been a great burden to the good folks here and should have been *at home* long ere this. Arrah will explain everything. I want, however, to say a word in her behalf. If there is a person in the world, that deserves the hearty co-operation of every friend of humanity, that person is Arrah Weems, who now, after a long series of self-sacrificing labor to aid others in their struggle for their God-given rights, solicits a small amount to redeem the last one of her own children in Slavery. Never have I had my sympathies so aroused in behalf of any object as in behalf of this most worthy family. She can tell you what I have done. And I do hope, that our friends in Philadelphia and New York will assist her to make up the full amount required for the purchase of the boy.

After she does what she can in P., will you give her the proper direction about getting to New York and to Mr. Tappan's? Inform him of what she has done, &c.

Please write me as soon as you can as to whether she arrived safely, &c. Give me your opinion, also, as to the proposal about the other. Had you not better keep the little one in P. till the other is taken there? Inform me also where E. is, how she is getting along, &c., who living with, &c.

Yours Truly,

E.L.S.

In this instance, also, as in the case of "J.B.," the care and anxiety of other souls, besides this child, crying for deliverance, weighed heavily on the mind of Mr. Stevens, as may be inferred from certain references in his letters. Mr. Stevens' love of humanity, and impartial freedom, even in those dark days of Slavery, when it was both unpopular and unsafe to allow the cries of the bondman to awaken the feeling of humanity to assist the suffering, was constantly leading him to take sides with the oppressed, and as he appears in this correspondence, so it was his wont daily to aid the helpless, who were all around him. Arrah Weems, who had the care of the child, alluded to so touchingly by Mr. Stevens, had known, to her heart's sorrow, how intensely painful it was to a mother's feelings to have her children torn from her by a cruel master and sold. For Arrah had had a number of children sold, and was at that very time striving diligently to raise money to redeem the last one of them. And through such kind-hearted friends as Mr. Stevens, the peculiar hardships of this interesting family of Weems' were brought to the knowledge of thousands of philanthropists in this country and England, and liberal contributions had already been made by friends of the Slave on both sides of the ocean. It may now be seen, that while this child had not been a conscious sufferer from the wicked system of Slavery, it had been the object of very great anxiety and suffering to several persons, who had individually perilled their own freedom for its redemption. This child, however, was safely brought to the Vigilance Committee, in Philadelphia, and was duly forwarded, *via* friends in New York, to its mother, in Syracuse, where she had stopped to work and wait for her little one, left behind at the time she escaped.

ESCAPE OF A YOUNG SLAVE MOTHER

LEFT HER LITTLE BABY-BOY, LITTLE GIRL AND HUSBAND BEHIND.

She anxiously waits their coming in Syracuse, N.Y. Not until after the foregoing story headed, the "Escape of a Child," etc., had been put into the hands of the printer and was in type, was the story of the mother discovered, although it was among the records preserved. Under changed names, in many instances, it has been found to be no easy matter to cull from a great variety of letters, records and advertisements, just when wanted, all the particulars essential to complete many of these narratives. The case of the child, alluded to above, is a case in point. Thus, however, while it is impossible to introduce the mother's story in its proper place, yet, since it has been found, it is too important and interesting to be left out. It is here given as follows:

$300 REWARD. – RAN AWAY from the subscriber on Saturday, the 30th of August, 1856, my SERVANT WOMAN, named EMELINE CHAPMAN, about 25 years of age; quite dark, slender built, speaks short, and stammers some; with two children, one a female about two and a half years old; the other a male, seven or eight months old, bright color. I will give the above reward if they are delivered to me in Washington.
MRS. EMILY THOMPSON,
Capitol Hill, Washington, D.C.

Emeline Chapman, so particularly described in the *Baltimore Sun* of the 23d of September, 1856, arrived by the regular Underground Rail Road train from Washington. In order to escape the responsibility attached to her original name, she adopted the name of Susan Bell. Thus for freedom she was willing to forgo her name, her husband, and even her little children. It was a serious sacrifice; but she had been threatened with the auction block, and she well understood what that meant. With regard to usage, having lived away from her owner, Emeline did not complain of any very hard times. True, she had been kept at work very constantly, and her owner had very faithfully received all her hire. Emeline had not even been allowed enough of her hire to find herself in clothing, or anything for the support of her two children – for these non-essentials, her kind mistress allowed her to seek elsewhere, as best she could. Emeline's husband was named John Henry; her little girl she called Margaret Ann, and her babe she had named after its father, all with the brand of Slavery upon them. The love of freedom, in the breast of this spirited young Slave-wife and mother, did not extinguish the love she bore to her husband and children, however otherwise her course, in leaving them, as she did, might appear. For it was just this kind of heroic and self-sacrificing struggle, that appealed to the hearts of men and compelled attention. The letters of Biglow and Stevens, relative to the little child, prove this fact, and additional testimony found in the appended letter from Rev. J.W. Loguen conclusively confirms the same. Indeed, who could close his eyes and ears to the plaintive cries of such a mother? Who could refrain from aiding on to freedom children honored in such a heroic parent?

> SYRACUSE,
> *Oct. 5, 1856.*

DEAR FRIEND STILL: – I write to you for Mrs. Susan Bell, who was at your city some time in September last. She is from Washington city. She left her dear little children behind (two children). She is stopping in our city, and wants to hear from her children very much indeed. She wishes to know if you have heard from Mr. Biglow, of Washington city. She will remain here until she can hear from you. She feels very anxious about her children, I will assure you. I should have written before this, but I have been from home much of the time since she came to our city. She wants to know if Mr. Biglow has heard anything about her husband. If you have not written to Mr. Biglow, she wishes you would. She sends her love to you and your dear family. She says that you were all kind to her, and she does not forget it. You will direct your letter to me, dear brother, and I will see that she gets it.

Miss F.E. Watkins left our house yesterday for Ithaca, and other places in that part of the State. Frederick Douglass, Wm. J. Watkins and others were with us last week; Gerritt Smith with others. Miss Watkins is doing great good in our part of the State. We think much indeed of her. She is such a good and glorious speaker, that we are all charmed with her. We have had thirty-one fugitives in the last twenty-seven days; but you, no doubt, have had many more than that. I hope the good Lord may bless you and spare you long to do good to the hunted and outraged among our brethren. Yours truly,

J.W. LOGUEN,

Agent of the Underground Rail Road.

"FLEEING GIRL OF FIFTEEN" IN MALE ATTIRE

PROFESSORS H. AND T. OFFER THEIR SERVICES – CAPTAINS B. ALSO ARE ENLISTED – SLAVE-TRADER GRASPING TIGHTLY HIS PREY, BUT SHE IS RESCUED – LONG CONFLICT, BUT GREAT TRIUMPH – ARRIVAL ON THANKSGIVING DAY, NOV. 25, 1855.

It was the business of the Vigilance Committee, as it was clearly understood by the friends of the Slave, to assist all needy fugitives, who might in any way manage to reach Philadelphia, but, for various reasons, not to send agents South to incite slaves to run away, or to assist them in so doing. Sometimes, however, this rule could not altogether be conformed to. Cases, in some instances, would appeal so loudly and forcibly to humanity, civilization, and Christianity, that it would really seem as if the very stones would cry out, unless something was done. As an illustration of this point, the story of the young girl, which is now to be related, will afford the most striking proof. At the same time it may be seen how much anxiety, care, hazard, delay and material aid, were required in order to effect the deliverance of some who were in close places, and difficult of access. It will be necessary to present a considerable amount of correspondence in this case, to bring to light the hidden mysteries of this narrative. The first letter, in explanation, is the following:

LETTER FROM J. BIGELOW, ESQ.

WASHINGTON, D.C.,
June 27, 1854.

MR. WM. STILL – *Dear Sir*: – I have to thank you for the prompt answer you had the kindness to give to my note of 22d inst. Having found a correspondence so quick and easy, and withal so very flattering, I address you again more fully.

The liberal appropriation for *transportation* has been made chiefly on account of a female child of ten or eleven years old, for whose purchase I have been authorized to offer $700 (refused), and for whose sister I have paid $1,600, and some $1,000 for their mother, &c.

This child sleeps in the same apartment with its master and mistress, which adds to the difficulty of removal. She is some ten or twelve miles from the city, so that really the chief hazard will be in bringing her safely to town, and in secreting her until a few days of *storm* shall have abated. All this, I think, is now provided for with entire safety.

The child has two cousins in the immediate vicinity: a young man of some twenty-two years of age, and his sister, of perhaps seventeen – *both Slaves*, but bright and clear-headed as anybody. The young man I have seen often – the services of *both* seem indispensable to the main object suggested; but having once rendered the service, they cannot, and ought not return to Slavery. They look for *freedom* as the reward of what they shall now do.

Out of the $300, cheerfully offered for the whole enterprise, I must pay some reasonable sum for transportation to the city and sustenance while here. It cannot be much; for the balance, I shall give a draft, which will be *promptly paid* on their arrival in New York.

If I have been understood to offer the whole $300, *it shall be paid*, though I have meant as above stated. Among the various ways that have been suggested, has been that of taking *all of them* into the cars here; that, I think, will be found impracticable. I find so much vigilance at the depot, that I would not deem it safe, though, in any kind of carriage they might leave in safety at any time.

All the rest I leave to the experience and sagacity of the gentleman who maps out the enterprise.

Now I will thank you to reply to this and let me know that it reaches you in safety, and is not put in a careless place, whereby I may be endangered; and state also, whether all my propositions are understood and acceptable, and whether, (pretty quickly after I shall inform you that *all things are ready*), the gentleman will make his appearance?

I live alone. My office and bed-room, &c., are at the corner of E. and 7th streets, opposite the east end of the General Post Office, where any one may call upon me.

It would, of course, be imprudent, that this letter, or any other *written* particulars, be in his pockets for fear of accident.

Yours very respectfully,

J. BIGELOW.

While this letter clearly brought to light the situation of things, its author, however, had scarcely begun to conceive of the numberless difficulties which stood in the way of success before the work could be accomplished. The information which Mr. Bigelow's letter contained of the painful situation of this young girl was submitted to different parties who could be trusted, with a view of finding a person who might possess sufficient courage to undertake to bring her away. Amongst those consulted were two or three captains who had on former occasions done good service in the cause. One of these captains was known in Underground Rail-Road circles as the "powder boy."[5] He was willing to undertake the work, and immediately concluded to make a visit to Washington, to see how the "land lay." Accordingly in company with another Underground Rail Road captain, he reported himself one day to Mr. Bigelow with as much assurance as if he were on an errand for an office under the government. The impression made on Mr. Bigelow's mind may be seen from the following letter; it may also be seen that he was fully alive to the necessity of precautionary measures.

SECOND LETTER FROM LAWYER BIGELOW

WASHINGTON, D.C.,
September 9th, 1855.

MR. WM. STILL, DEAR SIR: – I strongly hope the little matter of business so long pending and about which I have written you so many times, will take a move now. I have the promise that the merchandize shall be delivered in this city to-night. Like so many other promises, this also may prove a failure, though I have reason to believe that it will not. I shall, however, know before I mail this note. In case the goods arrive here I shall hope to see your long-talked of "Professional gentleman" in Washington, as soon as possible. He will find

---

5   He had been engaged at different times in carrying powder in his boat from a powder magazine, and from this circumstance, was familiarly called the "Powder Boy."

me by the enclosed card, which shall be a satisfactory introduction for him. You have never given me his name, nor am
I anxious to know it. But on a pleasant visit made last fall to
friend Wm. Wright, in Adams Co., I suppose I accidentally
learned it to be a certain Dr. H – – . Well, let him come.

I had an interesting call a week ago from two gentlemen,
masters of vessels, and brothers, one of whom, I understand,
you know as the "powder boy." I had a little light freight
for them; but not finding enough other freight to ballast their
craft, they went down the river looking for wheat, and promising to return soon. I hope to see them often.

I hope this may find you returned from your northern
trip,[6] as your time proposed was out two or three days ago.

I hope if the whole particulars of Jane Johnson's case[7]
are printed, you will send me the copy as proposed.

I forwarded some of her things to Boston a few days ago,
and had I known its importance in court, I could have sent
you one or two witnesses who would prove that her freedom
was intended by her before she left Washington, and that a
man was *engaged* here to go on to Philadelphia the same
day with her to give notice there of her case, though I think
he failed to do so. It was beyond all question her purpose,
before leaving Washington and provable too, that if Wheeler
should make her a free woman by taking her to a free state
"to use it rather."

Tuesday, 11th September. The attempt was made on

6　Mr. Bigelow's correspondent had been on a visit to the fugitives to
Canada.

7　Jane Johnson of the Passmore Williamson Slave Case.

Sunday to forward the merchandize, but failed through no fault of any of the parties that I now know of. It will be repeated soon, and you shall know the result.

"Whorra for Judge Kane." I feel so indignant at the man, that it is not easy to write the foregoing sentence, and yet who is helping our cause like Kane and Douglas, not forgetting Stringfellow. I hope soon to know that this reaches you in safety.

It often happens that light freight would be offered to Captain B., but the owners cannot by possibility *advance* the amount of freight. I wish it were possible in some such extreme cases, that after advancing *all they have*, some public fund should be found to pay the balance or at least lend it.

[I wish here to caution you against the supposition that I would do any act, or say a word towards helping servants to escape. Although I hate slavery so much, I keep my hands clear of any such wicked or illegal act.]

Yours, very truly,

J.B.

Will you recollect, hereafter, that in any of my future letters, in which I may use [] whatever words may be within the brackets are intended to have no signification whatever to you, only to blind the eyes of the uninitiated. You will find an example at the close of my letter.

Up to this time the chances seemed favorable of procuring the ready services of either of the above mentioned captains who visited Lawyer Bigelow for the removal of the merchandize to Philadelphia, providing the shipping master could have it in readiness to suit their convenience. But as these captains had a number of engagements at Richmond, Petersburg, &c., it was not deemed altogether safe to rely upon either of them, consequently in order to be prepared in case of an emergency, the matter was laid before two professional gentlemen who were each occupying chairs in one of the medical colleges of Philadelphia. They were known to be true friends of the slave, and had possessed withal some experience in Underground Rail Road matters. Either of these professors was willing to undertake the operation, provided arrangements could be completed in time to be carried out during the vacation. In this hopeful, although painfully indefinite position the matter remained for more than a year; but the correspondence and anxiety increased, and with them disappointments and difficulties multiplied. The hope of Freedom, however, buoyed up the heart of the young slave girl during the long months of anxious waiting and daily expectation for the hour of deliverance to come. Equally true and faithful also did Mr. Bigelow prove to the last; but at times he had some painfully dark seasons to encounter, as may be seen from the subjoined letter:

WASHINGTON, D.C.,
October 6th, 1855.

MR. STILL, DEAR SIR: – I regret exceedingly to learn by your favor of 4th instant, that all things are not ready. Although I cannot speak of any immediate and positive danger. [*Yet it is well known that the city is full of incendiaries.*]

Perhaps you are aware that any colored citizen is liable at any hour of day or night without any show of authority to have his house ransacked by constables, and if others do it and commit the most outrageous depredations none but white witnesses can convict them. Such outrages are always common here, and no kind of property exposed to colored protection only, can be considered safe. [I don't say that *much liberty* should not be given to constables on account of numerous runaways, but it don't always work for good.] Before advertising they go round and offer rewards to sharp colored men of perhaps *one or two hundred dollars*, to betray runaways, and having discovered their hiding-place, seize them and then cheat their informers out of the money.

[*Although a law-abiding man,*] I am anxious in this case of *innocence* to raise no conflict or suspicion. [*Be sure that the manumission is full and legal.*] And as I am *powerless* without your aid, *I pray you* don't lose a moment in giving me relief. The idea of waiting yet for weeks seems dreadful; do reduce it to days if possible, and give me notice of the *earliest possible time.*

The property is not yet advertised, but will be, [and if we delay too long, may be sold and lost.]

It was a great misunderstanding, though not your fault, that so much delay would be necessary. [I repeat again that I must have the thing done legally, therefore, please get a good lawyer to draw up the deed of manumission.]

Yours Truly,

J. BIGELOW.

Great was the anxiety felt in Washington. It is certainly not too much to say, that an equal amount of anxiety existed in Philadelphia respecting the safety of the merchandise. At this juncture Mr. Bigelow had come to the conclusion that it was no longer safe to write over his own name, but that he would do well to henceforth adopt the name of the renowned Quaker, Wm. Penn, (he was worthy of it) as in the case of the following letter.

WASHINGTON, D.C.,
November 10th, 1855.

DEAR SIR: – Doctor T. presented my card last night about half past eight which I instantly recognized. I, however, soon became suspicious, and afterwards confounded, to find the doctor using your name and the well known names of Mr. McK. and Mr. W. and yet, neither he nor I, could conjecture the object of his visit.

The doctor is agreeable and sensible, and doubtless a true-hearted man. He seemed to see the whole matter as I did, and was embarrassed. He had nothing to propose, no information to give of the "P. Boy," or of any substitute, and seemed to want no particular information from me concerning my anxieties and perils, though I stated them to him, but found him as powerless as myself to give me relief. I had an agreeable interview with the doctor till after ten, when he left, intending to take the cars at six, as I suppose he did do, this morning.

This morning after eight, I got your letter of the 9th, but it gives me but little enlightenment or satisfaction. You simply say that the doctor is a *true man*, which I cannot doubt, that you thought it best we should have an interview, and that you supposed I would meet the expenses. You informed me also that the "P. Boy" left for Richmond, on Friday, the 2d, to be gone *the length of time named in your last*, I must infer that to be *ten days* though in your last *you assured me* that the "P. Boy" would certainly start for *this place* (not Richmond) in two or three days, though the difficulty about freight might cause delay, and the whole enterprise might not be accomplished under ten days, &c., &c. That time having elapsed and I having agreed to an extra fifty dollars to ensure promptness. I have scarcely left my office since, except for my hasty meals, awaiting his arrival. You now inform me he has gone to Richmond, to be gone ten days, which will expire tomorrow, but you do not say he will return here or to Phila, or where, at the expiration of that time, and Dr. T. could tell me nothing whatever about him. Had he been able to tell me that this *best plan*, which I have so long rested upon, would fail, or was abandoned, I could then understand it, but he says no such thing, and you say, as you have twice before said, "ten days more."

Now, my dear sir, after this recapitulation, can you not see that I have reason for great embarrassment? I have given assurances, both here and in New York, founded on your assurances to me, and caused my friends in the latter place great anxiety, so much that I have had no way to explain my own letters but by sending your last two to Mr. Tappan.

I cannot doubt, I do not, but that you wish to help me, and the cause too, for which both of us have made many and large sacrifices with no hope of reward in this world. If in this case I have been very urgent since September Dr. T. can give you some of my reasons, they have not been selfish.

The whole matter is in a nutshell. Can I, in your opinion, depend on the "P. Boy," and when?

If he promises to come here next trip, will he come, or go to Richmond? This I think is the best way. Can I depend on it?

Dr. T. promised to write me some explanation and give some advice, and at first I thought to await his letter, but on second thought concluded to tell you how I feel, as I have done.

Will you answer my questions with some explicitness, and without delay?

I forgot to inquire of Dr. T. who is the head of your Vigilance Committee, whom I may address concerning other and further operations?

Yours very truly,

WM. PENN.

P.S. I ought to say, that I have no doubt but there were good reasons for the P. Boy's going to Richmond instead of W.; *but what can they be?*

Whilst there are a score of other interesting letters, bearing on this case, the above must suffice, to give at least, an idea of the perplexities and dangers attending its early history. Having accomplished this end, a more encouraging and pleasant phase of the transaction may now be introduced. Here the difficulties, at least very many of them, vanish, yet in one respect, the danger became most imminent. The following letter shows that the girl had been successfully rescued from her master, and that a reward of five hundred dollars had been offered for her.

WASHINGTON, D.C.,
October 12, 1855.

MR. WM. STILL: – AS YOU PICK UP ALL THE NEWS THAT IS STIRRING, I CONTRIBUTE A FEW SCRAPS TO YOUR STOCK, GOING TO SHOW THAT THE POOR SLAVE-HOLDERS HAVE THEIR TROUBLES AS WELL AS OTHER PEOPLE.

FOUR HEAVY LOSSES ON ONE SMALL SCRAP CUT FROM A SINGLE NUMBER OF THE "SUN!" HOW VEXATIOUS! HOW PROVOKING! ON THE OTHER HAND, THINK OF THE POOR, TIMID, BREATHLESS, FLYING CHILD OF FIFTEEN! **FIVE HUNDRED DOLLARS REWARD!** OH, FOR SUCCOR! TO WHOM IN ALL THIS WIDE LAND OF FREEDOM SHALL SHE FLEE AND FIND SAFETY? ALAS! – ALAS! – THE LAW POINTS TO NO ONE!

IS SHE STILL RUNNING WITH BLEEDING FEET?[8]

---

8   At the time this letter was written, she was then under Mr. B.'s protection in Washington, and had to be so kept for six weeks. His question, therefore, "is she still running with bleeding feet," etc., was simply a precautionary step to blind any who might perchance investigate the matter.

OR HIDES SHE IN SOME COLD CAVE, TO REST AND
STARVE? "$500 REWARD." YOURS, FOR THE WEAK
AND THE POOR. **PERISH** THE REWARD.

J.B.

Having thus succeeded in getting possession of, and secreting
this fleeing child of fifteen, as best they could, in Washington,
all concerned were compelled to "possess their souls in
patience," until the storm had passed. Meanwhile, the "child
of fifteen" was christened "Joe Wright," and dressed in male
attire to prepare for traveling as a lad. As no opportunity had
hitherto presented itself, whereby to prepare the "package"
for shipment, from Washington, neither the "powder boy" nor
Dr. T.[9] was prepared to attend to the removal, at this critical
moment. The emergency of the case, however, cried loudly
for aid. The other professional gentleman (Dr. H.), was now
appealed to, but his engagements in the college forbade his
absence before about Thanksgiving day, which was then six
weeks off. This fact was communicated to Washington, and
it being the only resource left, the time named was necessarily
acquiesced in. In the interim, "Joe" was to perfect herself in
the art of wearing pantaloons, and all other male rig. Soon
the days and weeks slid by, although at first the time for
waiting seemed long, when, according to promise, Dr. H. was
in Washington, with his horse and buggy prepared for duty.

---

9   Dr. T. was one of the professional gentlemen alluded to above, who
had expressed a willingness to act as an agent in the matter.

The impressions made by Dr. H., on William Penn's mind, at his first interview, will doubtless be interesting to all concerned, as may be seen in the following letter:

WASHINGTON, D.C.,
November 26, 1855.

MY DEAR SIR: – A recent letter from my friend, probably has led you to expect this from me. He was delighted to receive yours of the 23d, stating that the boy was *all right*. He found the "Prof. gentleman" a *perfect gentleman*; cool, quiet, thoughtful, and *perfectly competent to execute his undertaking*. At the first three minutes of their interview, he felt assured that all would be right. He, and all concerned, give you and that gentleman sincere thanks for what you have done. May the blessings of Him, who cares for the poor, be on your heads.

The especial object of this, is to inform you that there is a half dozen or so of packages here, *pressing for transportation*; twice or thrice that number are also pressing, but less so than the others. Their aggregate means will average, say, $10 each; besides these, we know of a few, say three or four, *able and smart*, but utterly destitute, and kept so purposely by their oppressors. For all these, we feel deeply interested; $10 each would not be enough for the "powder boy." Is there any fund from which a pittance could be spared to help these poor creatures? I don't doubt but that they would honestly repay a small loan as soon as they could earn it. I know full well, that if you begin with such cases, there is no boundary at which you can stop. For years, one half at least, of my friend's time here has been gratuitously given to cases of distress among this class. He never expects or desires to do less; he literally has the *poor always with him*. He knows that it is so with you also, therefore, he only states the case, being especially anxious for at least those to whom I have referred.

I think a small lot of hard coal might always be sold here *from the vessel* at a profit. Would not a like lot of Cumberland coal always sell in Philadelphia?

My friend would be very glad to see the powder boy here again, and if he brings coal, there are those here, who would try to help him sell.

Reply to your regular correspondent as usual.

WM. PENN.

By the presence of the Dr., confidence having been reassured that all would be right, as well as by the "inner light," William Penn experienced a great sense of relief. Everything having been duly arranged, the doctor's horse and carriage stood waiting before the White House (William Penn preferred this place as a starting point, rather than before his own office door). It being understood that "Joe" was to act as coachman in passing out of Washington, at this moment he was called for, and in the most polite and natural manner, with the fleetness of a young deer, he jumped into the carriage, took the reins and whip, whilst the doctor and William Penn were cordially shaking hands and bidding adieu. This done, the order was given to Joe, "drive on." Joe bravely obeyed. The faithful horse trotted off willingly, and the doctor sat in his carriage as composed as though he had succeeded in procuring an honorable and lucrative office from the White House, and was returning home to tell his wife the good news. The doctor had some knowledge of the roads, also some acquaintances in Maryland, through which State he had to travel; therefore, after leaving the suburbs of Washington, the doctor took the reins in his own hands, as he felt that he was more experienced as a driver than his young coachman. He was also mindful of the fact, that, before reaching Pennsylvania, his faithful beast would need feeding several times, and that they consequently would be obliged to pass one or two nights at least in Maryland, either at a tavern or farm-house.

In reflecting upon the matter, it occurred to the doctor, that in earlier days, he had been quite intimately acquainted with a farmer and his family (who were slave-holders), in Maryland, and that he would about reach their house at the end of the first day's journey. He concluded that he could do no better than to renew his acquaintance with his old friends on this occasion. After a very successful day's travel, night came on, and the doctor was safely at the farmer's door with his carriage and waiter boy; the doctor was readily recognized by the farmer and his family, who seemed glad to see him; indeed, they made quite a "fuss" over him. As a matter of strategy, the doctor made quite a "fuss" over them in return; nevertheless, he did not fail to assume airs of importance, which were calculated to lead them to think that he had grown older and wiser than when they knew him in his younger days. In casually referring to the manner of his traveling, he alluded to the fact, that he was not very well, and as it had been a considerable length of time since he had been through that part of the country, he thought that the drive would do him good, and especially the sight of old familiar places and people. The farmer and his family felt themselves exceedingly honored by the visit from the distinguished doctor, and manifested a marked willingness to spare no pains to render his night's lodging in every way comfortable.

The Dr. being an educated and intelligent gentleman, well posted on other questions besides medicine, could freely talk about farming in all its branches, and "niggers" too, in an emergency, so the evening passed off pleasantly with the Dr. in the parlor, and "Joe" in the kitchen. The Dr., however, had given "Joe" precept upon precept, "here a little, and there a little," as to how he should act in the presence of master white people, or slave colored people, and thus he was prepared to act his part with due exactness. Before the evening grew late, the Dr., fearing some accident, intimated that he was feeling a "little languid," and therefore thought that he had better "retire." Furthermore he added, that he was "liable to vertigo," when not quite well, and for this reason he must have his boy "Joe" sleep in the room with him. "Simply give him a bed quilt and he will fare well enough in one corner of the room," said the Dr. The proposal was readily acceded to, and carried into effect by the accommodating host. The Dr. was soon in bed, sleeping soundly, and "Joe," in his new coat and pants, wrapped up in the bed quilt, in a corner of the room quite comfortably.

The next morning the Dr. arose at as early an hour as was prudent for a gentleman of his position, and feeling refreshed, partook of a good breakfast, and was ready, with his boy, "Joe," to prosecute their journey. Face, eyes, hope, and steps, were set as flint, Pennsylvania-ward. What time the following day or night they crossed Mason and Dixon's line is not recorded on the Underground Rail Road books, but at four o'clock on Thanksgiving Day, the Dr. safely landed the "fleeing girl of fifteen" at the residence of the writer in Philadelphia. On delivering up his charge, the Dr. simply remarked to the writer's wife, "I wish to leave this young lad with you a short while, and I will call and see further about him." Without further explanation, he stepped into his carriage and hurried away, evidently anxious to report himself to his wife, in order to relieve her mind of a great weight of anxiety on his account. The writer, who happened to be absent from home when the Dr. called, returned soon afterwards. "The Dr. has been here" (he was the family physician), "and left this 'young lad,' and said, that he would call again and see about him," said Mrs. S. The "young lad" was sitting quite composedly in the dining-room, with his cap on. The writer turned to him and inquired, "I suppose you are the person that the Dr. went to Washington after, are you not?" "No," said "Joe." "Where are you from then?" was the next question. "From York, sir." "From York? Why then did the Dr. bring you here?" was the next query. "The Dr. went expressly to Washington after a young girl, who was to be brought away dressed up as a boy, and I took you to be the person." Without replying "the lad" arose and walked out of the house. The querist, somewhat mystified, followed him, and then when the two were alone, "the lad" said, "I am the one the Dr. went after." After congratulating her, the writer asked why she had said, that she was not from Washington, but from York. She explained, that the Dr. had strictly charged her not to own to any person, except the writer, that she was from Washington, but from York. As there were persons present (wife, hired girl, and a fugitive woman), when the questions were put to her, she felt that it would be a violation of her pledge to answer in the affirmative. Before this examination, neither of the individuals present for a moment entertained the slightest doubt but that she was a "lad," so well had she acted her part in every particular. She was dressed in a new suit, which fitted her quite nicely, and with her unusual amount of common sense, she appeared to be in no respect lacking. To send off a prize so rare and remarkable, as she was, without affording some of the stockholders and managers of the Road the pleasure of seeing her, was not to be thought of. In addition to the Vigilance Committee, quite a number of persons were invited to see her, and were greatly astonished. Indeed it was difficult to realize, that she was not a boy, even after becoming acquainted with the facts in the case.

The following is an exact account of this case, as taken from the Underground Rail Road records:

THANKSGIVING DAY,
Nov., 1855.

Arrived, Ann Maria Weems, alias "Joe Wright," alias "Ellen Capron," from Washington, through the aid of Dr. H. She is about fifteen years of age, bright mulatto, well grown, smart

and good-looking. For the last three years, or about that
length of time, she has been owned by Charles M. Price, a
negro trader, of Rockville, Maryland. Mr. P. was given to
"intemperance," to a very great extent, and gross "profanity."
He buys and sells many slaves in the course of the year.
"His wife is cross and peevish." She used to take great
pleasure in "torturing" one "little slave boy." He was the son
of his master (and was owned by him); this was the chief
cause of the mistress' spite.

Ann Maria had always desired her freedom from childhood,
and although not thirteen, when first advised to escape, she
received the suggestion without hesitation, and ever after that
time waited almost daily, for more than two years, the chance
to flee. Her friends were, of course, to aid her, and make
arrangements for her escape. Her owner, fearing that she might
escape, for a long time compelled her to sleep in the chamber
with "her master and mistress;" indeed she was so kept until
about three weeks before she fled. She left her parents living
in Washington. Three of her brothers had been sold South
from their parents. Her mother had been purchased for $1,000,
and one of her sisters for $1,600 for freedom. Before Ann
Maria was thirteen years of age $700 was offered for her by
a friend, who desired to procure her freedom, but the offer
was promptly refused, as were succeeding ones repeatedly
made. The only chance of procuring her freedom, depended
upon getting her away on the Underground Rail Road. She
was neatly attired in male habiliments, and in that manner
came all the way from Washington. After passing two or three
days with her new friends in Philadelphia, she was sent on

(in male attire) to Lewis Tappan, of New York, who had likewise been deeply interested in her case from the beginning,
and who held himself ready, as was understood, to cash a
draft for three hundred dollars to compensate the man who
might risk his own liberty in bringing her on from Washington.
After having arrived safely in New York, she found a home
and kind friends in the family of the Rev. A.N. Freeman, and
received quite an ovation characteristic of an Underground
Rail Road.

After having received many tokens of esteem and kindness
from the friends of the slave in New York and Brooklyn, she
was carefully forwarded on to Canada, to be educated at the
"Buxton Settlement."

An interesting letter, however, from the mother of Ann
Maria, conveying the intelligence of her late great struggle
and anxiety in laboring to free her last child from Slavery is
too important to be omitted, and hence is inserted in connection with this narrative.

LETTER FROM THE MOTHER

WASHINGTON, D.C.,
September 19th, 1857.

WM. STILL, ESQ., Philadelphia, Pa. SIR: – I have just sent
for my son Augustus, in Alabama. I have sent eleven hundred
dollars which pays for his body and some thirty dollars to
pay his fare to Washington. I borrowed one hundred and
eighty dollars to make out the eleven hundred dollars. I was

not very successful in Syracuse. I collected only twelve dollars, and in Rochester only two dollars. I did not know that the season was so unpropitious. The wealthy had all gone to the springs. They must have returned by this time. I hope you will exert yourself and help me get a part of the money I owe, at least. I am obliged to pay it by the 12th of next month. I was unwell when I returned through Philadelphia, or I should have called. I had been from home five weeks.

My son Augustus is the last of the family in Slavery. I feel rejoiced that he is soon to be free and with me, and of course feel the greatest solicitude about raising the one hundred and eighty dollars I have borrowed of a kind friend, or who has borrowed it for me at bank. I hope and pray you will help me as far as possible. Tell Mr. Douglass to remember me, and if he can, to interest his friends for me.

You will recollect that five hundred dollars of our money was taken to buy the sister of Henry H. Garnett's wife. Had I been able to command this I should not be necessitated to ask the favors and indulgences I do.

I am expecting daily the return of Augustus, and may Heaven grant him a safe deliverance and smile propitiously upon you and all kind friends who have aided in his return to me.

Be pleased to remember me to friends, and accept yourself the blessing and prayers of your dear friend,

EARRO WEEMS.

P.S. Direct your letter to E.L. Stevens, in Duff Green's Row, Capitol Hill, Washington, D.C.

E.W.

That William Penn who worked so faithfully for two years for the deliverance of Ann Maria may not appear to have been devoting all his time and sympathy towards this single object it seems expedient that two or three additional letters, proposing certain grand Underground Rail Road plans, should have a place here. For this purpose, therefore, the following letters are subjoined.

LETTERS FROM WILLIAM PENN

WASHINGTON, D.C.,
Oct. 3, 1854

DEAR SIR: – I address you to-day chiefly at the suggestion of the Lady who will hand you my letter, and who is a resident of your city.

After stating to you, that the case about which I have previously written, remains just as it was when I wrote last – full of difficulty – I thought I would call your attention to another enterprise; it is this: to find a man with a large heart for doing good to the oppressed, who will come to Washington to live, and who will *walk out to Penn'a., or a part of the way there, once or twice a week*. He will find parties who will *pay him for doing so*. Parties of say, two, three, five or so, who will pay him *at least* $5 each, for the privilege of following him, but *will never speak to him*; but will keep just in sight of him and obey any sign he may give; say, he takes off his hat and scratches his head as a sign for them to go to some barn or wood to rest, &c. No living being shall be found to say he ever spoke to them. A white man would be best, and then even parties led out by him could not, if they would, testify to any *understanding* or anything else against a white man. I think he might make a good living at it. Can it not be done?

If one or two safe stopping-places could be found on the way – such as a barn or shed, they could walk quite safely all night and then sleep all day – about two, or *easily* three nights would convey them to a place of safety. The traveler might be a peddler or huckster, with an old horse and cart, and bring us in eggs and butter if he pleases.

Let him once plan out his route, and he might then take ten or a dozen at a time, and they are often able and willing to pay $10 a piece.

I have a hard case now on hand; a brother and sister 23 to 25 years old, whose mother lives in your city. They are cruelly treated; they want to go, they *ought* to go; but they are utterly destitute. Can nothing be done for such cases? If you can think of anything let me know it. I suppose you know me?

WASHINGTON, D.C.,
April 3, 1856.

DEAR SIR: – I sent you the recent law of Virginia, under which all vessels are to be searched for fugitives within the waters of that State.

It was long ago suggested by a sagacious friend, that the "powder boy" might find a better port in the Chesapeake bay, or in the Patuxent river to communicate with this vicinity, than by entering the Potomac river, even were there no such law.

Suppose he opens a trade with some place south-west of Annapolis, 25 or 30 miles from here, or less. He might carry wood, oysters, &c., and all his customers from this vicinity might travel in *that direction* without any of the suspicions that might attend their journeyings *towards this city*. In this way, doubtless, a good business might be carried on without interruption or competition, and provided the plan was conducted without affecting the inhabitants along that shore, no suspicion would arise as to the manner or magnitude of his business operations. How does this strike you? What does the "powder boy" think of it?

I heretofore intimated a *pressing necessity* on the part of several females – they are variously situated – two have children, say a couple each; some have none – of the latter, one can raise $50, another, say 30 or 40 dollars – another who was gazetted last August (a copy sent you), can raise, through her friends, 20 or 30 dollars, &c., &c. None of these can walk so far or so fast as scores of *men* that are constantly leaving. I cannot shake off my anxiety for these poor creatures. Can you think of anything for any of these? Address your other correspondent in answer to this at your leisure.

Yours,

WM. PENN.

P.S. – April 3d. Since writing the above, I have received yours of 31st. I am rejoiced to hear that business is so successful and prosperous – may it continue till *the article* shall cease to be merchandize.

I spoke in my last letter of the departure of a "few friends." I have since heard of their good health in Penn'a. Probably you may have seen them.

In reference to the expedition of which you think you can "hold out some little encouragement," I will barely remark, that I shall be glad, if it is undertaken, to have all the notice of the *time and manner* that is possible, so as to make ready.

A friend of mine says, anthracite coal will always pay here from Philadelphia, and thinks a small vessel might run often – that she never would be searched in the Potomac, unless she went outside.

You advise caution towards Mr. P. I am precisely of your opinion about him, that he is a "queer stick," and while I advised him carefully in reference to his own undertakings, I took no counsel of him concerning mine.

Yours,

W.P.

**FIVE YEARS
AND ONE MONTH
SECRETED**

*JOHN HENRY, HEZEKIAH, AND JAMES HILL.
JOHN MAKES A DESPERATE RESISTANCE
AT THE SLAVE AUCTION AND ESCAPES
AFTER BEING SECRETED NINE MONTHS.
HEZEKIAH ESCAPED FROM A TRADER AND
WAS SECRETED THIRTEEN MONTHS
BEFORE HIS FINAL DELIVERANCE. JAMES
WAS SECRETED THREE YEARS IN A PLACE
OF GREAT SUFFERING, AND ESCAPED. IN
ALL FIVE YEARS AND ONE MONTH.*

Many letters from John Henry show how incessantly his mind ran out towards the oppressed, and the remarkable intelligence and ability he displayed with the pen, considering that he had no chance to acquire book knowledge. After having fled for refuge to Canada and having become a partaker of impartial freedom under the government of Great Britain, to many it seemed that the fugitive should be perfectly satisfied. Many appeared to think that the fugitive, having secured freedom, had but little occasion for anxiety or care, even for his nearest kin. "Change your name." "Never tell any one how you escaped." "Never let any one know where you came from." "Never think of writing back, not even to your wife; you can do your kin no good, but may do them harm by writing." "Take care of yourself." "You are free, well, be satisfied then." "It will do you no good to fret about your wife and children; that will not get them out of Slavery." Such was the advice often given to the fugitive. Men who had been slaves themselves, and some who had aided in the escape of individuals, sometimes urged these sentiments on men and women whose hearts were almost breaking over the thought that their dearest and best friends were in chains in the prison house. Perhaps it was thoughtlessness on the part of some, and a wish to inspire due cautiousness on the part of others, that prompted this advice. Doubtless some did soon forget their friends. They saw no way by which they could readily communicate with them. Perhaps Slavery had dealt with them so cruelly, that little hope or aspiration was left in them.

It was, however, one of the most gratifying facts connected with the fugitives, the strong love and attachment that they constantly expressed for their relatives left in the South; the undying faith they had in God as evinced by their touching appeals on behalf of their fellow-slaves. But few probably are aware how deeply these feelings were cherished in the breasts of this people. Forty, fifty, or sixty years, in some instances elapsed, but this ardent sympathy and love continued warm and unwavering as ever. Children left to the cruel mercy of slave-holders, could never be forgotten. Brothers and sisters could not refrain from weeping over the remembrance of their separation on the auction block: of having seen innocent children, feeble and defenceless women in the grasp of a merciless tyrant, pleading, groaning, and crying in vain for pity. Not to remember those thus bruised and mangled, it would seem alike unnatural, and impossible. Therefore it is a source of great satisfaction to be able, in relating these heroic escapes, to present the evidences of the strong affections of this greatly oppressed race.

John Henry never forgot those with whom he had been a fellow-sufferer in Slavery; he was always fully awake to their wrongs, and longed to be doing something to aid and encourage such as were striving to get their Freedom. He wrote many letters in behalf of others, as well as for himself, the tone of which was always marked by the most zealous devotion to the slave, a high sense of the value of Freedom, and unshaken confidence that God was on the side of the oppressed, and a strong hope, that the day was not far distant, when the slave power would be "suddenly broken and that without remedy."

Notwithstanding the literary imperfections of these letters, they are deemed well suited to these pages. Of course, slaves were not allowed book learning. Virginia even imprisoned white women for teaching free colored children the alphabet. Who has forgotten the imprisonment of Mrs. Douglass for this offense? In view of these facts, no apology is needed on account of Hill's grammar and spelling.

In these letters, may be seen, how much liberty was valued, how the taste of Freedom moved the pen of the slave; how the thought of fellow-bondmen, under the heel of the slave-holder, aroused the spirit of indignation and wrath; how importunately appeals were made for help from man and from God; how much joy was felt at the arrival of a fugitive, and the intense sadness experienced over the news of a failure or capture of a slave. Not only are the feelings of John Henry Hill represented in these epistles, but the feelings of very many others amongst the intelligent fugitives all over the country are also represented to the letter. It is more with a view of doing justice to a brave, intelligent class, whom the public are ignorant of, than merely to give special prominence to John and his relatives as individuals, that these letters are given.

ESCAPE OF JOHN HENRY HILL FROM THE SLAVE AUCTION IN RICHMOND, ON THE FIRST DAY OF JANUARY, 1853

JOHN HENRY at that time, was a little turned of twenty-five years of age, full six feet high, and remarkably well proportioned in every respect. He was rather of a brown color, with marked intellectual features. John was by trade, a carpenter, and was considered a competent workman. The year previous to his escape, he hired his time, for which he paid his owner $150. This amount John had fully settled up the last day of the year. As he was a young man of steady habits, a husband and father, and withal an ardent lover of Liberty; his owner, John Mitchell, evidently observed these traits in his character, and concluded that he was a dangerous piece of property to keep; that his worth in money could be more easily managed than the man. Consequently, his master unceremoniously, without intimating in any way to John, that he was to be sold, took him to Richmond, on the first day of January (the great annual sale day), and directly to the slave-auction. Just as John was being taken into the building, he was invited to submit to hand-cuffs. As the thought flashed upon his mind that he was about to be sold on the auction-block, he grew terribly desperate. "Liberty or death" was the watchword of that awful moment. In the twinkling of an eye, he turned on his enemies, with his fist, knife, and feet, so tiger-like, that he actually put four or five men to flight, his master among the number. His enemies thus suddenly baffled, John wheeled, and, as if assisted by an angel, strange as it may appear, was soon out of sight of his pursuers, and securely hid away. This was the last hour of John Henry's slave life, but not, however, of his struggles and sufferings for freedom, for before a final chance to escape presented itself, nine months elapsed. The mystery as to where, and how he fared, the following account, in his own words, must explain –

Nine months I was trying to get away. I was secreted for a long time in a kitchen of a merchant near the corner of Franklyn and 7th streets, at Richmond, where I was well taken care of, by a lady friend of my mother. When I got Tired of staying in that place, I wrote myself a pass to pass myself to Petersburg, here I stopped with a very prominent Colored person, who was a friend to Freedom stayed here until two white friends told other friends if I was in the city to tell me to go at once, and stand not upon the order of going, because they had hard a plot. I wrot a pass, started for Richmond, Reached Manchester, got off the Cars walked into Richmond, once more got back into the same old Den, Stayed here from the 16th of Aug. to 12th Sept. On the 11th of Sept. 8 o'clock P.M. a message came to me that there had been a State Room taken on the steamer *City of Richmond* for my benefit, and I assured the party that it would be occupied if God be willing. Before 10 o'clock the next morning, on the 12th, a beautiful Sept. day, I arose early, wrote my pass for Norfolk left my old Den with a many a good bye, turned out the back way to 7th St., thence to Main, down Main behind 4 night waich to old Rockett's and after about 20 minutes of delay I succeed in Reaching the State Room. My Conductor was very much Excited, but I felt as Composed as I do at this moment, for I had started from my Den that morning for Liberty or for Death providing myself with a Brace of Pistels.

Yours truly

J.H. HILL.

A private berth was procured for him on the steamship City of Richmond, for the amount of $125, and thus he was brought on safely to Philadelphia. While in the city, he enjoyed the hospitalities of the Vigilance Committee, and the greetings of a number of friends, during the several days of his sojourn. The thought of his wife, and two children, left in Petersburg, however, naturally caused him much anxiety. Fortunately, they were free, therefore, he was not without hope of getting them; moreover, his wife's father (Jack McCraey), was a free man, well known, and very well to do in the world, and would not be likely to see his daughter and grandchildren suffer. In this particular, Hill's lot was of a favorable character, compared with that of most slaves leaving their wives and children.

FIRST LETTER
ON ARRIVING IN CANADA

TORONTO,
October 4th, 1853.

DEAR SIR: – I take this method of informing you that I am well, and that I got to this city all safe and sound, though I did not get here as soon as I expect. I left your city on Saterday and I was on the way untel the Friday following. I got to New York the same day that I left Philadelphia, but I had to stay there untel Monday evening. I left that place at six o'clock. I got to Albany next morning in time to take the half past six o'clock train for Rochester, here I stay untel Wensday night. The reason I stay there so long Mr. Gibbs given me a letter to Mr Morris at Rochester. I left that place Wensday, but I only got five miles from that city that night. I got to Lewiston on Thurday

afternoon, but too late for the boat to this city. I left
Lewiston on Friday at one o'clock, got to this city at five.
Sir I found this to be a very handsome city. I like it better
than any city I ever saw. It are not as large as the city that
you live in, but it is very large place much more so than
I expect to find it. I seen the gentleman that you given me
letter to. I think him much of a gentleman. I got into work
on Monday. The man whom I am working for is name
Myers; but I expect to go to work for another man by name
of Tinsly, who is a master workman in this city. He says
that he will give me work next week and everybody advises
me to work for Mr. Tinsly as there more surity in him.

Mr. Still, I have been looking and looking for my friends
for several days, but have not seen nor heard of them. I
hope and trust in the Lord Almighty that all things are well
with them. My dear sir I could feel so much better sattisfied
if I could hear from my wife. Since I reached this city I
have talagraphed to friend Brown to send my thing to me,
but I cannot hear a word from no one at all. I have written
to Mr. Brown two or three times since I left the city. I trust
that he has gotten my wife's letters, that is if she has written.
Please direct your letters to me, near the corner Sarah and
Edward street, until I give you further notice. You will tell
friend B. how to direct his letters, as I forgotten it when I
writt to him, and ask him if he has heard anything from
Virginia. Please to let me hear from him without delay for
my very soul is trubled about my friends whom I expected
to of seen here before this hour. Whatever you do please
to write. I shall look for you paper shortly.

Believe me sir to be your well wisher.

JOHN H. HILL.

SECOND LETTER

Expressions of gratitude – The Custom House refuses to charge him duty – He is greatly concerned for his wife

TORONTO,
October 30th, 1853.

MY DEAR FRIEND: – I now write to inform you that I have received my things all safe and sound, and also have shuck hand with the friend that you send on to this place one of them is stopping with me. His name is Chas. Stuert, he seemes to be a tolerable smart fellow. I Rec'd my letters. I have taken this friend to see Mr. Smith. However will give him a place to board untell he can get to work. I shall do every thing I can for them all that I see the gentleman wish you to see his wife and let her know that he arrived safe, and present his love to her and to all the friend. Mr. Still, I am under ten thousand obligation to you for your kindness when shall I ever repay? S. speek very highly of you. I will state to you what Custom house master said to me. He ask me when he Presented my efects are these your efects. I answered yes. He then ask me was I going to settle in Canada. I told him I was. He then ask me of my case. I told all about it. He said I am happy to see you and all that will come. He ask me how much I had to pay for my Paper. I told him half dollar. He then told me that I should have my money again. He a Rose from his seat and got my money. So my friend you can see the people and tell them all this is a land of liberty and believe they will find friends here. My best love to all.

My friend I must call upon you once more to do more kindness for me that is to write to my wife as soon as you get this, and tell her when she gets ready to come she will pack and consign her things to you. You will give her some instruction, but not to your expenses but to her own.

When you write direct your letter to Phillip Ubank, Petersburg, Va. My Box arrived here the 27th.

My dear sir I am in a hurry to take this friend to church, so I must close by saying I am your humble servant in the cause of liberty and humanity.

JOHN H. HILL.

THIRD LETTER

Canada is highly praised – The Vigilance Committee is implored to send all the Fugitives there – "Farmers and Mechanics wanted" – "No living in Canada for Negroes," as argued by "Masters," flatly denied, &c., &c., &c.

So I ask you to send the fugitives to Canada. I don't know much of this Province but I beleaves that there is Rome enough for the colored and whites of the United States. We wants farmers mechanic men of all qualification &c., if they are not made we will make them, if we cannot make the old, we will make our children.

Now concerning the city toronto this city is Beautiful and Prosperous Levele city. Great many wooden codages more than what should be but I am in hopes there will be more of the Brick and Stonn. But I am not done about your Republicanism. Our masters have told us that there was no living in Canada for a Negro but if it may Please your gentlemanship to publish these facts that we are here able to earn our bread and money enough to make us comftable. But I say give me freedom, and the United States may have all her money and her Luxtures, yeas give Liberty or Death. I'm in America, but not under Such a Government that I cannot express myself, speak, think or write So as I am able, and if my master had allowed me to have an education I would make them American Slave-holders feel me, Yeas I would make them tremble when I spoke, and when I take my Pen in hand their knees smote together. My Dear Sir suppose I was an educated man. I could write you something worth reading, but you know we poor fugitives whom has just come over from the South are not able to write much on no subject whatever, but I hope by the aid of my God I will try to use my midnight lamp, untel I can have some influence upon the American Slavery. If some one would say to me, that they would give my wife bread untel I could be Educated I would stoop my trade this day and take up my books.

But a crisis is approaching when assential requisite to the American Slaveholders when blood Death or Liberty will be required at their hands. I think our people have depened too long and too much on false legislator let us now look for ourselves. It is true that England however the Englishman is our best friend but we as men ought not to depened upon her Remonstrace with the Americans because she loves her commercial trade as any Nations do. But I must say, while we look up and acknowledge the Power greatness and honor of old England, and believe that while we sit beneath the Silken folds of her flag of Perfect Liberty, we are secure, beyond the reach of the aggressions of the Blood hounds and free from the despotism that would wrap around our limbs by the damable Slaveholder. Yet we would not like spoiled childeren depend upon her, but upon ourselves and as one means of strengthening ourselves, we should agitate the emigration to Canada. I here send you a paragraph which I clipted from the weekly *Glob*. I hope you will publish so that Mr. Williamson may know that men are not chattel here but reather they are men and if he wants his chattle let him come here after it or his thing. I wants you to let the whole United States know we are satisfied here because I have seen more Pleasure since I came here then I saw in the U.S. the 24 years that I served my master. Come Poor distress men women and come to Canada where colored men are free. Oh how sweet the word do sound to me yeas when I contemplate of these things, my very flesh creaps my heart thrub when I think of my beloved friends whom I left in that cursid hole. Oh my God what can I do for them or shall I do for them. Lord help them. Suffer them to be no longer depressed beneath the Bruat Creation but may they be looked upon as men made of the Bone and Blood as the Anglo-Americans. May God in his mercy Give Liberty to all this world. I must close as it am late hour at night. I Remain your friend in the cause of Liberty and humanity,

JOHN H. HILL, a fugitive.

If you know any one who would give me an education write and let me know for I am in want of it very much.

Your with Respect,

J.H.H.

If the sentiments in the above letter do not indicate an uncommon degree of natural intelligence, a clear perception of the wrongs of Slavery, and a just appreciation of freedom, where shall we look for the signs of intellect and manhood?

FOURTH LETTER

Longs for his wife – In hearing of the return of a Fugitive from Philadelphia is made sorrowful – His love of Freedom increases, &c., &c.

TORONTO,
November 12th, 1853.

MY DEAR STILL: – Your letter of the 3th came to hand thursday and also three copes all of which I was glad to Received they have taken my attention all together Every Time I got them. I also Rec'd. a letter from my friend Brown. Mr. Brown stated to me that he had heard from my wife but he did not say what way he heard. I am looking for my wife every day. Yes I want her to come then I will be better satisfied. My friend I am a free man and feeles alright about that matter. I am doing tolrable well in my line of business, and think I will do better after little. I hope you all will never stop any of our Brotheran that makes their Escep from the South but send them on to this Place where they can be free man and woman. We want them here and not in your State where they can be taken away at any hour. Nay but let him come here where he can Enjoy the Rights of a human being and not to be trodden under the feet of men like themselves. All the People that comes here does well. Thanks be to God that I came to this place. I would like very well to see you all but never do I expect to see you in the United States. I want you all to come to this land of Liberty where the bondman can be free. Come one come all come to this place, and I hope my dear friend you will send on here. I shall do for them as you all done for me when I came on here however I will do the best I can for them if they can they shall do if they will do, but some comes here that can't do well because they make no efford. I hope my friend you will teach them such lessons as Mrs. Moore Give me before I left your city. I hope she may live a hundred years longer and enjoy good health. May God bless her for the good cause which she are working in. Mr. Still you ask me to remember you to Nelson. I will do so when I see him, he are on the lake so is Stewart. I received a letter to-day for Stewart from your city which letter I will take to him when he comes to the city. He are not stoping with us at this time. I was very sorry a few days ago when I heard that a man was taken from your city.

Send them over here, then let him come here and take them away and I will try to have a finger in the Pie myself. You said that you had written to my wife ten thousand thanks for what you have done and what you are willing to do. My friend whenever you hear from my wife please write to me. Whenever she come to your city please give instruction how to travel. I wants her to come the faster way. I wish she was here now. I wish she could get a ticket through to this place. I have mail a paper for you to day.

We have had snow but not to last long. Let me hear from you. My Respect friend Brown. I will write more when I have the opportunity.

Yours with Respect,

JOHN H. HILL.

P.S. My dear Sir. Last night after I had written the above, and had gone to bed, I heard a strange voice in the house, Saying to Mr. Myers to come quickly to one of our colod Brotheran out of the street. We went and found a man a Carpenter laying on the side walk woltun in his Blood. Done by some unknown Person as yet but if they stay on the earth the law will deteck them. It is said that party of colord people done it, which party was seen to come out an infame house.

Mr. Myers have been down to see him and Brought the Sad news that the Poor fellow was dead. Mr. Scott for Henry Scott was the name, he was a fugitive from Virginia he came here from Pittsburg Pa. Oh, when I went where he laid what a shock, it taken my Sleep altogether night. When I got to

Sopt his Body was surrounded by the Policeman. The law has taken the woman in cusidy. I write and also send you a paper of the case when it comes out.

J.H. HILL.

FIFTH LETTER

He rejoices over the arrival of his wife – but at the same time, his heart is bleeding over a dear friend whom he had promised to help before he left Slavery.

TORONTO,
December 29th, 1853.

MY DEAR FRIEND: – It affords me a good deel of Pleasure to say that my wife and the Children have arrived safe in this City. But my wife had very bad luck. She lost her money and the money that was belonging to the children, the whole amount was 35 dollars. She had to go to the Niagara falls and Telegraph to me come after her. She got to the falls on Sat'dy and I went after her on Monday. We saw each other once again after so long an Abstance, you may know what sort of metting it was, joyful times of corst. My wife are well Satisfied here, and she was well Pleased during her stay in your city. My Trip to the falls cost Ten Eighty Seven and half. The things that friend Brown Shiped to me by the Express costed $24¼. So you can see fiting out a house Niagara falls and the cost for bringing my things to this place, have got me out of money, but for all I am a free man.

The weather are very cold at Present, the snow continue to fall though not as deep here as it is in Boston. The people haves their own Amousements, the weather as it is now, they don't care for the snow nor ice, but they are going from Ten A.M. until Twelve P.M., the hous that we have open don't take well because we don't Sell Spirits, which we are trying to avoid if we can.

Mr. Still, I hold in my hand A letter from a friend of South, who calls me to promise that I made to him before I left. My dear Sir, this letter have made my heart Bleed, since I Received it, he also desires of me to remember him to his beloved Brethren and then to Pray for him and his dear friends who are in Slavery. I shall Present his letter to the churches of this city. I forward to your care for Mrs. Moore, a few weeks ago. Mrs. Hill sends her love to your wife and yourself.

Please to write, I Sincerely hope that our friends from Petersburg have reached your city before this letter is dated. I must close by saying, that I Sir, remain humble and obedient Servant,

J.H.H.

SIXTH LETTER

He is now earnestly appealing in behalf of a friend in Slavery, with a view to procuring aid and assistance from certain parties, by which this particular friend in bondage might be rescued.

Toranto,
March 8th, 1854.

My Dear Friend Still: – We will once more truble you opon this great cause of freedom, as we know that you are a man, that are never fatuged in Such a glorious cause. Sir, what I wish to Say is this. Mr. Forman has Received a letter from his wife dated the 29th ult. She States to him that She was Ready at any time, and that Everything was Right with her, and she hoped that he would lose no time in sending for her for she was Ready and awaiting for him. Well friend Still, we learnt that Mr. Minkens could not bring her the account of her child. We are very sorry to hear Such News, however, you will please to read this letter with care, as we have learnt that Minkens Cannot do what we wishes to be done; we perpose another way. There is a white man that Sale from Richmond to Boston, that man are very Safe, he will bring F's wife with her child. So you will do us a favour will take it upon yourself to transcribe from this letter what we shall write. I.E. this there is a Colored gen. that workes on the basin in R – – this man's name is Esue Poster, he can tell Mrs. forman all about this Saleor. So you can place the letter in the hands of M. to take to forman's wife, She can read it for herself. She will find Foster at ladlum's warehouse on the Basin, and when you write call my name to him and he will trust it. this foster are a member of the old Baptist Church. When you have done all you can do let us know what you have done, if you hears anything of my uncle let me know.

SEVENTH LETTER.

He laments over his uncle's fate, who was suffering in a dungeon-like place of concealment daily waiting for the opportunity to escape.

Toronto,
March 18th, 1864.

My Dear Still: – Yours of the 15th Reached on the 11th, found myself and family very well, and not to delay no time in replying to you, as there was an article in your letter which article Roused me very much when I read it; that was you praying to me to be cautious how I write down South. Be so kind as to tell me in your next letter whether you have at any time apprehended any danger in my letters however, in those bond southward; if there have been, allow me to beg ten thousand pardon before God and man, for I am not design to throw any obstacle in the way of those whom I left in South, but to aide them in every possible way. I have done as you Requested, that to warn the friends of the dager of writing South. I have told all you said in yours that Mr. Minkins would be in your city very soon, and you would see what you could do for me, do you mean or do speak in reference to my dear uncle. I am hopes that you will use every ifford to get him from the position in which he now stand. I know how he feels at this time, for I have felt the same when I was a runway. I was bereft of all participation with my family for nearly nine months, and now that poor fellow are place in same position. Oh God help I pray, what a pitty it is that I cannot do him no good, but I sincerely hope that you will not get fatigued at doing good in such cases, nay, I think other wises of you, however, I Say no more on this subject at present, but leave it for you to judge.

On the 13th inst. you made Some Remarks concerning friend Forman's wife, I am Satisfied that you will do all you can for her Release from Slavery, but as you said you feels for them, so do I, and Mr. Foreman comes to me very often to know if I have heard anything from you concerning his wife, they all comes to for the same.

God Save the Queen. All my letters Southward have passed through your hands with an exception of one.

JOHN H. HILL.

EIGHTH LETTER.

Death has snatched away one of his children and he has cause to mourn. In his grief he recounts his struggles for freedom, and his having to leave his wife and children. He acknowledges that he had to "work very hard for comforts," but he declares that he would not "exchange with the comforts of ten thousand slaves."

TORONTO,
Sept. 14th, 1854.

MY DEAR FRIEND STILL: – this are the first oppertunity that I have had to write you since I Reed your letter of the 20th July, there have been sickness and Death in my family since your letter was Reed, our dear little Child have been taken from us one whom we loved so very Dear, but the almighty God knows what are best for us all.

Louis Henry Hill, was born in Petersburg Va May 7th 1852. and Died Toronto August 19th 1854 at five o'clock P.M.

Dear Still I could say much about the times and insidince that have taken place since the coming of that dear little angle jest spoken of. it was 12 months and 3 days from the time that I took departure of my wife and child to proceed to Richmond to awaite a conveyance up to the day of his death.

it was thursday the 13th that I lift Richmond, it was Saturday the 15th that I land to my great joy in the city of Phila. then I put out for Canada. I arrived in this city on Friday the 30th and to my great satisfaction. I found myself upon Briton's free land, not only free for the white man bot for all.

this day 12 months I was not out of the reach the slave-holders, but this 14th day of Sept. I am as Free as your President Pearce. only I have not been free so long However the 30th of the month I will have been free only 12 months.

It is true that I have to work very hard for comfort but I would not exchange with ten thousand slave that are equel with their masters. I am Happy, Happy.

Give love to Mrs. Still. My wife laments her child's death too much, wil you be so kind as to see Mr. Brown and ask him to write to me, and if he have heard from Petersburg Va.

Yours truely

J.H. HILL.

NINTH LETTER

He is anxiously waiting for the arrival of friends from the South. Hints that slaveholders would be very unsafe in Canada, should they be foolish enough to visit that country for the purpose of enticing slaves back.

TORONTO,
Jan. 19th, 1854.

MY DEAR STILL: – Your letter of the 16th came to hand just in time for my perpose I perceivs by your statement that the money have not been to Petersburg at all done just what was right and I would of sent the money to you at first, but my dear friend I have called upon you for so many times that I have been ashamed of myself to call any more So you may perceive by the above written my obligations to you, you said that you had written on to Petersburg, you have done Right which I believes is your general way of doing your business, the money are all right I only had to pay a 6d on the Ten dollars. this money was given to by a friend in the city N. york, the friend was from Richmond Virginia (a white man) the amount was fifteen dollars, I forward a letter to you yesterday which letter I forgot to date. my friend I wants to hear from virginia the worst of all things. you know that we expect some freneds on and we cannot hear any thing from them which makes us uneasy for fear that they have attempt to come away and been detected. I have ears open at all times, listen at all hours expecting to hear from them Please to see friend Brown and know from him if he has heard anything from our friends, if he have not. tell him write and inquiare into the matter why it is that they have not come over, then let me hear from you all.

We are going to have a grand concert &c I mean the Abolisnous Socity. I will attend myself and also my wife if the Lord be willing you will perceive in previous letter that I mension something concerning Mr Forman's wife if there be any chance whatever please to proceed, Mr Foreman sends his love to you Requested you to do all you can to get his wife away from Slavery.

Our best respects to your wife. You promised me that you would write somthing concerning our arrival in Canada but I suppose you have not had the time as yet, I would be very glad to read your opinion on that matter I have notice several articles in the freeman one of the Canada weaklys concerning the Christiana prisoners respecting Castnor Hanway and also Mr. Rauffman. if I had one hundred dollars to day I would give them five each, however I hope that I may be able to subscribe something for their Relefe. in Regards to the letters have been written from Canada to the South the letters was not what they thought them to be and if the slave-holders know when they are doing well they had better keep their side for if they comes over this side of the lake I am under the impression they will not go back with somethin that their mother boned them with whether thiar slaves written for them or not. I know some one here that have written his master to come after him, but not because he expect to go with him home but because he wants to retaleate upon his persecutor, but I would be sorry for man that have written for his master expecting to return with him because the people here would kill them. Sir I cannot write enough to express myself so I must close by saying I Remain yours.

JOHN H. HILL.

TENTH LETTER

Great joy over an arrival – Twelve months praying for the deliverance of an Uncle groaning in a hiding-place, while the Slave-hunters are daily expected – Strong appeals for aid, &c., &c.

TORONTO,
January 7th, 1855.

MY DEAR FRIEND: – It is with much pleasure that I take this opportunity of addressing you with these few lines hoping when they reeches you they may find yourself and family enjoying good health as they leaves us at present.

And it is with much happiness that I can say to you that Mrs. Mercer arrived in this city on yesterday. Mr. Mercer was at my house late in the evening, and I told him that when he went home if hear anything from Virginia, that he must let me know as soon as possible. He told me that if he went home and found any news there he would come right back and inform me thereof. But little did he expect to find his dearest there. You may judge what a meeting there was with them, and may God grant that there may be some more meetings with our wives and friends. I had been looking for some one from the old sod for several days, but I was in good hopes that it would be my poor Uncle. But poor fellow he are yet groaning under the sufferings of a horrid sytam, Expecting every day to Receive his Doom. Oh, God, what shall I do, or what can I do for him? I have prayed for him more than 12 months, yet he is in that horrid condition. I can never hear anything Directly from him or any of my people.

Once more I appeal to your Humanity. Will you act for him, as if you was in slavery yourself, and I sincerely believe that he will come out of that condition? Mrs. M. have told me that she given some directions how he could be goten at, but friend Still, if this conductor should not be success-full this time, will you mind him of the Poor Slave again. I hope you will as Mrs. Mercer have told the friend what to do I cannot do more, therefore I must leve it to the Mercy of God and your Exertion.

The weather have been very mile Ever since the 23rd of Dec. I have thought considerable about our condition in this country Seeing that the weather was so very faverable to us. I was thinking a few days ago, that nature had giving us A country & adopted all things Sutable.

You will do me the kindness of telling me in your next whether or not the ten slaves have been Brought out from N.C.

I have not hard from Brown for Nine month he have done some very Bad letting me alone, for what cause I cannot tell. Give my Best Respect to Mr. B. when you see him. I wish very much to hear from himself and family. You will please to let me hear from you. My wife Joines me in love to yourself and family.

Yours most Respectfully,

JOHN H. HILL.

P.S. Every fugitive Regreated to hear of the Death of Mrs. Moore. I myself think that there are no other to take her Place.

yours
J.H.H.

ELEVENTH LETTER
[Extract]

Rejoices at hearing of the success of the Underground Rail Road – Inquires particularly after the "fellow" who "cut off the Patrol's head in Maryland."

HAMILTON,
August 15th, 1856.

DEAR FRIEND: – I am very glad to hear that the Underground Rail Road is doing such good business, but tell me in your next letter if you have seen the heroic fellow that cut off the head of the Patrol in Maryland. We wants that fellow here, as John Bull has a great deal of fighting to do, and as there is a colored Captain in this city, I would seek to have that fellow Promoted, Provided he became a soldier.

Great respect,

JOHN H. HILL.

P.S. – Please forward the enclosed to Mr. McCray.

TWELFTH LETTER
[Extract]

Believes in praying for the Slave – but thinks "fire and sword" would be more effective with Slave-holders.

HAMILTON,
Jan. 5th, 1857.

MR. STILL: – Our Pappers contains long details of insurrectionary movements among the slaves at the South and one paper adds that a great Nomber of Generals, Captains with other officers had being arrested. At this day four years ago I left Petersburg for Richmond to meet the man whom called himself my master, but he wanted money worser that day than I do this day, he took me to sell me, he could not have done a better thing for me for I intended to leave any how by the first convaiance. I hard some good Prayers put up for the suffers on last Sunday evening in the Baptist Church. Now friend still I believe that Prayers affects great good, but I beleve that the fire and sword would affect more good in this case. Perhaps this is not your thoughts, but I must acknowledge this to be my Polacy. The world are being turned upside down, and I think we might as well take an active part in it as not. We must have something to do as other people, and I hope this moment among the Slaves are the beginning. I wants to see something go on while I live.

Yours truly,

JOHN H. HILL.

THIRTEENTH LETTER

Sad tidings from Richmond – Of the arrest of a Captain with Slaves on board as Underground Rail Road passengers.

HAMILTON,
June 5th, 1858.

DEAR FRIEND STILL: – I have just heard that our friend Capt. B. have being taken Prisoner in Virginia with slaves on board of his vessel. I hard this about an hour ago. the Person told me of this said he read it in the newspaper, if this be so it is awfull. You will be so kind as to send me some information. Send me one of the Virginia Papers. Poor fellow if they have got him, I am sorry, sorry to my heart. I have not heard from my Uncle for a long time if have heard or do hear anything from him at any time you will oblige me by writing. I wish you to inquire of Mr. Anderson's friends (if you know any of them), if they have heard anything from him since he was in your city. I have written to him twice since he was here according to his own directions, but never received an answer. I wants to hear from my mother very much, but cannot hear one word. You will present my best regards to the friend. Mrs. Hill is quite sick.

Yours truly,

J.H. HILL.

P.S. – I have not received the Anti-Slavery Standard for several weeks. Please forward any news relative to the Capt.

J.H.H.

THE ESCAPE OF HEZEKIAH HILL (UNCLE OF JOHN HENRY HILL)

Impelled by the love of freedom Hezekiah resolved that he would work no longer for nothing; that he would never be sold on the auction block: that he no longer would obey the bidding of a master, and that he would die rather than be a slave. This decision, however, had only been entertained by him a short time prior to his escape. For a number of years Hezekiah had been laboring under the pleasing thought that he should succeed in obtaining freedom through purchase, having had an understanding with his owner with this object in view. At different times he had paid on account for himself nineteen hundred dollars, six hundred dollars more than he was to have paid according to the first agreement. Although so shamefully defrauded in the first instance, he concluded to bear the disappointment as patiently as possible and get out of the lion's mouth as best he could.

He continued to work on and save his money until he had actually come within one hundred dollars of paying two thousand. At this point instead of getting his free papers, as he firmly believed that he should, to his surprise one day he saw a notorious trader approaching the shop where he was at work. The errand of the trader was soon made known. Hezekiah simply requested time to go back to the other end of the shop to get his coat, which he seized and ran. He was pursued but not captured. This occurrence took place in Petersburg, Va., about the first of December, 1854. On the night of the same day of his escape from the trader, Hezekiah walked to Richmond and was there secreted under a floor by a friend. He was a tall man, of powerful muscular strength, about thirty years of age just in the prime of his manhood with enough pluck for two men.

A heavy reward was offered for him, but the hunters failed to find him in this hiding-place under the floor. He strongly hoped to get away soon; on several occasions he made efforts, but only to be disappointed. At different times at least two captains had consented to afford him a private passage to Philadelphia, but like the impotent man at the pool, some one always got ahead of him. Two or three times he even managed to reach the boat upon the river, but had to return to his horrible place under the floor. Some were under the impression that he was an exceedingly unlucky man, and for a time captains feared to bring him. But his courage sustained him unwaveringly.

Finally at the expiration of thirteen months, a private passage was procured for him on the steamship *Pennsylvania*, and with a little slave boy, seven years of age (the son of the man who had secreted him), though placed in a very hard berth, he came safely to Philadelphia, greatly to the astonishment of the Vigilance Committee, who had waited for him so long that they had despaired of his ever coming.

The joy that filled Hezekiah's bosom may be imagined but never described. None but one who had been in similar straits could enter into his feelings.

He had left his wife Louisa, and two little boys, Henry and Manuel. His passage cost one hundred dollars.

Hezekiah being a noted character, a number of the true friends were invited to take him by the hand and to rejoice with him over his noble struggles and his triumph; needing rest and recruiting, he was made welcome to stay, at the expense of the committee, as long as he might feel disposed so to do. He remained several days, and then went on to Canada rejoicing. After arriving there he returned his acknowledgment for favors received, &c., in the following letter:

TORONTO
Jan 24th 1856.

MR. STILL: – this is to inform you that Myself and little boy, arrived safely in this city this day the 24th, at ten o'clock after a very long and pleasant trip. I had a great deal of attention paid to me while on the way.

I owes a great deel of thanks to yourself and friends. I will just say hare that when I arrived at New York, I found Mr. Gibbs sick and could not be attended to there. However, I have arrived alright.

You will please to give my respects to your friend that writes in the office with you, and to Mr Smith, also Mr Brown, and the friends, Mrs Still in particular.

Friend Still you will please to send the enclosed to John Hill Petersburg I want him to send some things to me you will be so kind as to send your direction to them, so that the things to your care. if you do not see a convenient way to send it by hands, you will please direct your letter to Phillip Ubank Petersburg.

Yours Respectfully
H HILL.

JAMES – (BROTHER OF JOHN HENRY HILL)

For three years James suffered in a place of concealment, before he found the way opened to escape. When he resolved on having his freedom he was much under twenty-one years of age, a brave young man, for three years, with unfailing spirit, making resistance in the city of Richmond to the slave Power!

Such heroes in the days of Slavery, did much to make the infernal system insecure, and to keep alive the spirit of freedom in liberty-loving hearts the world over, wherever such deeds of noble daring were made known. But of his heroism, but little can be reported here, from the fact, that such accounts as were in the possession of the Committee, were never transferred from the loose slips of paper on which they were first written, to the regular record book. But an important letter from the friend with whom he was secreted, written a short while before he escaped (on a boat), gives some idea of his condition:

RICHMOND, VA.,
February 16th, 1861.

DEAR BROTHER STILL: – I received a message from brother Julius anderson, asking me to send the bundle on but I has no way to send it, I have been waiting and truly hopeing that you would make some arrangement with some person, and send for the parcel. I have no way to send it, and I cannot communicate the subject to a stranger there is a Way by the N.y. line, but they are all strangers to me, and of course I could not approach them With this subject for I would be indangered myself greatly. this business is left to you and to you alone to attend to in providing the way for me to send on the parcel, if you only make an arrangement with some person and let me know the said person and the article which they is to be sent on then I can send the parcel. unless you do make an arrangement with some person, and assure them that they will receive the funs for delivering the parcel this Business cannot be accomplished. it is in your power to try to make some provision for the article to be sent but it is not in my power to do so, the bundle has been on my hands now going on 3 years, and I have suffered a great deal of danger, and is still suffering the same. I have understood Sir that there were no difficul about the mone that you had it in your possession Ready for the bundle whenever it is delivered. But Sir as I have said I can do nothing now. Sir I ask you please through sympathy and feelings on my part & his try to provide a way for the bundle to be sent and relieve me of the danger in which I am in. you might succeed in making an arrangement with those on the New york Steamers for they dose such things but please let me know the man that the arrangement is made with – please give me an answer by the bearer.

yours truly friend

C.A.

At last, the long, dark night passed away, and this young slave safely made his way to freedom, and proceeded to Boston, where he now resides. While the Committee was looked to for aid in the deliverance of this poor fellow, it was painful to feel that it was not in their power to answer his prayers – not until after his escape, was it possible so to do. But his escape to freedom gave them a satisfaction which no words can well express. At present, John Henry Hill is a justice of the peace in Petersburg. Hezekiah resides at West Point, and James in Boston, rejoicing that all men are free in the United States, at last.

FOUR ARRIVALS

*CHARLOTTE AND HARRIET ESCAPE IN DEEP MOURNING
– MASTER IN THE SAME CAR HUNTING FOR THEM, SEES
THEM, BUT DOES NOT KNOW THEM – WHITE LADY AND
CHILD WITH A COLORED COACHMAN, TRAVELING – AT
CHAMBERSBUEG AT A HOTEL, THE PROPRIETOR
DETECTS THEM AS U.G.R.R. PASSENGERS – THREE
"LIKELY" YOUNG MEN FROM BALTIMORE – "FOUR
LARGE AND TWO SMALL HAMS" – POLICE OFFICES
IMPARTING INFORMATION AT THE ANTI-SLAVERY
OFFICE – U.G.R.R. PASSENGERS TRAVELING WITH THEIR
MASTERS' HORSES AND CARRIAGES – "BREAK DOWN" –
CONFLICT WITH WHITE MEN – SIX PASSENGERS RIDING
TWO HORSES, &c.*

About the 31st of May, 1856, an exceedingly anxious state of feeling existed with the active Committee in Philadelphia. In the course of twenty-four hours four arrivals had come to hand from different localities. The circumstances connected with the escape of each party, being so unusual, there was scarcely ground for any other conclusion than that disaster was imminent, if not impossible to be averted.

It was a day long to be remembered. Aside from the danger, however, a more encouraging hour had never presented itself in the history of the Road. The courage, which had so often been shown in the face of great danger, satisfied the Committee that there were heroes and heroines among these passengers, fully entitled to the applause of the liberty-loving citizens of Brotherly Love. The very idea of having to walk for days and nights in succession, over strange roads, through by-ways, and valleys, over mountains, and marshes, was fitted to appal the bravest hearts, especially where women and children were concerned.

Being familiar with such cases, the Committee was delighted beyond measure to observe how wisely and successfully each of these parties had managed to overcome these difficulties.

Party No. 1 consisted of Charlotte Giles and Harriet Eglin, owned by Capt. Wm. Applegarth and John Delahay. Neither of these girls had any great complaint to make on the score of ill-treatment endured.

So they contrived each to get a suit of mourning, with heavy black veils, and thus dressed, apparently absorbed with grief, with a friend to pass them to the Baltimore depot (hard place to pass, except aided by an individual well known to the R.R. company), they took a direct course for Philadelphia.

While seated in the car, before leaving Baltimore (where slaves and masters both belonged), who should enter but the master of one of the girls! In a very excited manner, he hurriedly approached Charlotte and Harriet, who were apparently weeping. Peeping under their veils, "What is your name," exclaimed the excited gentleman. "Mary, sir," sobbed Charlotte. "What is your name?" (to the other mourner) "Lizzie, sir," was the faint reply. On rushed the excited gentleman as if moved by steam – through the cars, looking for his property; not finding it, he passed out of the cars, and to the delight of Charlotte and Harriet soon disappeared. Fair business men would be likely to look at this conduct on the part of the two girls in the light of a "sharp practice." In military parlance it might be regarded as excellent strategy. Be this as it may, the Underground Rail Road passengers arrived safely at the Philadelphia station and were gladly received.

A brief stay in the city was thought prudent lest the hunters might be on the pursuit. They were, therefore, retained in safe quarters.

In the meantime, Arrival No. 2 reached the Committee. It consisted of a colored man, a white woman and a child, ten years old. This case created no little surprise. Not that quite a number of passengers, fair enough to pass for white, with just a slight tinge of colored blood in their veins, even sons and daughters of some of the F.F.V., had not on various occasions come over the U.G.R.R. But this party was peculiar. An explanation was sought, which resulted in ascertaining that the party was from Leesburg, Virginia; that David, the colored man, was about twenty-seven years of age, intelligent, and was owned, or claimed by Joshua Pusey. David had no taste for Slavery, indeed, felt that it would be impossible for him to adapt himself to a life of servitude for the special benefit of others; he had, already, as he thought, been dealt with very wrongfully by Pusey, who had deprived him of many years of the best part of his life, and would continue thus to wrong him, if he did not make a resolute effort to get away. So after thinking of various plans, he determined not to run off as a slave with his "budget on his back," but to "travel as a coachman," under the "protection of a white lady." In planning this pleasant scheme, David was not blind to the fact that neither himself nor the "white lady," with whom he proposed to travel, possessed either horse or carriage.

But his master happened to have a vehicle that would answer for the occasion. David reasoned that as Joshua, his so called master, had deprived him of his just dues for so many years, he had a right to borrow, or take without borrowing, one of Joshua's horses for the expedition. The plan was submitted to the lady, and was approved, and a mutual understanding here entered into, that she should hire a carriage, and take also her little girl with them. The lady was to assume the proprietorship of the horse, carriage and coachman. In so doing all dangers would be, in their judgment, averted. The scheme being all ready for execution, the time for departure was fixed, the carriage hired, David having secured his master Joshua's horse, and off they started in the direction of Pennsylvania. White people being so accustomed to riding, and colored people to driving, the party looked all right. No one suspected them, that they were aware of, while passing through Virginia.

On reaching Chambersburg, Pa., in the evening, they drove to a hotel, the lady alighted, holding by the hand her well dressed and nice-looking little daughter, bearing herself with as independent an air as if she had owned twenty such boys as accompanied her as coachman. She did not hesitate to enter and request accommodations for the night, for herself, daughter, coachman, and horse. Being politely told that they could be accommodated, all that was necessary was, that the lady should show off to the best advantage possible. The same duty also rested with weight upon the mind of David.

The night passed safely and the morning was ushered in with bright hopes which were overcast but only for a moment, however. Breakfast having been ordered and partaken of, to the lady's surprise, just as she was in the act of paying the bill, the proprietor of the hotel intimated that he thought that matters "looked a little suspicious," in other words, he said plainly, that he "believed that it was an Underground Rail Road movement;" but being an obliging hotel-keeper, he assured her at the same time, that he "would not betray them." Just here it was with them as it would have been on any other rail road when things threaten to come to a stand; they could do nothing more than make their way out of the peril as best they could. One thing they decided to do immediately, namely, to "leave the horse and carriage," and try other modes of travel. They concluded to take the regular passenger cars. In this way they reached Philadelphia. In Harrisburg, they had sought and received instructions how to find the Committee in Philadelphia.

What relations had previously existed between David and this lady in Virginia, the Committee knew not. It looked more like the time spoken of in Isaiah, where it is said, "And a little child shall lead them," than any thing that had ever been previously witnessed on the Underground Rail Road. The Underground Rail Road never practised the proscription governing other roads, on account of race, color, or previous condition. All were welcome to its immunities, white or colored, when the object to be gained favored freedom, or weakened Slavery. As the sole aim apparent in this case was freedom for the slave the Committee received these travellers as Underground Rail Road passengers.

Arrival No. 3. Charles H. Ringold, Robert Smith, and John Henry Richards, all from Baltimore. Their ages ranged from twenty to twenty-four years. They were in appearance of the class most inviting to men who were in the business of buying and selling slaves. Charles and John were owned by James Hodges, and Robert by Wm. H. Normis, living in Baltimore. This is all that the records contain of them. The exciting and hurrying times when they were in charge of the Committee probably forbade the writing out of a more detailed account of them, as was often the case.

With the above three arrivals on hand, it may be seen how great was the danger to which all concerned were exposed on account of the bold and open manner in which these parties had escaped from the land of the peculiar institution. Notwithstanding, a feeling of very great gratification existed in view of the success attending the new and adventurous modes of traveling. Indulging in reflections of this sort, the writer on going from his dinner that day to the anti-slavery office, to his surprise found an officer awaiting his coming. Said officer was of the mayor's police force. Before many moments had been allowed to pass, in which to conjecture his errand, the officer, evidently burdened with the importance of his mission, began to state his business substantially as follows:

"I have just received a telegraphic despatch from a slave-holder living in Maryland, informing me that six slaves had escaped from him, and that he had reason to believe that they were on their way to Philadelphia, and would come in the regular train direct from Harrisburg; furthermore I am requested to be at the depot on the arrival of the train to arrest the whole party, for whom a reward of $1,300 is offered. Now I am not the man for this business. I would have nothing to do with the contemptible work of arresting fugitives. I'd rather help them off. What I am telling you is confidential. My object in coming to the office is simply to notify the Vigilance Committee so that they may be on the look-out for them at the depot this evening and get them out of danger as soon as possible. This is the way I feel about them; but I shall telegraph back that I will be on the look-out."

While the officer was giving this information he was listened to most attentively, and every word he uttered was carefully weighed. An air of truthfulness, however, was apparent; nevertheless he was a stranger and there was cause for great cautiousness. During the interview an unopened telegraphic despatch which had come to hand during the writer's absence, lay on the desk. Impressed with the belief that it might shed light on the officer's story, the first opportunity that offered, it was seized, opened, and it read as follows (copied from the original):

> HARRISBURG,
> *May 31st, 1856.*

> WM. STILL, N. 5th St.: – I have sent via at two o'clock four large and two small hams.

> JOS. C. BUSTILL.

Here there was no room for further doubt, but much need for vigilance. Although the despatch was not read to the officer, not that his story was doubted, but purely for prudential reasons, he was nevertheless given to understand, that it was about the same party, and that they would be duly looked after. It would hardly have been understood by the officer, had he been permitted to read it so guardedly was it worded, it was indeed dead language to all save the initiated. In one particular especially, relative to the depot where they were expected to arrive, the officer was in the dark, as his despatch pointed to the regular train, and of course to the depot at Eleventh and Market streets. The Underground Rail Road despatch on the contrary pointed to Broad and Callowhill streets "Via," *i.e.* Reading.

As notified, that evening the "four large and two small hams" arrived, and turned out to be of the very finest quality, just such as any trader would have paid the highest market price for. Being mindful of the great danger of the hour, there was felt to be more occasion just then for anxiety and watchfulness, than for cheering and hurrahing over the brave passengers. To provide for them in the usual manner, in view of the threatening aspect of affairs, could not be thought of. In this critical hour it devolved upon a member of the Committee, for the safety of all parties, to find new and separate places of accommodation, especially for the six known to be pursued. To be stored in other than private families would not answer. Three or four such were visited at once; after learning of the danger much sympathy was expressed, but one after another made excuses and refused. This was painful, for the parties had plenty of house room, were identified with the oppressed race, and on public meeting occasions made loud professions of devotion to the cause of the fugitive, &c. The memory of the hour and circumstances is still fresh.

Accommodations were finally procured for a number of the fugitives with a widow woman (Ann Laws), whose opportunities for succor were far less than at the places where refusals had been met with. But Mrs. L. was kind-hearted, and nobly manifested a willingness to do all that she could for their safety. Of course the Committee felt bound to bear whatever expense might necessarily be incurred. Here some of the passengers were kept for several days, strictly private, long enough to give the slave-hunters full opportunity to tire themselves, and give up the chase in despair. Some belonging to the former arrivals had also to be similarly kept for the same reasons. Through careful management all were succored and cared for. Whilst much interesting information was obtained from these several arrivals: the incidents connected with their lives in Slavery, and when escaping were but briefly written out. Of this fourth arrival, however, the following intelligence will doubtless be highly gratifying to the friends of freedom, wherever the labors of the Underground Rail Road may be appreciated. The people round about Hagerstown, Maryland, may like to know how these "articles" got off so successfully, the circumstances of their escape having doubtless created some excitement in that region of the country.

Arrival No. 4. Charles Bird, George Dorsey, Angeline Brown, Albert Brown, Charles Brown and Jane Scott.

Charles was twenty-four years of age, quite dark, of quick motion, and ready speech, and in every way appearing as though he could take care of himself. He had occupied the condition of a farm laborer. This calling he concluded to forsake, not because he disliked farming, but simply to get rid of David Clargart, who professed to own him, and compelled him to work without pay, "for nothing." While Charles spoke favorably of Clargart as a man, to the extent, at all events, of testifying that he was not what was called a hard man, nevertheless Charles was so decidedly opposed to Slavery that he felt compelled to look out for himself. Serving another man on the no pay principle, at the same time liable to be flogged, and sold at the pleasure of another, Charles felt was worse than heathenish viewed in any light whatsoever. He was prepared therefore, to leave without delay. He had four sisters in the hands of Clargart, but what could he do for them but leave them to Providence.

The next on the list was George Dorsey, a comrade of Charles. He was a young man, of medium size, mixed blood, intelligent, and a brave fellow as will appear presently.

This party in order to get over the road as expeditiously as possible, availed themselves of their master's horses and wagon and moved off civilly and respectably. About nine miles from home on the road, a couple of white men, finding their carriage broken down approached them, unceremoniously seized the horses by the reins and were evidently about to assume authority, supposing that the boys would surrender at once. But instead of so doing, the boys struck away at them with all their might, with their large clubs, not even waiting to hear what these superior individuals wanted. The effect of the clubs brought them prostrate in the road, in an attitude resembling two men dreaming (it was in the night). The victorious passengers, seeing that the smashed up carriage could be of no further use to them, quickly conceived the idea of unhitching and attempting further pursuit on horseback. Each horse was required to carry three passengers. So up they mounted and off they galloped with the horses' heads turned directly towards Pennsylvania. No further difficulty presented itself until after they had traveled some forty miles. Here the poor horses broke down, and had to be abandoned. The fugitives were hopeful, but of the difficulties ahead they wot not; surely no flowery beds of ease awaited them. For one whole week they were obliged to fare as they could, out in the woods, over the mountains, &c. How they overcame the trials in this situation we cannot undertake to describe. Suffice it to say, at the end of the time above mentioned they managed to reach Harrisburg and found assistance as already intimated.

George and Angeline (who was his sister) with her two boys had a considerable amount of white blood in their veins, and belonged to a wealthy man by the name of George Schaeffer, who was in the milling business. They were of one mind in representing him as a hard man. "He would often threaten to sell, and was very hard to please." George and Angeline left their mother and ten brothers and sisters.

Jane was a well-grown girl, smart, and not bad-looking, with a fine brown skin, and was also owned by Schaeffer.

Letters from the enterprising Charlotte and Harriet (arrival No. 1), brought the gratifying intelligence, that they had found good homes in Western New York, and valued their freedom highly. Three out of quite a number of letters received from them from time to time are subjoined.

SENNETT,
June, 1856.

MR. WILLIAM STILL: – *Dear Sir*: – I am happy to tell you that Charlotte Gildes and myself have got along thus far safely. We have had no trouble and found friends all the way along, for which we feel very thankful to you and to all our friends on the road since we left. We reached Mr. Loguen's in Syracuse, on last Tuesday evening & on Wednesday two gentlemen from this community called and we went with them to work in their families. What I wish you would do is to be so kind as to send our clothes to this place if they should fall into your hands. We hope our uncle in Baltimore will get the letter Charlotte wrote to him last Sabbath, while we were at your house, concerning the clothes. Perhaps the best would be to send them to Syracuse to the *care of Mr. Loguen* and he will send them to us. This will more certainly ensure our getting them. If you hear anything that would be interesting to Charlotte or me from Baltimore, please direct a letter to us to this place, to the care of Revd. Chas. Anderson, Sennett, Cayuga Co., N.Y. Please give my love and Charlotte's to Mrs. Still and thank her for her kindness to us while at your house.

Your affectionate friend,

HARRIET EGLIN.

SECOND LETTER

SENNETT,
July 31st, 1856.

MR. WM. STILL: – *My Dear Friend*: – I have just received your note of 29th inst. and allow me dear sir, to assure you that the only letter I have written, is the one you received, an answer to which you sent me. I never wrote to Baltimore, nor did any person write for me there, and it is with *indescribable grief*, that I hear what your letter communicates to me, of those who you say have gotten into difficulty on my account. My Cousin Charlotte who came with me, got into a good place in this vicinity, but she could not content herself to stay here but just *one week* – she then went to Canada – and she is the one who by writing (if any one), has brought this trouble upon those to whom you refer in Baltimore.

She has written me two letters from Canada, and by neither of them can I ascertain *where she lives* – her letters are mailed at Suspension Bridge, but she does not live there as her letters show. In the first she does not even sign her name. She has evidently employed some person to write, who is nearly as ignorant as herself. If I knew where to find her I would find out *what* she has written.

I don't know but she has told where I live, and may yet get me and my friends here, in trouble too, as she has some in other places. I don't wish to have you trouble yourself about my clothes, I am in a place where I can get all the clothes I want or need. Will you please write me when convenient and tell me what you hear about those who I fear are suffering as the result of their kindness to me? May God, in some way, grant them deliverance. Oh the misery, the sorrow, which this cursed system of Slavery is constantly bringing upon millions in this land of boasted freedom!

Can you tell me where Sarah King is, who was at your house when I was there? She was going to Canada to meet her husband. Give my love to Mrs. Still & accept the same yourself. Your much indebted & obliged friend,

HARRIET EGLIN.

The "difficulty" about which Harriet expressed so much regret in the above letter, had reference to a letter supposed to have been written by her friend Charlotte to Baltimore, about her clothing. It had been intercepted, and in this way, a clue was obtained by one of the owners as to how they escaped, who aided them, etc. On the strength of the information thus obtained, a well-known colored man, named Adams, was straightway arrested and put in prison at the instance of one of the owners, and also a suit was at the same time instituted against the Rail Road Company for damages – by which steps quite a huge excitement was created in Baltimore. As to the colored man Adams, the prospect looked simply hopeless. Many hearts were sad in view of the doom which they feared would fall upon him for obeying a humane impulse (he had put the girls on the cars). But with the Rail Road Company it was a different matter; they had money, power, friends, etc., and could defy the courts. In the course of a few months, when the suit against Adams and the Rail Road Company came up, the Rail Road Company proved in court, in defense, that the prosecutor entered the cars in search of his runaway, and went and spoke to the two young women in "mourning" the day they escaped, looking expressly for the identical parties, for which he was seeking damages before the court, and that he declared to the conductor, on leaving the cars, that the said "two girls in mourning, were not the ones he was looking after," or in other words, that "neither" belonged to him. This positive testimony satisfied the jury, and the Rail Road Company and poor James Adams escaped by the verdict not guilty. The owner of the lost property had the costs to pay of course, but whether he was made a wiser or better man by the operation was never ascertained.

THIRD LETTER.

SENNETT,
October 28th, 1856.

DEAR MR. STILL: – I am happy to tell you that I am well and happy. I still live with Rev. Mr. Anderson in this place, I am learning to read and write. I do not like to trouble you too much, but I would like to know if you have heard anything more about my friends in Baltimore who got into trouble on our account. Do be pleased to write me if you can give me any information about them. I feel bad that they should suffer for me. I wish all my brethren and sisters in bondage, were as well off as I am. The girl that came with me is in Canada, near the Suspension Bridge. I was glad to see Green Murdock, a colored young man, who stopped at your house about six weeks ago, he knew my folks at the South. He has got into a good place to work in this neighborhood. Give my love to Mrs Still, and believe me your obliged friend,

HARRIET EGLIN.

P.S. I would like to know what became of Johnson,[1] the man whose foot was smashed by jumping off the cars, he was at your house when I was there.

H.E.

---

1   Johnson was an unfortunate young fugitive, who, while escaping, beheld his master or pursuer in the cars, and jumped therefrom, crushing his feet shockingly by the bold act.

CHARLES GILBERT

*FLEEING FROM DAVIS A NEGRO
TRADER, SECRETED UNDER A
HOTEL, UP A TREE, UNDER
A FLOOR, IN A THICKET, ON
A STEAMER.*

In 1854 Charles was owned in the city of Richmond by Benjamin Davis, a notorious negro trader. Charles was quite a "likely-looking article," not too black or too white, but rather of a nice "ginger-bread color." Davis was of opinion that this "article" must bring him a tip-top price. For two or three months the trader advertised Charles for sale in the papers, but for some reason or other Charles did not command the high price demanded.

While Davis was thus daily trying to sell Charles, Charles was contemplating how he might escape. Being uncommonly shrewd he learned something about a captain of a schooner from Boston, and determined to approach him with regard to securing a passage. The captain manifested a disposition to accommodate him for the sum of ten dollars, provided Charles could manage to get to Old Point Comfort, there to embark. The Point was about one hundred and sixty miles distant from Richmond.

A man of ordinary nerve would have declined this condition unhesitatingly. On the other hand it was not Charles' intention to let any offer slide; indeed he felt that he must make an effort, if he failed. He could not see how his lot could be made more miserable by attempting to flee. In full view of all the consequences he ventured to take the hazardous step, and to his great satisfaction he reached Old Point Comfort safely. In that locality he was well known, unfortunately too well known, for he had been raised partly there, and, at the same time, many of his relatives and acquaintances were still living there. These facts were evidently well known to the trader, who unquestionably had snares set in order to entrap

Charles should he seek shelter among his relatives, a reasonable supposition. Charles had scarcely reached his old home before he was apprised of the fact that the hunters and watch dogs of Slavery were eagerly watching for him. Even his nearest relatives, through fear of consequences had to hide their faces as it were from him. None dare offer him a night's lodging, scarcely a cup of water, lest such an act might be discovered by the hunters, whose fiendish hearts would have found pleasure in meting out the most dire punishments to those guilty of thus violating the laws of Slavery. The prospect, if not utterly hopeless, was decidedly discouraging. The way to Boston was entirely closed. A "reward of $200" was advertised for his capture. For the first week after arriving at Old Point he entrusted himself to a young friend by the name of E.S. The fear of the pursuers drove him from his hiding-place at the expiration of the week. Thence he sought shelter neither with kinfolks, Christians, nor infidels, but in this hour of his calamity he made up his mind that he would try living under a large hotel for a while. Having watched his opportunity, he managed to reach Higee hotel, a very large house without a cellar, erected on pillars three or four feet above the ground. One place alone, near the cistern, presented some chance for a hiding-place, sufficient to satisfy him quite well under the circumstances. This dark and gloomy spot he at once willingly occupied rather than return to Slavery. In this refuge he remained four weeks. Of course he could not live without food; but to communicate with man or woman would inevitably subject him to danger. Charles' experience in the neighborhood of his old home left no ground for him to hope that he would be likely to find friendly aid anywhere under the shadow of Slavery. In consequence of these fears he received his food from the "slop tub," securing this diet in the darkness of night after all was still and quiet around the hotel. To use his own language, the meals thus obtained were often "sweet" to his taste.

One evening, however, he was not a little alarmed by the approach of an Irish boy who came under the hotel to hunt chickens. While prowling around in the darkness he appeared to be making his way unconsciously to the very spot where Charles was reposing. How to meet the danger was to Charles' mind at first very puzzling, there was no time now to plan. As quick as thought he feigned the bark of a savage dog accompanied with a furious growl and snarl which he was confident would frighten the boy half out of his senses, and cause him to depart quickly from his private apartment. The trick succeeded admirably, and the emergency was satisfactorily met, so far as the boy was concerned, but the boy's father hearing the attack of the dog, swore that he would kill him. Charles was a silent listener to the threat, and he saw that he could no longer remain in safety in his present quarter. So that night he took his departure for Bay Shore; here he decided to pass a day in the woods, but the privacy of this place was not altogether satisfactory to Charles' mind; but where to find a more secure retreat he could not, – dared not venture to ascertain that day. It occurred to him, however, that he would be much safer up a tree than hid in the bushes and undergrowth. He therefore climbed up a large acorn tree and there passed an entire day in deep meditation. No gleam of hope appeared, yet he would not suffer himself to think of returning to bondage. In this dilemma he remembered a poor washer-woman named Isabella, a slave who had charge of a wash-house. With her he resolved to seek succor. Leaving the woods he proceeded to the wash-house and was kindly received by Isabella, but what to do with him or how to afford him any protection she could see no way whatever. The schooling which Charles had been receiving a number of weeks in connection with the most fearful looking-for of the threatened wrath of the trader made it much easier for him than for her to see how he could be provided for. A room and comforts he was not accustomed to. Of course he could not expect such comforts now. Like many another escaping from the relentless tyrant, Charles could contrive methods which to his venture-some mind would afford hope, however desperate they might appear to others. He thought that he might be safe under the floor. To Isabella the idea was new, but her sympathies were strongly with Charles, and she readily consented to accom-modate him under the floor of the wash-house. Isabella and a friend of Charles, by the name of John Thomas, were the only persons who were cognizant of this arrangement. The kindness of these friends, manifested by their willingness to do anything in their power to add to the comfort of Charles, was proof to him that his efforts and sufferings had not been altogether in vain. He remained under the floor two weeks, accessible to kind voices and friendly ministrations. At the end of this time his repose was again sorely disturbed by reports from without that suspicion had been awakened towards the wash-house. How this happened neither Charles nor his friends could conjecture. But the arrival of six officers whom he could hear talking very plainly in the house, whose errand was actually to search for him, convinced him that he had never for a single moment been in greater danger. The officers not only searched the house, but they offered his friend John Thomas $25 if he would only put them on Charles' track. John professed to know nothing; Isabella was equally ignorant. Discouraged with their efforts on this occasion, the officers gave up the hunt and left the house. Charles, however, had had enough of the floor accommodations. He left that night and returned to his old quarters under the hotel. Here he stayed one week, at the expiration of which time the need of fresh air was so imperative, that he resolved to go out at night to Allen's cottage and spend a day in the woods. He had knowledge of a place where the undergrowth and bushes were almost impenetrable. To rest and refresh himself in this thicket he felt would be a great comfort to him. Without serious difficulty he reached the thicket, and while pondering over the all-absorbing matter as to how he should ever manage to make his escape, an old man approached. Now while Charles had no reason to think that he was sought by the old intruder, his very near approach admonished him that it would neither be safe nor agreeable to allow him to come nearer. Charles remembering that his trick of playing the dog, when previously in danger under the hotel, had served a good end, thought that it would work well in the thicket. So he again tried his power at growling and barking hideously for a moment or two, which at once caused the man to turn his course. Charles could hear him distinctly retreating, and at the same time cursing the dog.

The owner of the place had the reputation of keeping "bad dogs," so the old man poured out a dreadful threat against "Stephens' dogs," and was soon out of the reach of the one in the thicket.

Notwithstanding his success in frightening off the old man, Charles felt that the thicket was by no means a safe place for him. He concluded to make another change. This time he sought a marsh; two hours' stay there was sufficient to satisfy him, that that too was no place to tarry in, even for a single night. He, therefore, left immediately. A third time, he returned to the hotel, where he remained only two days. His appeals had at last reached the heart of his mother – she could no longer bear to see him struggling, and suffering, and not render him aid, whatever the consequences might be. If she at first feared to lend him a helping hand, she now resolutely worked with a view of saving money to succor him. Here the prospect began to brighten.

A passage was secured for him on a steamer bound for Philadelphia. One more day, and night must elapse, ere he could be received on board. The joyful anticipations which now filled his breast left no room for fear; indeed, he could scarcely contain himself; he was drunk with joy. In this state of mind he concluded that nothing would afford him more pleasure before leaving, than to spend his last hours at the wash house, "under the floor." To this place he went with no fear of hunters before his eyes. Charles had scarcely been three hours in this place, however, before three officers came in search of him. Two of them talked with Isabella, asked her about her "boarders," etc.; in the meanwhile, one of them uninvited, made his way up stairs. It so happened, that Charles was in this very portion of the house. His case now seemed more hopeless than ever. The officer up stairs was separated from him simply by a thin curtain. Women's garments hung all around. Instead of fainting or surrendering, in the twinkling of an eye, Charles' inventive intellect, led him to enrobe himself in female attire. Here, to use his own language, a "thousand thoughts" rushed into his mind in a minute. The next instant he was going down stairs in the presence of the officers, his old calico dress, bonnet and rig, attracting no further attention than simply to elicit the following simple questions: "Whose gal are you?" "Mr. Cockling's, sir." "What is your name?" "Delie, sir." "Go on then!" said one of the officers, and on Charles went to avail himself of the passage on the steamer which his mother had procured for him for the sum of thirty dollars.

In due time, he succeeded in getting on the steamer, but he soon learned, that her course was not direct to Philadelphia, but that some stay would be made in Norfolk, Va. Although disappointed, yet this being a step in the right direction, he made up his mind to be patient. He was delayed in Norfolk four weeks. From the time Charles first escaped, his owner (Davis the negro trader) had kept a standing reward of $550 advertised for his recovery. This showed that Davis was willing to risk heavy expenses for Charles as well as gave evidence that he believed him still secreted either about Richmond, Petersburg, or Old Point Comfort. In this belief he was not far from being correct, for Charles spent most of his time in either of these three places, from the day of his escape until the day that he finally embarked. At last, the long looked-for hour arrived to start for Philadelphia.

He was to leave his mother, with no hope of ever seeing her again, but she had purchased herself and was called free. Her name was Margaret Johnson. Three brothers likewise were ever in his thoughts (in chains), "Henry," "Bill," and "Sam," (half brothers). But after all the hope of freedom outweighed every other consideration, and he was prepared to give up all for liberty. To die rather than remain a slave was his resolve.

Charles arrived per steamer, from Norfolk, on the 11th day of November, 1854. The Richmond papers bear witness to the fact, that Benjamin Davis advertised Charles Gilbert, for mouths prior to this date, as has been stated in this narrative. As to the correctness of the story, all that the writer has to say is, that he took it down from the lips of Charles, hurriedly, directly after his arrival, with no thought of magnifying a single incident. On the contrary, much that was of interest in the story had to be omitted. Instead of being overdrawn, not half of the particulars were recorded. Had the idea then been entertained, that the narrative of this young slave-warrior was to be brought to light in the manner and time that it now is, a far more thrilling account of his adventures might have been written. Other colored men who knew both Davis and Charles, as well as one man ordinarily knows another, rejoiced at seeing Charles in Philadelphia, and they listened with perfect faith to his story. So marvellous were the incidents of his escape, that his sufferings in Slavery, previous to his heroic struggles to throw off the yoke, were among the facts omitted from the records. While this may be regretted it is, nevertheless, gratifying on the whole to have so good an account of him as was preserved. It is needless to say, that the Committee took especial pleasure in aiding him, and listening to so remarkable a story narrated so intelligently by one who had been a slave.

LIBERTY
OR DEATH
JIM BOW-LEGS

ALIAS BILL PAUL

In 1855 a traveler arrived with the above name, who, on examination, was found to possess very extraordinary characteristics. As a hero and adventurer some passages of his history were most remarkable. His schooling had been such as could only be gathered on plantations under brutal overseers; – or while fleeing, – or in swamps, – in prisons, – or on the auction-block, etc.; in which condition he was often found. Nevertheless in these circumstances his mind got well stored with vigorous thoughts – neither books nor friendly advisers being at his command. Yet his native intelligence as it regarded human nature, was extraordinary. His resolution and perseverance never faltered. In all respects he was a remarkable man. He was a young man, weighing about one hundred and eighty pounds, of uncommon muscular strength. He was born in the State of Georgia, Oglethorpe county, and was owned by Dr. Thomas Stephens, of Lexington. On reaching the Vigilance Committee in Philadelphia, his story was told many times over to one and another. Hour after hour was occupied by friends in listening to the simple narrative of his struggles for freedom. A very full account of "Jim," was forwarded in a letter to M.A. Shadd, the then Editress of the *Provincial Freeman*. Said account has been carefully preserved, and is here annexed as it appeared in the columns of the above named paper:

> I must now pass to a third adventurer. The one to whom I allude, is a young man of twenty-six years of age, by the name of "Jim," who fled from near Charleston, S.C. Taking all the facts and circumstances into consideration respecting the courageous career of this successful adventurer for freedom, his case

is by far more interesting than any I have yet referred to. Indeed, for the good of the cause, and the honor of one who gained his liberty by periling his life so frequently: – shot several times, – making six unsuccessful attempts to escape from the far South, – numberless times chased by bloodhounds, – captured, imprisoned and sold repeatedly, – living for months in the woods, swamps and caves, subsisting mainly on parched corn and berries, &c., &c., his narrative ought, by all means, to be published, though I doubt very much whether many could be found who could persuade themselves to believe one-tenth part of this marvellous story.

Though this poor Fugitive was utterly ignorant of letters, his natural good sense and keen perception qualified him to arrest the attention and interest the heart in a most remarkable degree.

His master finding him not available, on account of his absconding propensities, would gladly have offered him for sale. He was once taken to Florida, for that purpose; but, generally, traders being wide awake, on inspecting him, would almost invariably pronounce him a "d – – n rascal," because he would never fail to eye them sternly, as they inspected him. The obedient and submissive slave is always recognized by hanging his head and looking on the ground, when looked at by a slave-holder. This lesson Jim had never learned, hence he was not to be trusted.

His head and chest, and indeed his entire structure, as solid as a rock, indicated that he was physically no ordinary man; and not being under the influence of the spirit of "non-resistance," he had occasionally been found to be a rather formidable customer.

His father was a full-blooded Indian, brother to the noted Indian Chief, Billy Bowlegs; his mother was quite black and of unmixed blood.

For five or six years, the greater part of Jim's time was occupied in trying to escape, and in being in prison for sale, to punish him for running away.

His mechanical genius was excellent, so were his geographical abilities. He could make shoes or do carpenter's work very handily, though he had never had the chance to learn. As to traveling by night or day, he was always road-ready and having an uncommon memory, could give exceedingly good accounts of what he saw, etc.

When he entered a swamp, and had occasion to take a nap he took care first to decide upon the posture he must take, so that if come upon unexpectedly by the hounds and slave-hunters, he might know in an instant which way to steer to defeat them. He always carried a liquid, which he had prepared, to prevent hounds from scenting him, which he said had never failed. As soon as the hounds came to the place where he had rubbed his legs and feet with said liquid, they could follow him no further, but howled and turned immediately.

Quite a large number of the friends of the slave saw this noble-hearted fugitive, and would sit long and listen with the most undivided attention to his narrative – none doubting for a moment, I think, the entire truthfulness of his story. Strange as his story was, there was so much natural simplicity in his manner and countenance, one could not refrain from believing him.

AN IRISH GIRL'S DEVOTION TO FREEDOM

IN LOVE WITH A SLAVE – GETS HIM OFF TO CANADA – FOLLOWS HIM – MARRIAGE, &C.

Having dwelt on the sad narratives of Samuel Green and his son in the preceding chapter, it is quite a relief to be able to introduce a traveler whose story contains incidents less painful to contemplate. From the record book the following brief account is taken:

"April 27, 1855. John Hall arrived safely from Richmond, Va., per schooner, (Captain B). One hundred dollars were paid for his passage." In Richmond he was owned by James Dunlap, a merchant. John had been sold several times, in consequence of which, he had possessed very good opportunities of experiencing the effect of change of owners. Then, too, the personal examination made before sale, and the gratification afforded his master when he (John), brought a good price – left no very pleasing impressions on his mind.

By one of his owners, named Burke, John alleged that he had been "cruelly used." When quite young, both he and his sister, together with their mother, were sold by Burke. From that time he had seen neither mother nor sister – they were sold separately. For three or four years the desire to seek liberty had been fondly cherished, and nothing but the want of a favorable opportunity had deterred him from carrying out his designs. He considered himself much "imposed upon" by his master, particularly as he was allowed "no choice about living" as he "desired." This was indeed ill-treatment as John viewed the matter. John may have wanted too much. He was about thirty-five years of age, light complexion – tall – rather handsome-looking, intelligent, and of good manners. But notwithstanding these prepossessing features, John's owner valued him at only $1,000. If he had been a few shades

darker and only about half as intelligent as he was, he would
have been worth at least $500 more. The idea of having had
a white father, in many instances, depreciated the pecuniary
value of male slaves, if not of the other sex. John emphatically
was one of this injured class; he evidently had blood in his
veins which decidedly warred against submitting to the yoke.
In addition to the influence which such rebellious blood
exerted over him, together with a considerable amount of
intelligence, he was also under the influence and advice of a
daughter of old Ireland. She was heart and soul with John in
all his plans which looked Canada-ward. This it was that
"sent him away."

It is very certain, that this Irish girl was not annoyed by
the kinks in John's hair. Nor was she overly fastidious about
the small percentage of colored blood visible in John's
complexion. It was, however, a strange occurrence and very
hard to understand. Not a stone was left unturned until John
was safely on the Underground Rail Road. Doubtless she
helped to earn the money which was paid for his passage.
And when he was safe off, it is not too much to say, that John
was not a whit more delighted than was his intended Irish
lassie, Mary Weaver. John had no sooner reached Canada than
Mary's heart was there too.

Circumstances, however, required that she should remain
in Richmond a number of months for the purpose of winding
up some of her affairs. As soon as the way opened for her,
she followed him. It was quite manifest, that she had not
let a single opportunity slide, but seized the first chance
and arrived partly by means of the Underground Rail Road

and partly by the regular train. Many difficulties were surmounted before and after leaving Richmond, by which they earned their merited success. From Canada, where they anticipated entering upon the matrimonial career with mutual satisfaction, it seemed to afford them great pleasure to write back frequently, expressing their heartfelt gratitude for assistance, and their happiness in the prospect of being united under the favorable auspices of freedom! At least two or three of these letters, bearing on particular phases of their escape, etc., are too valuable not to be published in this connection:

FIRST LETTER

HAMILTON,
March 25th, 1856.

Mr. Still: – Sir and Friend – I take the liberty of addressing you with these few lines hoping that you will attend to what I shall request of you.

I have written to Virginia and have not received an answer yet. I want to know if you can get any one of your city to go to Richmond for me. If you can, I will pay the expense of the whole. The person that I want the messenger to see is a white girl. I expect you know who I allude to, it is the girl that sent me away. If you can get any one to go, you will please write right away and tell me the cost, &c. I will forward the money and a letter. Please use your endeavors.

Yours Respectfuliy,

JOHN HALL.

Direct yours to Mr. Hill.

SECOND LETTER

HAMILTON,
Sept. 15th, 1856.

To Mr. Still, Dear Sir: – I take this opportunity of addressing these few lines to you hoping to find you in good health I am happy to inform you that Miss Weaver arrived here on Tuesday last, and I can assure you it was indeed a happy day. As for your part that you done I will not attempt to tell you how thankful I am, but I hope that you can imagine what my feelings are to you. I cannot find words sufficient to express my gratitude to you, I think the wedding will take place on Tuesday next, I have seen some of the bread from your house, and she says it is the best bread she has had since she has been in America. Sometimes she has impudence enough to tell me she would rather be where you are in Philadelphia than to be here with me. I hope this will be no admiration to you for no honest hearted person ever saw you that would not desire to be where you are, No flattery, but candidly speaking, you are worthy all the praise of any person who has ever been with you, I am now like a deserted Christian, but yet I have asked so much, and all has been done yet I must ask again, My love to Mrs. Still. Dear Mr.

Still I now ask you please to exercise all your influence to get this young man Willis Johnson from Richmond for me It is the young man that Miss Weaver told you about, he is in Richmond I think he is at the corner of Fushien Street, & Grace in a house of one Mr. Rutherford, there is several Rutherford in the neighborhood, there is a church call'd the third Baptist Church, on the R.H. side going up Grace street, directly opposite the Baptist church at the corner, is Mrs. Meads Old School at one corner, and Mr. Rutherfords is at the other corner. He can be found out by seeing Fountain Tombs who belongs to Mr. Rutherford and if you should not see him, there is James Turner who lives at the Governors, Please to see Captain Bayliss and tell him to take these directions and go to John Hill, in Petersburgh, and he may find him. Tell Captain Bayliss that if he ever did me a friendly thing in his life which he did do one friendly act, if he will take this on himself, and if money should be lacking I will forward any money that he may require, I hope you will sympathize with the poor young fellow, and tell the captain to do all in his power to get him and the costs shall be paid. He lies now between death or victory, for I know the man he belongs to would just as soon kill him as not, if he catches him, I here enclose to you a letter for Mr. Wm. C. Mayo, and please to send it as directed. In this letter I have asked him to send a box to you for me, which you will please pay the fare of the express upon it, when you get it please to let me know, and I will send you the money to pay the expenses of the carriage clear through. Please to let Mr. Mayo know how to direct a box to you, and the best way to send it from Richmond to Philadelphia. You will greatly oblige me by so doing. In this letter I have enclosed a trifle for postage which you will please to keep on account of my letters I hope you wont think hard of me but I simply send it because I know you have done enough, and are now doing more, without imposing in the matter I have done it a great many more of our people who you have done so much fore. No more from your humble and oldest servant.

JOHN HALL, Norton's Hotel, Hamilton.

THIRD LETTER

MONDAY,
Sept. 29, 56.

Sir: – I take this opportunity of informing you that we are in excellent health, and hope you are the same, I wrote a letter to you about 2 weeks ago and have not yet had an answer to it I wish to inform you that the wedding took place on Tuesday last, and Mrs. Hall now sends her best love to you, I enclose a letter which I wish you to forward to Mr. Mayo, you will see in his letter what I have said to him and I wish you would furnish him with such directions as it requires for him to send them things to you. I have told him not to pay for them but to send them to you so when you get them write me word what the cost of them are, and I will send you the money for them. Mary desires you to give her love to Mrs. Still. If any letters come for me please to send to me at Nortons Hotel, Please to let me know if you had a letter from me about 12 days ago. You will please

Direct the enclosed to Mr. W.C. Mayo, Richmond, Va. Let me know if you have heard anything of Willis Johnson Mr. & Mrs. Hill send their kind love to you, they are all well, no more at present from your affect.,

JOHN HALL

Nortons Hotel.

FOURTH LETTER

HAMILTON,
December 23d, 1856.

DEAR SIR: – I am happy to inform you that we are both enjoying good health and hope you are the same. I have been expecting a letter from you for some time but I suppose your business has prevented you from writing. I suppose you have not heard from any of my friends at Richmond. I have been longing to hear some news from that part, you may think "Out of sight and out of mind," but I can assure you, no matter how far I may be, or in what distant land, I shall never forget you, if I can never reach you by letters you may be sure I shall always think of you. I have found a great many friends in my life, but I must say you are the best one I ever met with, except one, you must know who that is, 'tis one who if I did not consider a friend, I could not consider any other person a friend, and that is Mrs. Hall. Please to let me know if the navigation between New York & Richmond is closed. Please to let me know whether it would be convenient to you to go to New York if it is please let me know what is the expense. Tell Mrs Still that my wife would be very happy to receive a letter from her at some moment when she is at leisure, for I know from what little I have seen of domestic affairs it keeps her pretty well employed, And I know she has not much time to write but if it were but two lines, she would be happy to receive it from her, my reason for wanting you to go to New York, there is a young man named Richard Myers and I should like for you to see him. He goes on board the *Orono* to Richmond and is a particular friend of mine and by seeing him I could get my clothes from Richmond, I expect to be out of employ in a few days, as the hotel is about to close on the 1st January and I hope you will write to me soon I want you to send me word how you and all the family are and all the news you can, you must excuse my short letter, as it is now near one o'clock and I must attend to business, but I have not written half what I intended to, as time is short, hoping to hear from you soon I remain yours sincerely,

JOHN HALL.

Mr. and Mrs. Hill desire their best respects to you and Mrs. Still.

It cannot be denied that this is a most extraordinary occurrence. In some respects it is without a parallel. It was, however, no uncommon thing for white men (slave-holders) in the South to have colored wives and children whom they did not hesitate to live with and acknowledge by their actions, with their means, and in their wills as the rightful heirs of their substance. Probably there is not a state in the Union where such relations have not existed. Seeing such usages, Mary might have reasoned that she had as good a right to marry the one she loved most as anybody else, particularly as she was in a "free country."

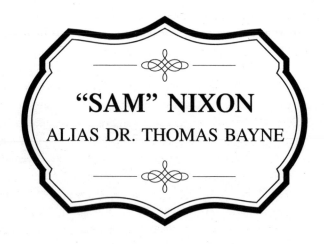

"SAM" NIXON
ALIAS DR. THOMAS BAYNE

*THE ESCAPE OF A DENTIST ON THE
U.G.R.R. – HE IS TAKEN FOR AN
IMPOSTOR – ELECTED A MEMBER
OF CITY COUNCIL IN NEW BEDFORD
– STUDYING MEDICINE, ETC.*

But few could be found among the Underground Rail Road passengers who had a stronger repugnance to the unrequited labor system, or the recognized terms of "master and slave," than Dr. Thomas Bayne. Nor were many to be found who were more fearless and independent in uttering their sentiments. His place of bondage was in the city of Norfolk, Va., where he was held to service by Dr. C.F. Martin, a dentist of some celebrity. While with Dr. Martin, "Sam" learned dentistry in all its branches, and was often required by his master, the doctor, to fulfil professional engagements, both at home and at a distance, when it did not suit his pleasure or convenience to appear in person. In the mechanical department, especially, "Sam" was called upon to execute the most difficult tasks. This was not the testimony of "Sam" alone; various individuals who were with him in Norfolk, but had moved to Philadelphia, and were living there at the time of his arrival, being invited to see this distinguished professional piece of property, gave evidence which fully corroborated his. The master's professional practice, according to "Sam's" calculation, was worth $3,000 per annum. Full $1,000 of this amount in the opinion of "Sam" was the result of his own fettered hands. Not only was "Sam" serviceable to the doctor in the mechanical and practical branches of his profession, but as a sort of ready reckoner and an apt penman, he was obviously considered by the doctor, a valuable "article." He would frequently have "Sam" at his books instead of a book-keeper. Of course, "Sam" had never received, from Dr. M., an hour's schooling in his life, but having perceptive faculties naturally very large, combined with much self-esteem, he could hardly help learning readily. Had his master's design to keep him in ignorance been ever so great, he would have found it a labor beyond his power. But there is no reason to suppose that Dr. Martin was opposed to Sam's learning to read and write. We are pleased to note that no charges of ill-treatment are found recorded against Dr. M. in the narrative of "Sam."

True, it appears that he had been sold several times in his younger days, and had consequently been made to feel keenly, the smarts of Slavery, but nothing of this kind was charged against Dr. M., so that he may be set down as a pretty fair man, for aught that is known to the contrary, with the exception of depriving "Sam" of the just reward of his labor, which, according to St. James, is pronounced a "fraud." The doctor did not keep "Sam" so closely confined to dentistry and book-keeping that he had no time to attend occasionally to outside duties. It appears that he was quite active and successful as an Underground Rail Road agent, and rendered important aid in various directions. Indeed, Sam had good reason to suspect that the slave-holders were watching him, and that if he remained, he would most likely find himself in "hot water up to his eyes." Wisdom dictated that he should "pull up stakes" and depart while the way was open. He knew the captains who were then in the habit of taking similar passengers, but he had some fears that they might not be able to pursue the business much longer. In contemplating the change which he was about to make, "Sam" felt it necessary to keep his movements strictly private. Not even was he at liberty to break his mind to his wife and child, fearing that it would do them no good, and might prove his utter failure. His wife's name was

Edna and his daughter was called Elizabeth; both were slaves and owned by E.P. Tabb, Esq., a hardware merchant of Norfolk.

No mention is made on the books, of ill-treatment, in connection with his wife's servitude; it may therefore be inferred, that her situation was not remarkably hard. It must not be supposed that "Sam" was not truly attached to his wife. He gave abundant proof of true matrimonial devotion, notwith-standing the secrecy of his arrangements for flight. Being naturally hopeful, he concluded that he could better succeed in securing his wife after obtaining freedom himself, than in undertaking the task beforehand.

The captain had two or three other Underground Rail Road male passengers to bring with him, besides "Sam," for whom, arrangements had been previously made – no more could be brought that trip. At the appointed time, the passengers were at the disposal of the captain of the schooner which was to bring them out of Slavery into freedom. Fully aware of the dangerous consequences should he be detected, the captain, faithful to his promise, secreted them in the usual manner, and set sail northward. Instead of landing his passengers in Philadelphia, as was his intention, for some reason or other (the schooner may have been disabled), he landed them on the New Jersey coast, not a great distance from Cape Island. He directed them how to reach Philadelphia. Sam knew of friends in the city, and straightway used his ready pen to make known the distress of himself and partners in tribulation. In making their way in the direction of their destined haven, they reached Salem, New Jersey, where they were discovered to be strangers and fugitives, and were directed to Abigail

Goodwin, a Quaker lady, an abolitionist, long noted for her devotion to the cause of freedom, and one of the most liberal and faithful friends of the Vigilance Committee of Philadelphia.

This friend's opportunities of witnessing fresh arrivals had been rare, and perhaps she had never before come in contact with a "chattel" so smart as "Sam." Consequently she was much embarrassed when she heard his story, especially when he talked of his experience as a "Dentist." She was inclined to suspect that he was a "shrewd impostor" that needed "watching" instead of aiding. But her humanity forbade a hasty decision on this point. She was soon persuaded to render him some assistance, notwithstanding her apprehensions. While tarrying a day or two in Salem, "Sam's" letter was received in Philadelphia. Friend Goodwin was written to in the meantime, by a member of the Committee, directly with a view of making inquires concerning the stray fugitives, and at the same time to inform her as to how they happened to be coming in the direction found by her. While the mind of the friend was much relieved by the letter she received, she was still in some doubt, as will be seen by the appended extract from a letter on the subject:

LETTER FROM A. GOODWIN

SALEM,
3 mo., 25, '55.

DEAR FRIEND: – Thine of the 22d came to hand yesterday noon.

I do not believe that any of them are the ones thee wrote about, who wanted Dr. Lundy to come for them, and promised they would pay his expenses. They had no money, the minister said, but were pretty well off for clothes. I gave him all I had and more, but it seemed very little for four travelers – only a dollar for each – but they will meet with friends and helpers on the way. He said they expected to go away to-morrow. I am afraid, it's so cold, and one of them had a sore foot, they will not get away – it's dangerous staying here. There has been a slave-hunter here lately, I was told yesterday, in search of a woman; he tracked her to our Alms-house – she had lately been confined and was not able to go – he will come back for her and his infant – and will not wait long I expect. I want much to get her away first – and if one had a C.C. Torney here no doubt it would be done; but she will be well guarded. How much I wish the poor thing could be secreted in some safe place till she is able to travel Northward; but where that could be it's not easy to see. I presume the Carolina freed people have arrived ere now. I hope they will meet many friends, and be well provided for. Mary Davis will be then paid – her cousins have sent her twenty-four dollars, as it was not wanted for the purchase money – it was to be kept for them when they arrive. I am glad thee did keep the ten for the fugitives.

Samuel Nixon is now here, just come – a smart young man – they will be after him soon. I advise him to hurry on to Canada; he will leave here to-morrow, but don't say that he will go straight to the city. I would send this by him if he did. I am afraid he will loiter about and be taken – do make them go on fast – he has left. I could not hear much he said

– some who did don't like him at all – think him an impostor – a great brag – said he was a dentist ten years. He was asked where he came from, but would not tell till he looked at the letter that lay on the table and that he had just brought back. I don't feel much confidence in him – don't believe he is the one thee alluded to. He was asked his name – he looked at the letter to find it out. Says nobody can make a better set of teeth than he can. He said they will go on to-morrow in the stage – he took down the number and street of the Anti-slavery office – you will be on your guard against imposition – he kept the letter thee sent from Norfolk. I had then no doubt of him, and had no objection to it. I now rather regret it. I would send it to thee if I had it, but perhaps it is of no importance.

He wanted the names taken down of nine more who expected to get off soon and might come here. He told us to send them to him, but did not seem to know where he was going to. He was well dressed in fine broad-cloth coat and overcoat, and has a very active tongue in his head.

But I have said enough – don't want to prejudice thee against him, but only be on thy guard, and do not let him deceive thee, as I fear he has some of us here.

With kind regards,

A. GOODWIN.

In due time Samuel and his companions reached Philadelphia, where a cordial welcome awaited them. The confusion and difficulties into which they had fallen, by having to travel an indirect route, were fully explained, and to the hearty merriment of the Committee and strangers, the dilemma of their good Quaker friend Goodwin at Salem was alluded to. After a sojourn of a day or two in Philadelphia, Samuel and his companions left for New Bedford. Canada was named to them as the safest place for all Refugees; but it was in vain to attempt to convince "Sam" that Canada or any other place on this Continent, was quite equal to New Bedford. His heart was there, and there he was resolved to go – and there he did go too, bearing with him his resolute mind, determined, if possible, to work his way up to an honorable position at his old trade, Dentistry, and that too for his own benefit.

Aided by the Committee, the journey was made safely to the desired haven, where many old friends from Norfolk were found. Here our hero was known by the name of Dr. Thomas Bayne – he was no longer "Sam." In a short time the Dr. commenced his profession in an humble way, while, at the same time, he deeply interested himself in his own improve-ment, as well as the improvement of others, especially those who had escaped from Slavery as he himself had. Then, too, as colored men were voters and, therefore, eligible to office in New Bedford, the Doctor's naturally ambitious and intel-ligent turn of mind led him to take an interest in politics, and before he was a citizen of New Bedford four years, he was duly elected a member of the City Council. He was also an outspoken advocate of the cause of temperance, and was likewise a ready speaker at Anti-slavery meetings held by his race. Some idea of his abilities, and the interest he took in the Underground Rail Road, education, etc., may be gathered from the appended letters:

NEW BEDFORD,
June 23d, 1855.

W. Still: – Sir – I write you this to inform you that I has received my things and that you need not say any thing to Bagnul about them – I see by the Paper that the under ground Rail Road is in operation. Since 2 weeks a go when Saless Party was betrayed by that Capt whom we in mass. are so anxious to Learn his name – There was others started last Saturday night – They are all my old friends and we are waiting their arrival, we hope you will look out for them they may come by way of Salem, N.J. if they be not overtaken. They are from Norfolk – Times are very hard in Canada 2 of our old friends has left Canada and come to Bedford for a living. Every thing are so high and wages so low They cannot make a living (owing to the War) others are Expected shortly – let me hear from Sales and his Party. Get the Name of the Capt. that betrayed him let me know if Mrs. Goodwin of Salem are at the same place yet – John Austin are with us. C. Lightfoot is well and remembers you and family. My business increases more since I has got an office. Send me a Norfolk Paper or any other to read when convenient.

Let me hear from those People as soon as possible. They consist of woman and child 2 or 3 men belonging to Marsh Bottimore, L. Slosser and Herman & Co – and Turner – all of Norfolk, Va.

Truly yours,

THOS. BAYNE.

Direct to Box No. 516, New Bedford, Mass. Don't direct my letters to my office. Direct them to my Box 516. My office is 66-1/2 William St. The same street the Post office is near the city market.

The Doctor, feeling his educational deficiency in the enlightened city of New Bedford, did just what every uncultivated man should, devoted himself assiduously to study, and even applied himself to abstruse and hard subjects, medicine, etc., as the following letters will show:

NEW BEDFORD,
Jan., 1860.

No. 22, Cheapside, opposite City Hall.

My Dear Friend: – Yours of the 3d inst. reached me safely in the midst of my misfortune. I suppose you have learned that my office and other buildings burned down during the recent fire. My loss is $550, insured $350.

I would have written you before, but I have been to R.I. for some time and soon after I returned before I examined the books, the fire took place, and this accounts for my delay. In regard to the books I am under many obligations to you and all others for so great a piece of kindness, and shall ever feel indebted to you for the same. I shall esteem them very highly for two reasons, first, The way in which they come, that is through and by your Vigilance as a colored man helping a colored man to get such knowledge as will give the lie to our enemies. Secondly – their contents being just the thing I needed at this time. My indebtedness to you and all concerned for me in this direction is inexpressible. There are some books the Doctor says I must have, such as the Medical Dictionary, Physician's Dictionary, and a work on Anatomy. These I will have to get, but any work that may be of use to a student of anatomy or medicine will be thankfully received. You shall hear from me again soon.

Truly Yours,

THOS. BAYNE.

NEW BEDFORD,
March 18th, 1861.

Mr. Wm. Still: – Dear Sir – Dr. Powell called to see me and informed me that you had a medical lexicon (Dictionary) for me. If you have such a book for me, it will be very thankfully received, and any other book that pertains to the medical or dental profession. I am quite limited in means as yet and in want of books to prosecute my studies. The books I need most at present is such as treat on midwifery, anatomy, &c. But any book or books in either of the above mentioned cases will be of use to me. You can send them by Express, or by any friend that may chance to come this way, but by Express will be the safest way to send them. Times are quite dull. This leaves me well and hope it may find you and family the same. My regards to your wife and all others.

Yours, &c.,

THOMAS BAYNE,

22 Cheapside, opposite City Hall.

Thus the doctor continued to labor and improve his mind until the war removed the hideous institution of Slavery from the nation; but as soon as the way opened for his return to his old home, New Bedford no longer had sufficient attractions to retain him. With all her faults he conceived that "Old Virginia" offered decided inducements for his return. Accordingly he went directly to Norfolk, whence he escaped. Of course every thing was in the utmost confusion and disorder when he returned, save where the military held sway. So as soon as the time drew near for reorganizing, elections, &c., the doctor was found to be an aspirant for a seat in Congress, and in "running" for it, was found to be a very difficult candidate to beat. Indeed in the first reports of the election his name was amongst the elected; but subsequent counts proved him to be among the defeated by only a very slight majority.

At the time of the doctor's escape, in 1855, he was thirty-one years of age, a man of medium size, and about as purely colored, as could readily be found, with a full share of self-esteem and pluck.

SUNDRY ARRIVALS

FROM LOUDON CO., VA., NORFOLK, BALTIMORE, MD., PETERSBURG, VA., &C., ABOUT THE MONTH OF JUNE, 1855.

The first arrival to be here noticed consisted of David Bennett, and his wife Martha, with their two children, a little boy named George, and a nameless babe one month old. This family journeyed from Loudon county, Va. David, the husband, had been in bonds under Captain James Taylor. Martha, the wife, and her two children were owned by George Carter. Martha's master was represented as a very barbarous and cruel man to the slaves. He made a common practice of flogging females when stripped naked. This was the emphatic testimony of Martha. Martha declared that she had been so stripped, and flogged by him after her marriage. The story of this interesting young mother, who was about twenty-seven years of age, was painful to the ear, particularly as the earnestness and intelligence of this poor, bruised, and mangled soul bore such strong evidence to the truthfulness of her statements. During the painful interview the mind would involuntarily picture this demon, only as the representative of thousands in the South using the same relentless sway over men and women; and this fleeing victim and her little ones, before escaping, only as sharers of a common lot with many other mothers and children, whose backs were daily subjected to the lash. If on such an occasion it was hard to find fitting words of sympathy, or adequate expressions of indignation, the pleasure of being permitted to give aid and comfort to such was in part a compensation and a relief. David, the husband of this woman, was about thirty-two years of age. No further notice was made of him.

Arrival No. 2 consisted of Henry Washington, alias Anthony Hanly, and Henry Stewart. Henry left Norfolk and a "very mild master," known by the name of "Seth March," out of sheer disgust for the patriarchal institution. Directly after speaking of his master in such flattering terms he qualified the "mild," &c. by adding that he was excessively close in money matters. In proof of this assertion, Henry declared, that out of his hire he was only allowed $1.50 per week to pay his board, clothe himself, and defray all other expenses; leaving no room whatever for him to provide for his wife. It was, therefore, a never-failing source of unhappiness to be thus debarred, and it was wholly on this account that he "took out," as he did, and at the time that he did. His wife's name was "Sally." She too was a slave, but "had not been treated roughly."

For fifty long years Henry had been in the grasp of this merciless system – constrained to toil for the happiness of others, to make them comfortable, rich, indolent, and tyrannical. To say that he was like a bird out of a cage, conveys in no sense whatever the slightest idea of his delight in escaping from the prison house. And yet, his pleasure was sadly marred by the reflection that his bosom companion was still in bondage in the gloomy prison-house. Henry was a man of dark color, well made, and of a reflective turn of mind. On arriving in Canada, he manifested his gratitude through Rev. H. Wilson, as follows –

ST. CATHARINES,
Aug. 20th, 1855.

DEAR BR. STILL: – I am requested by Henry Washington to inform you that he got through safe, and is here in good business. He returns to you his sincere thanks for your attention to him on his way. I had the pleasure of receiving seven fugitives last week. Send them on, and may God speed them in the flight. I would like to have a miracle-working power, that I could give wings to them all so that they could come faster than by Railroads either underground or above.

Yours truly,

HIRAM WILSON.

While he was thus hopefully succeeding in Canada, separated from his companion by many hundreds of miles, death came and liberated her from the yoke, as the subjoined letter indicates –

ST. CATHARINES, C.W.
Nov. 12, 1855.

MR. WILLIAM STILL: – *Dear Sir*: – I have received a letter from Joseph G. Selden a friend in Norfolk, Va., informing me of the death of my wife, who deceased since I saw you here; he also informs me that my clothing will be forwarded to you by Jupiter White, who now has it in his charge. You will therefore do me a great favor, if you will be so good as to forward them to me at this place St. Catharines, C.W.

The accompanying letter is the one received from Mr. Selden which I send you, that you may see that it is all right. You will please give my respects to Mrs. Still and family. Most respectfully yours,

HENRY WASHINGTON.

Henry Stewart, who accompanied the above mentioned traveler to Canada, had fled a short while before from Plymouth, North Carolina. James Monroe Woodhouse, a farmer, claimed Stewart as his property, and "hired him out" for $180 per annum. As a master, Woodhouse was considered to be of the "moderate" type, according to Stewart's judgment. But respecting money matters (when his slaves wanted a trifle), "he was very hard. He did not flog, but would not give a slave a cent of money upon any consideration."

It was by procuring a pass to Norfolk, that Henry managed to escape. Although a father and a husband, having a wife (Martha) and two children (Mary Ann and Susan Jane), he felt that his lot as a slave utterly debarred him from discharging his duty to them; that he could exercise no rights or privileges whatever, save as he might obtain permission from his master. In the matter of separation, even although the ties of husband and wife, parents and children were most closely knit, his reason dictated that he would be justified in freeing himself if possible; indeed, he could not endure the pressure of Slavery any longer. Although only twenty-three years of age, the burdens that he had been called upon to bear, made his naturally intelligent mind chafe to an unusual degree, especially when reflecting upon a continued life of Slavery. When the time decided upon for his flight arrived, he said nothing to his wife on the subject, but secured his pass and took his departure for Norfolk. On arriving there, he sought out an Underground Rail Road captain, and arranged with him to bring him to Philadelphia. Whether the sorrow-stricken wife ever afterwards heard of her husband, or the father of his two little children, the writer is unable to say. It is possible that this narrative may reveal to the mother and her offspring (if they are still living), the first ray of light concerning the missing one. Indeed it is not unreasonable to suppose, that thousands of anxious wives, husbands and children, who have been scattered in every direction by Slavery, will never be able to learn as much of their lost ones as is contained in this brief account of Henry Stewart.

Arrival No. 3, brought William Nelson, his wife, Susan, and son, William Thomas, together with Louisa Bell, and Elias Jasper. These travelers availed themselves of the schooner of Captain B. who allowed them to embark at Norfolk, despite the search laws of Virginia. It hardly need be said, however, that it was no trifling matter in those days, to evade the law. Captains and captives, in order to succeed, found that it required more than ordinary intelligence and courage, shrewdness and determination, and at the same time, a very ardent appreciation of liberty, without which, there could be no success. The simple announcement then, that a party of this number had arrived from Norfolk, or Richmond, or Petersburg, gave the Committee unusual satisfaction. It made them quite sure that there was pluck and brain some-where.

These individuals, in a particularly marked degree, possessed the qualities that greatly encouraged the efforts of the Committee. William Nelson was a man of a dark chestnut color, medium size, with more than an ordinary degree of what might be termed "mother wit." Apparently, William possessed well settled convictions, touching the questions of morals and religion, despite the overflowing tide of corruption and spurious religious teachings consequent on the existing pro-slavery usages all around him. He was a member of the Methodist Church, under the charge of the Rev. Mr. Jones. For twenty years, William had served in the capacity of a "packer" under Messrs. Turner and White, who held a deed for William as their legal property. While he declared that he had been very "tightly worked" he nevertheless admitted that he had been dealt with in a mild manner in some respects. For his board and clothing, William had been allowed $1.50 per week. Truly a small sum for a hard-working man with a family – yet this was far more than many slaves received from their masters. In view of receiving this small pittance, he had toiled hard – doing over-work in order to make "buckle and strap meet." Once he had been sold on the auction-block. A sister of his had also shared the same fate. While seriously contemplating his life as a slave, he was soon led to the conclusion that it was his duty to bend his entire energies towards freeing himself and his family if possible. The idea of not being able to properly provide for his family rendered him quite unhappy; he therefore resolved to seek a passage North, via the Underground Rail Road. To any captain who would aid him in the matter, he resolved to offer a large reward, and determined that the amount should only be limited by his inability to increase it. Finally, after much anxious preparation, agreement was entered into with Captain B., on behalf of himself, wife, child, and Louisa Bell, which was mutually satisfactory to all concerned, and afforded great hope to

William. In due time the agreement was carried into effect, and all arrived safely and were delivered into the hands of the Committee in Philadelphia. The fare of the four cost $240, and William was only too grateful to think, that a Captain could be found who would risk his own liberty in thus aiding a slave to freedom.

The Committee gladly gave them aid and succor, and agreed with William that the Captain deserved all that he received for their deliverance. The arrival of William, wife, and child in Canada was duly announced by the agent at St. Catharines, Rev. H. Wilson, as follows:

ST. CATHARINES, C.W.,
June 28th, 1855.

MR. WM. STILL: – *My Dear Friend:* – I am happy to announce the safe arrival of Thomas Russell with his wife and child. They have just arrived. I am much pleased with their appearance. I shall do what I can for their comfort and encouragement. They stopt at Elmira from Monday night till this morning, hoping that Lucy Bell would come up and join them at that place. They are very anxious to hear from her, as they have failed of meeting with her on the way or finding her here in advance of them. They wish to hear from you as soon as you can write, and would like to know if you have forwarded Lucy on, and if so, what route you sent her. They send their kind respects to you and your family and many thanks for your kindness to them.

They wish you to inquire after Lucy if any harm has befallen her after her leaving Philadelphia. Please write promptly in my care.

Yours truly in the love of freedom,

HIRAM WILSON.

The man who came to us as Wm. Nelson, is now known only as "Thomas Russell." It may here be remarked, that, owing to the general custom of changing names, as here instanced, it is found difficult to tell to whom the letters severally refer. Where the old and new names were both carefully entered on the book there is no difficulty, of course, but it was not always thus.

Susan Bell, the wife of William, was about thirty years of age, of a dark color, rather above medium size, well-made, good-looking, and intelligent – quite equal to her husband, and appeared to have his affections undividedly. She was owned by Thomas Baltimore, with whom she had lived for the last seven years. She stated that during a part of her life she had been treated in a "mild manner." She had no complaint to make until after the marriage of her master. Under the new wife and mistress, Susan found a very marked change for the worse. She fared badly enough then. The mistress, on every trifling occasion for complaint, was disposed to hold the auction-block up to Susan, and would likewise influence her husband to do the same. From the fact, that four of Susan's sisters had been sold away to "parts unknown," she was not prepared to relish these almost daily threats from her irritable mistress, so she became as anxious for a trip on the Underground Rail Road as was her husband.

About one hundred miles away in the country, her father, mother, three brothers, and one sister were living; but she felt that she could not remain a slave on their account. Susan's owner had already fixed a price on her and her child, twenty-two months old, which was one thousand dollars. From this fate she was saved only by her firm resolution to seek her freedom.

Louisa Bell was also of Wm. Nelson's party, and a fair specimen of a nice-looking, wide awake woman; of a chestnut color, twenty-eight years of age. She was the wife of a free man, but the slave of L. Stasson, a confectioner. The almost constant ringing in her ears of the auction-block, made her most miserable, especially as she had once suffered terribly by being sold, and had likewise seen her mother, and five sisters placed in the same unhappy situation, the thought of which never ceased to be most painful. In reflecting upon the course which she was about to pursue in order to free herself from the prison-house, she felt more keenly than ever for her little children, and readily imagined how sadly she would mourn while thinking of them hundreds of miles distant, growing up only to be slaves. And particularly would her thoughts dwell upon her boy, six years of age; full old enough to feel deeply the loss of his mother, but without hope of ever seeing her again.

Heart-breaking as were these reflections, she resolved to leave Robert and Mary in the hands of God, and escape, if possible from her terrible thraldom. Her plan was submitted to her husband; he acquiesced fully and promised to follow her as soon as an opportunity might present itself. Although the ordeal that she was called upon to pass through was of the most trying nature she bravely endured the journey through to Canada. On her arrival there the Rev. H. Wilson wrote on behalf of herself, and the cause as follows:

ST. CATHERINES, C.W.
July 6th, 1855.

DEAR BR. STILL: – I have just received your letters touching U.G.R.R. operations. All is right. Jasper and Mrs. Bell got here on Saturday last, and I think I dropt you a line announcing the fact. I write again thus soon because two more by name of Smith, John and Wm., have arrived the present week and were anxious to have me inform you that they are safely landed and free in this refuge land. They wish me to communicate their kind regards to you and others who have aided them. They have found employment and are likely to do well. The 5 of last week have gone over to Toronto. I gave them letters to a friend there after furnishing them as well as I could with such clothing as they required. I am afraid that I am burdening you too much with postage, but can't help doing so unless I fail to write at all, as my means are not half equal to the expenses to which I am subject.

Faithfully and truly yours,

HIRAM WILSON.

Elias Jasper, who was also a fellow-passenger with Wm. Nelson and Co., was noticed thus on the Underground Rail Road: Age thirty-two years, color dark, features good, and gifted both with his tongue and hands. He had worked more or less at the following trades: Rope-making, carpentering, engineering, and photographing. It was in this latter calling that he was engaged when the Underground Rail Road movement first arrested his attention, and so continued until his departure.

For several years he had been accustomed to hire his time, for which he had been required to pay $10 per month. In acquiring the above trades he had been at no expense to his master, as he had learned them solely by his own perseverance, endowed as he was with a considerable share of genius. Occasionally he paid for lessons, the money being earned by his over-work. His master, Bayham, was a "retired gentleman."

Elias had been sold once, and had suffered in various other ways, particularly from being flogged. He left his wife, Mary, but no child. Of his intention to leave Elias saw not how to impart to his wife, lest she should in some way let the "cat out of the bag." She was owned by a Miss Portlock, and had been treated "tolerably well," having had the privilege of hiring her time. She had $55 to pay for this favor, which amount she raised by washing, etc. Elias was a member of the Methodist Church, as were all of his comrades, and well did they remember the oft-repeated lesson, "Servants obey your masters," etc. They soon understood this kind of preaching after breathing free air. The market value of Elias was placed at $1,200.

Arrival, No. 4. Maria Joiner. Captain F. arrived, from Norfolk, with the above named passenger, the way not being open to risk any other on that occasion. This seemed rather slow business with this voyager, for he was usually accustomed to bringing more than one. However, as this arrival was only one day later than the preceding one noticed, and came from the same place, the Committee concluded, that they had much reason for rejoicing nevertheless. As in the case of a great number among the oppressed of the South, when simply looking at Maria, no visible marks of ill usage in any way were discernible. Indeed, as she then appeared at the age of thirty-three, a fine, fresh, and healthy-looking mulatto woman, nine out of every ten would have been impressed with the idea, that she had never been subjected to hard treatment; in other words, that she had derived her full share of advantages from the "Patriarchal Institution." The appearance of just such persons in Southern cities had often led Northerners, when traveling in those parts, to regard the lot of slaves as quite comfortable. But the story of Maria, told in an earnest and intelligent manner, was at once calculated to dissipate the idea of a "comfortable" existence in a state of bondage. She frankly admitted, however, that prior to the death of her old master, she was favorably treated, compared with many others; but, unfortunately, after his death, she had fallen into the hands of one of the old man's daughters, from whom, she declared, that she had received continued abuse, especially when said daughter was under the influence of liquor. At such times she was very violent. Being spirited, Maria could not consent to suffer on as a slave in this manner. Consequently she began to cogitate how she might escape from her mistress (Catharine Gordon), and reach a free State. None other than the usual trying and hazardous ways could be devised – which was either to be stowed away in the hold of a schooner, or concealed amongst the rubbish of a steamer, where, for the time being, the extreme suffering was sure to tax every nerve even of the most valiant-hearted men. The daily darkening prospects constrained her to decide, that she was willing to suffer, not only in adopting this mode of travel, but on the other hand, that she had better be dead than remain under so cruel a woman as her mistress. Maria's husband and sister (no other relatives are noticed) were naturally formidable barriers in the way of her escape. Notwithstanding her attachment to them, she fully made up her mind to be free. Immediately she took the first prerequisite step, which was to repair to a place of concealment with a friend in the city, and there, like the man at the pool, wait until her turn came to be conveyed thence to a free State. In this place she was obliged to wait eight long months, enduring daily suffering in various ways, especially during the winter season. But, with martyr-like faith, she endured to the end, and was eventually saved from the hell of Slavery. Maria was appraised at $800.

Arrival No. 5. Richard Green, alias Wm. Smith, and his brother George. These young brothers fled from George Chambers of Baltimore. The elder brother was twenty-five, the younger twenty-three. Both were tall and well made and of a chestnut color, and possessed a good degree of natural ability. When desiring to visit their parents, their request was positively refused by their owner. Taking offence at this step, both mutually resolved to run away at the earliest opportunity. Thus in accordance with well premeditated plans, they set out and unobstructedly arrived in Philadelphia. At first it was simply very pleasant to take them by the hand and welcome them; then to listen for a few moments to their intelligent narration of how they escaped, the motives that prompted them, etc. But further inquiries soon brought out incidents of the most thrilling and touching nature – not with regard to hardships which they had personally experienced, but in relation to outrages which had been perpetrated upon their mother. Such simple facts as were then written are substantially as follows: Nearly thirty years prior to the escape of Richard and his brother their mother was in very bad health, so much so that physicians regarded her incurable. Her owner was evidently fully impressed with the belief that instead of being profitable to him, she might be an expense, which he could not possibly obviate, while he retained her as a slave. Now there was a way to get out of this dilemma. He could emancipate her and throw the responsibility of her support upon herself. Accordingly he drew up papers, called for his wife's mother to witness them, then formally put them into the hands of the invalid slave woman (Dinah), assuring her at the same time, that she was free – being fully released as set forth in her papers. "Take notice I have no more claim on you nor you on me from this time." Marvellous liberality! After working the life out of a woman, in order that he should not have her to bury, he becomes hastily in favor of freedom. He is, however, justified by the laws of Maryland. Complaint, therefore, would simply amount to nothing. In the nature of the case Dinah was now free, but she was not wholly alone in the world. She had a husband, named Jacob Green, who was owned by Nathan Childs for a term of years only, at the expiration of which time he was to be free. All lived then in Talbot county, Md. At the appointed time Jacob's bondage ended, and he concluded that he might succeed better by moving to Baltimore. Indeed the health of his wife was so miserable that nothing in his old home seemed to offer any inducement in the way of a livelihood. So off they moved to Baltimore. After a time, under careful and kind treatment, the faithful Jacob was greatly encouraged by perceiving that the health of his companion was gradually improving – signs indicated, that she might yet become a well woman. The hopes of husband and wife, in this particular, were, in the lapse of time, fully realized. Dinah was as well as ever, and became the mother of another child – a little boy. Everything seemed to be going on happily, and they had no apparent reason to suspect any troubles other than such as might naturally have to be encountered in a state of poverty and toil.

The unfettered boy was healthy, and made rapid advance in a few years. That any one should ever claim him was never for a moment feared.

The old master, however, becoming tired of country life, had also moved to Baltimore. How, they knew not, but he had heard of the existence of this boy.

That he might satisfy himself on this point, he one day very slyly approached the house with George. No sooner was the old man within the enclosures than he asked Dinah, "Whose child is that?" pointing to the boy. "Ask Jacob," was the reply of the mother. The question was then put to Jacob, the father of the boy. "I did not think that you would ask such a question, or that you would request anything like that," Jacob remarked, naturally somewhat nervous, but he added, "I have the privilege of having any one I please in my house." "Where is he from?" again demanded the master. The father repeated, "I have a right to have," etc., "I am my own man," etc. "I have found out whose he is," the hunter said. "I am going presently to take him home with me." At this juncture he seized the little fellow, at the same time calling out, "Dinah, put his clothes on." By this time the father too had seized hold of the child. Mustering courage, the father said, "Take notice that you are not in the country, pulling and hauling people about." "I will have him or I will leave my heart's blood in the house," was the savage declaration of the master. In his rage he threatened to shoot the father. In the midst of the excitement George called in two officers to settle the trouble. "What are you doing here?" said the officers to the slave-holder. "I am after my property – this boy," he exclaimed. "Have you ever seen it before?" they inquired. "No," said the slave-holder. "Then how do you know that he belongs to you?" inquired the officers. "I believe he is mine," replied the slave-holder.

All the parties concerned were then taken by the officers before an Alderman. The father owned the child but the mother denied it. The Alderman then decided that the child should be given to the father.

The slave-holder having thus failed, was unwilling, nevertheless, to relinquish his grasp. Whereupon he at once claimed the mother. Of course he was under the necessity of resorting to the Courts in order to establish his claim. Fortunately the mother had securely preserved the paper given her by her master so many years before, releasing her. Notwithstanding this the suit was pending nearly a year before the case was decided. Everything was so clear the mother finally gained the suit. This decision was rendered only about two months prior to the escape of Richard and George.

Arrival No. 6. Henry Cromwell. This passenger fled from Baltimore county, Md. The man that he escaped from was a farmer by the name of William Roberts, who also owned seven other young slaves. Of his treatment of his slaves nothing was recorded.

Henry was about six feet high, quite black, visage thin, age twenty-five. He left neither wife, parents, brothers nor sisters to grieve after him. In making his way North he walked of nights from his home to Harrisburg, Pa., and there availed himself of a passage on a freight car coming to Philadelphia.

Arrival No. 7. Henry Bohm. Henry came from near Norfolk, Va. He was about twenty-five years of age, and a fair specimen of a stout man, possessed of more than ordinary physical strength. As to whom he fled from, how he had been treated, or how he reached Philadelphia, the record book is silent. Why this is the case cannot now be accounted for, unless the hurry of getting him off forbade sufficient delay to note down more of the particulars.

Arrival No. 8. Ralph Whiting, James H. Forman, Anthony Atkinson, Arthur Jones, Isaiah Nixon, Joseph Harris, John Morris, and Henry Hodges. A numerous party like this had the appearance of business. They were all young and hopeful, and belonged to the more intelligent and promising of their race. They were capable of giving the best of reasons for the endeavors they were making to escape to a free country.

They imparted to the Committee much information respecting their several situations, together with the characters of their masters in relation to domestic matters, and the customs and usages under which they had been severally held to service – all of which was listened to with deep interest. But it was not an easy matter, after having been thus entertained, to write out the narratives of eight such persons. Hundreds of pages would hardly have contained a brief account of the most interesting portion of their histories. It was deemed sufficient to enter their names and their forsaken homes, etc., as follows:

"Ralph was twenty-six years of age, five feet ten inches high, dark, well made, intelligent, and a member of the Methodist Church. He was claimed by Geo. W. Kemp, Esq., cashier of the Exchange Bank of Norfolk, Va. Ralph gave Mr. Kemp the credit of being a 'moderate man' to his slaves. Ralph was compelled to leave his wife, Lydia, and two children, Anna Eliza, and Cornelius."

"James was twenty-three years of age, dark mulatto, nearly six feet high, and of prepossessing appearance. He fled from James Saunders, Esq. Nothing, save the desire to be free, prompted James to leave his old situation and master. His parents and two sisters he was obliged to leave in Norfolk."

Two brief letters from James, one concerning his "sweet-heart," whom he left in Norfolk, the other giving an account of her arrival in Canada and marriage thereafter will, doubtless, be read with interest. They are here given as follows:

NIAGARA FALLS, June 5th, 1856. MR. STILL: – Sir – I take my pen in hand to write you theas few lines to let you know that I am well at present and hope theas few lines may find you the same. Sir my object in writing to you is that I expect a young Lady by the name of Miss Mariah Moore, from Norfolk, Virginia. She will leave Norfolk on the 13th of this month in the Steamship *Virginia* for Philadelphia you will oblige me very much by seeing her safely on the train of cars that leaves Philadelphia for the Suspension Bridge Niagara Falls pleas to tell the Lady to telegraph to me what time she will leave Philadelphia so i may know what time to meet her at the Suspension Bridge my Brother Isaac Porman send his love also his family to you and your family they are all well at present pleas to give my respects to Mr. Harry Londay, also Miss Margaret Cunigan, no more at present.

I remain your friend,

JAMES H. FORMAN.

When you telegraph to me direct to the International Hotel, Niagara Falls, N.Y.

NIAGARA FALLS,
July 24th, 1856.

DEAR SIR: – I take this opportunity of writing these few lines to you hoping that they may find you enjoying good health as these few lines leave me at present. I thank you for your kindness. Miss Moore arrived here on the 30th of June and I was down to the cars to receive her. I thought I would have written to you before, but I thought I would wait till I got married. I got married on the 22d of July in the English Church Canada about 11 o'clock my wife sends all her love to you and your wife and all enquiring friends please to kiss your two children for her and she says she is done crying and I am glad to hear she enjoyed herself so well in Philadelphia give my respects to Miss Margaret Cuningham and I am glad to hear her sister arrived my father sends his respects to you no more at present but remain your friend,

JAMES H. FORMAN.

Direct your letter to the International Hotel, Niagara Falls.

Anthony was thirty-six years of age, and by blood, was quite as nearly related to the Anglo-Saxon as the Anglo-African. He was nevertheless, physically a fine specimen of a man. He was about six feet high, and bore evidence of having picked up a considerable amount of intelligence considering his opportunities. He had been sold three times. Anthony was decidedly opposed to having to pass through this ordeal a fourth time, therefore, the more he meditated over his condition, the more determined he became to seek out an Underground Rail Road agent, and make his way to Canada.

Concluding that Josiah Wells, who claimed him, had received a thousand times too much of his labor already, Anthony was in a fit state of mind to make a resolute effort to gain his freedom. He had a wife, but no children. His father, one sister, and two brothers were all dear to him, but all being slaves "one could not help the other," Anthony reasoned, and wisely too. So, at the command of the captain, he was ready to bear his part of the suffering consequent upon being concealed in the hold of a vessel, where but little air could penetrate.

Arthur was forty-one years of age, six feet high – chestnut color, well made, and possessed good native faculties needing cultivation. He escaped from a farmer, by the name of John Jones, who was classed, as to natural temperament, amongst "moderate slave-holders."

"I wanted my liberty," said Arthur promptly and emphatically, and he declared that was the cause of his escape. He left his mother, two sisters, and three brothers in Slavery.

Isaiah was about twenty-two, small of stature, but smart, and of a substantially black complexion. He had been subjected to very hard treatment under Samuel Simmons who claimed him, and on this account he was first prompted to leave. His mother and three brothers he left in bondage.

Joseph was twenty-three years of age, and was, in every way, "likely-looking." According to the laws of Slavery, he was the property of David Morris, who was entitled to be ranked amongst the more compassionate slave-holders of the South. Yet, Joseph was not satisfied, deprived of his freedom. He had not known hardships as many had, but it was not in him notwithstanding, to be contented as a slave. In leaving, he had to "tear himself away" from his parents, three brothers, and two sisters.

Henry escaped from S. Simmons of Plymouth, North Carolina, and was a fellow-servant with Isaiah. Simmons was particularly distinguished for his tyrannical rule and treatment of his slaves – so Henry and Isaiah had the good sense to withdraw from under his yoke, very young in life; Henry being twenty-three.

John was about twenty-one years of age, five feet eight inches high, dark color, and well-grown for his years. Before embarking, he had endured seven months of hard suffering from being secreted, waiting for an opportunity to escape. It was to keep his master from selling him, that he was thus induced to secrete himself. After he had remained away some months, he resolved to suffer on until his friends could manage to procure him a passage on the Underground Rail Road. With this determined spirit he did not wait in vain.

Arrival No. 9. Robert Jones and wife: – In the majority of cases, in order to effect the escape of either, sad separations between husbands and wives were unavoidable. Fortunately, it was not so in this case. In journeying from the house of bondage, Robert and his wife were united both in sympathies and in struggles. Robert had experienced "hard times," just in what way, however, was not recorded; his wife had been differently treated, not being under the same taskmaster as her husband. At the time of their arrival all that was recorded of their bondage is as follows –

August 2d, 1855, Robert Jones and wife, arrived from Petersburg, Va. Robert is about thirty-five, chestnut color, medium size, of good manners, intelligent, had been owned by Thomas N. Lee, "a very hard man." Robert left because he "wanted his liberty – always had from a boy." Eliza, his wife, is about forty years of age, chestnut color, nice-looking, and well-dressed. She belonged to Eliza H. Richie, who was called a "moderate woman" towards her slaves. Notwithstanding the limited space occupied in noting them on the record book, the Committee regarded them as being among the most worthy and brave travelers passing over the Underground Rail Road, and felt well satisfied that such specimens of humanity would do credit in Canada, not only to themselves, but to their race.

Robert had succeeded in learning to read and write tolerably well, and had thought much over the condition and wrongs of the race, and seemed to be eager to be where he could do something to lift his fellow-sufferers up to a higher plane of liberty and manhood. After an interview with Robert and his wife, in every way so agreeable, they were forwarded on in the usual manner, to Canada. While enjoying the sweets of freedom in Canada, he was not the man to keep his light under a bushel. He seemed to have a high appreciation of the potency of the pen, and a decidedly clear idea that colored men needed to lay hold of many enterprises with resolution, in order to prove themselves qualified to rise equally with other branches of the human family. Some of his letters, embracing his views, plans and suggestions, were so encouraging and sensible, that the Committee was in the habit of showing them to friendly persons, and indeed, extracts of some of his letters were deemed of sufficient importance to publish. One alone, taken from many letters received from him, must here suffice to illustrate his intelligence and efforts as a fugitive and citizen in Canada.

Hamilton, C.W.,
August 9th, 1856.

MR. WM. STILL; – *Dear Friend*: – I take this opportunity of writing you these few lines to inform you of my health, which is good at present, &c. * * * *

I was talking to you about going to Liberia, when I saw you last, and did intend to start this fall, but I since looked at the condition of the colored people in Canada. I thought I would try to do something for their elevation as a nation, to place them in the proper position to stand where they ought to stand. In order to do this, I have undertaken to get up a military company amongst them. They laughed at me to undertake such a thing; but I did not relax my energies. I went and had an interview with Major J.T. Gilepon, told him what my object was, he encouraged me to go on, saying that he would do all he could for the accomplishment of my object. He referred to *Sir Allan McNab, &c.* * * * * I took with me Mr. J.H. Hill to see him – he told me that it should be done, and required us to write a petition to the *Governor General*, which has been done. * * * * The company is already organized. Mr. Howard was elected Captain; J.H. Hill, 1st Lieutenant; Hezekiah Hill, Ensign; Robert Jones, 1st Sergeant. The company's name is, Queen Victoria's Rifle Guards. You may, by this, see what I have been doing since I have been in Canada. When we receive our appointments by the Government. I will send by express, my daguerreotype in uniform.

My respects, &c. &c., Robert Jones.

HEAVY REWARD

When this arrival made its appearance, it was at first sight quite evident that one of the company was a man of more than ordinary parts, both physically and mentally. Likewise, taking them individually, their appearance and bearing tended largely to strengthen the idea that the spirit of freedom was rapidly gaining ground in the minds of the slaves, despite the efforts of the slave-holders to keep them in darkness. In company with the three men, for whom the above large reward was offered, came a woman by the name of Eliza Nokey.

As soon as the opportunity presented itself, the Active Committee feeling an unusual desire to hear their story, began the investigation by inquiring as to the cause of their escape, etc., which brought simple and homely but earnest answers from each. These answers afforded the best possible means of seeing Slavery in its natural, practical workings – of obtaining such testimony and representations of the vile system, as the most eloquent orator or able pen might labor in vain to make clear and convincing, although this arrival had obviously been owned by men of high standing. The fugitives themselves innocently stated that one of the masters, who was in the habit of flogging adult females, was a "moderate man." Josiah Bailey was the leader of this party, and he appeared well-qualified for this position. He was about twenty-nine years of age, and in no particular physically, did he seem to be deficient. He was likewise civil and polite in his manners, and a man of good common sense. He was held and oppressed by William H. Hughlett, a farmer and dealer in ship timber, who had besides invested in slaves to the number of forty head. In his habits he was generally taken for a "moderate" and "fair" man, "though he was in the habit of flogging the slaves – females as well as males," after they had arrived at the age of maturity. This was not considered strange or cruel in Maryland. Josiah was the "foreman" on the place, and was entrusted with the management of hauling the ship-timber, and through harvesting and busy seasons was required to lead in the fields. He was regarded as one of the most valuable hands in that part of the country, being valued at $2,000. Three weeks before he escaped, Joe was "stripped naked," and "flogged" very cruelly by his master, simply because he had a dispute with one of the fellow-servants, who had stolen, as Joe alleged, seven dollars of his hard earnings. This flogging produced in Joe's mind, an unswerving determination to leave Slavery or die: to try his luck on the Underground Rail Road at all hazards. The very name of Slavery made the fire fairly burn in his bones. Although a married man, having a wife and three children (owned by Hughlett), he was not prepared to let his affection for them keep him in chains – so Anna Maria, his wife, and his children Ellen, Anna Maria, and Isabella, were shortly widowed and orphaned by the slave lash.

William Bailey was owned by John C. Henry, a large slave-holder, and a very "hard" one, if what William alleged of him was true. His story certainly had every appearance of truthfulness. A recent brutal flogging had "stiffened his back-bone," and furnished him with his excuse for not being willing to continue in Maryland, working his strength away to enrich his master, or the man who claimed to be such. The memorable flogging, however, which caused him to seek flight on the

Underground Rail Road, was not administered by his master or on his master's plantation. He was hired out, and it was in this situation that he was so barbarously treated. Yet he considered his master more in fault than the man to whom he was hired, but redress there was none, save to escape.

The hour for forwarding the party by the Committee, came too soon to allow time for the writing of any account of Peter Pennington and Eliza Nokey. Suffice it to say, that in struggling through their journey, their spirits never flagged; they had determined not to stop short of Canada. They truly had a very high appreciation of freedom, but a very poor opinion of Maryland.

SLAVE TRADER HALL IS FOILED

ROBERT McCOY
alias WILLIAM DONAR

In October, 1854, the Committee received per steamer, directly from Norfolk, Va., Robert McCoy and Elizabeth Saunders. Robert had constantly been in the clutches of the negro-trader Hall, for the last sixteen years, previous to his leaving, being owned by him. He had, therefore, possessed very favorable opportunities for varied observation and experience relative to the trader's conduct in his nefarious business, as well as for witnessing the effects of the auction-block upon all ages – rending asunder the dearest ties, despite the piteous wails of childhood or womanhood, parental or conjugal relations. But no attempt will be made to chronicle the deeds of this dealer in human flesh. Those stories fresh from the lips of one who had just escaped, were painful in the extreme, but in the very nature of things some of the statements are too revolting to be published. In lieu of this fact, except the above allusions to the trader's business, this sketch will only refer to Robert's condition as a slave, and finally as a traveler on the Underground Rail Road.

Robert was a man of medium size, dark mulatto, of more than ordinary intelligence. His duties had been confined to the house, and not to the slave pen. As a general thing, he had managed, doubtless through much shrewdness, to avoid very severe outrages from the trader. On the whole, he had fared "about as well" as the generality of slaves.

Yet, in order to free himself from his "miserable" life, he was willing, as he declared, to suffer almost any sacrifice. Indeed, his conduct proved the sincerity of this declaration, as he had actually been concealed five months in a place in the city, where he could not possibly avoid daily suffering of the most trying kind. His resolve to be free was all this while maturing. The trader had threatened to sell Robert, and to prevent it Robert (thus) "took out." Successfully did he elude the keen scent and grasp of the hunters, who made diligent efforts to recapture him. Although a young man – only about twenty-eight years of age – his health was by no means good. His system had evidently been considerably shattered by Slavery, and symptoms of consumption, together with chronic rheumatism, were making rapid headway against the physical man. Under his various ills, he declared, as did many others from the land of bondage, that his faith in God afforded him comfort and hope. He was obliged to leave his wife, Eliza, in bonds, not knowing whether they should ever meet again on earth, but he was somewhat hopeful that the way would open for her escape also.

After reaching Philadelphia, where his arrival had long been anticipated by the Vigilance Committee, his immediate wants were met, and in due order he was forwarded to New Bedford, where, he was led to feel, he would be happy in freedom.

Scarcely had he been in New Bedford one month, before his prayers and hopes were realized with regard to the deliverance of his wife. On hearing of the good news of her coming he wrote as follows –

NEW BEDFORD,
Nov. 3, 1859.

DEAR SIR: – i embrace this opertunity to inform you that i received your letter with pleasure, i am enjoying good health and hope that these few lines will find you enjoying the same blessing. i rejoise to hear from you i feel very much indetted to you for not writing before but i have been so bissy that is the cause, i rejoise to heare of the arrival of my wife, and hope she is not sick from the roling of the sea and if she is not, pleas to send her on here Monday with a six baral warlian and a rifall to gard her up to my residance i thank you kindly for the good that you have don for me. Give my respects to Mrs. Still, tell her i want to see her very bad and you also i would come but i am afraid yet to venture, i received your letter the second, but about the first of spring i hope to pay you a visit or next summer. i am getting something to do every day. i will write on her arrivall and tell you more. Mr. R. White sends his love to you and your famerly and says that he is very much indetted to you for his not writing and all so he desires to know wheather his cloths has arived yet or not, and if they are please to express them on to him or if at preasant by Mrs. Donar. Not any more at preasent. i remain your affectionate brother,

WILLIAM DONAR.

By the same arrival, and similarly secreted, Elizabeth Frances, alias Ellen Saunders, had the good luck to reach Philadelphia. She was a single young woman, about twenty-two, with as pleasant a countenance as one would wish to see. Her manners were equally agreeable. Perhaps her joy over her achieved victory added somewhat to her personal appearance. She had, however, belonged to the more favored class of slaves. She had neither been over-worked nor badly abused. Elizabeth was the property of a lady a few shades lighter than herself (Elizabeth was a mulatto) by the name of Sarah Shephard, of Norfolk. In order the more effectually to profit by Elizabeth's labor, the mistress resorted to the plan of hiring her out for a given sum per month. Against this usage Elizabeth urged no complaint. Indeed the only very serious charge she brought was to the effect, that her mistress sold her mother away from her far South, when she was a child only ten years old. She had also sold a brother and sister to a foreign southern market. The reflections consequent upon the course that her mistress had thus pursued, awakened Elizabeth to much study relative to freedom, and by the time that she had reached womanhood she had very decided convictions touching her duty with regard to escaping. Thus growing to hate slavery in every way and manner, she was prepared to make a desperate effort to be free. Having saved thirty-five dollars by rigid economy, she was willing to give every cent of it (although it was all she possessed), to be aided from Norfolk to Philadelphia. After reaching the city, having suffered severely while coming, she was invited to remain until somewhat recruited. In the healthy air of freedom she was soon fully restored, and ready to take her departure for New Bedford, which place she reached without difficulty and was cordially welcomed. The following letter, expressive of her obligations for aid received, was forwarded soon after her arrival in New Bedford:

NEW BEDFORD, Mass.,
October 16th, 1854.

MR. STILL: – Dear Sir – I now take my pen in my hand to inform you of my health which is good at present all except a cold I have got but I hope when these few lines reach you you may be enjoying good health. I arrived in New Bedford Thursday morning safely and what little I have seen of the city I like it very much my friends were very glad to see me. I found my sister very well. Give my love to Mrs. Still and also your dear little children. I am now out at service. I do not think of going to Canada now. I think I shall remain in this city this winter. Please tell Mrs. Still I have not met any person who has treated me any kinder than she did since I left. I consider you both to have been true friends to me. I hope you will think me the same to you. I feel very thankful to you indeed. It might been supposed, out of sight out of mind, but it is not so. I never forget my friends. Give my love to Florence. If you come to this city I would be very happy to see you. Kiss your dear little children for me. Please to answer this as soon as possible, so that I may know you received this. No more at present. I still remain your friend,

ELLEN SAUNDERS.

ELIZA MCCOY – the wife of Robert McCoy, whose narrative has just been given, and who was left to wait in hope when her husband escaped – soon followed him to freedom. It is a source of great satisfaction to be able to present her narrative in so close proximity to her husband's. He arrived about the first of October – she about the first of November, following. From her lips testimony of much weight and interest was listened to by several friends relative to her sufferings as a slave – on the auction-block, and in a place of concealment seven months, waiting and praying for an opportunity to escape. But it was thought sufficient to record merely a very brief outline of her active slave life, which consisted of the following noticeable features.

Eliza had been owned by Andrew Sigany, of Norfolk – age about thirty-eight – mulatto, and a woman whose appearance would readily command attention and respect anywhere outside of the barbarism of Slavery. She stated that her experience as a sufferer in cruel hands had been very trying, and that in fretting under hardships, she had "always wanted to be free." Her language was unmistakable on this point. Neither mistress nor servant was satisfied with each other; the mistress was so "queer" and "hard to please," that Eliza became heartily sick of trying to please her – an angel would have failed with such a woman. So, while matters were getting no better, but, on the contrary, were growing worse and worse, Eliza thought she would seek a more pleasant atmosphere in the North. In fact she felt that it would afford her no little relief to allow her place to be occupied by another. When she went into close quarters of concealment, she fully understood what was meant and all the liabilities thereto. She had pluck enough to endure unto the end without murmuring. The martyrs in olden times who dwelt in "dens and caves of the earth," could hardly have fared worse than some of these way-worn travelers.

After the rest, needed by one who had suffered so severely until her arrival in Philadelphia, she was forwarded to her anxiously waiting husband in New Bedford, where she was gladly received.

ESCAPING
IN A CHEST

$150 REWARD. Ran away from the subscriber, on Sunday night, 27th inst., my NEGRO GIRL, Lear Green, about 18 years of age, black complexion, round-featured, good-looking and ordinary size; she had on and with her when she left, a tan-colored silk bonnet, a dark plaid silk dress, a light mouslin delaine, also one watered silk cape and one tan colored cape. I have reason to be confident that she was persuaded off by a negro man named Wm. Adams, black, quick spoken, 5 feet 10 inches high, a large scar on one side of his face, running down in a ridge by the corner of his mouth, about 4 inches long, barber by trade, but works mostly about taverns, opening oysters, &c. He has been missing about a week; he had been heard to say he was going to marry the above girl and ship to New York, where it is said his mother resides. The above reward will be paid if said girl is taken out of the State of Maryland and delivered to me; or fifty dollars if taken in the State of Maryland.

JAMES NOBLE.

No. 153 Broadway, Baltimore.

Lear Green, so particularly advertised in the *Baltimore Sun* by "James Noble," won for herself a strong claim to a high place among the heroic women of the nineteenth century. In regard to description and age the advertisement is tolerably accurate, although her master might have added, that her countenance was one of peculiar modesty and grace. Instead of being "black," she was of a "dark-brown color." Of her bondage she made the following statement: She was owned

by "James Noble, a Butter Dealer" of Baltimore. He fell heir
to Lear by the will of his wife's mother, Mrs. Rachel Howard,
by whom she had previously been owned. Lear was but a
mere child when she came into the hands of Noble's family.
She, therefore, remembered but little of her old mistress. Her
young mistress, however, had made a lasting impression upon
her mind; for she was very exacting and oppressive in regard
to the tasks she was daily in the habit of laying upon Lear's
shoulders, with no disposition whatever to allow her any liber-
ties. At least Lear was never indulged in this respect. In this
situation a young man by the name of William Adams proposed
marriage to her. This offer she was inclined to accept, but
disliked the idea of being encumbered with the chains of
slavery and the duties of a family at the same time.

After a full consultation with her mother and also her
intended upon the matter, she decided that she must be free
in order to fill the station of a wife and mother. For a time
dangers and difficulties in the way of escape seemed utterly
to set at defiance all hope of success. Whilst every pulse was
beating strong for liberty, only one chance seemed to be left,
the trial of which required as much courage as it would to
endure the cutting off the right arm or plucking out the right
eye. An old chest of substantial make, such as sailors
commonly use, was procured. A quilt, a pillow, and a few
articles of raiment, with a small quantity of food and a bottle
of water were put in it, and Lear placed therein; strong ropes
were fastened around the chest and she was safely stowed
amongst the ordinary freight on one of the Erricson line of
steamers. Her intended's mother, who was a free woman,

agreed to come as a passenger on the same boat. How could she refuse? The prescribed rules of the Company assigned colored passengers to the deck. In this instance it was exactly where this guardian and mother desired to be – as near the chest as possible. Once or twice, during the silent watches of the night, she was drawn irresistibly to the chest, and could not refrain from venturing to untie the rope and raise the lid a little, to see if the poor child still lived, and at the same time to give her a breath of fresh air. Without uttering a whisper, that frightful moment, this office was successfully performed. That the silent prayers of this oppressed young woman, together with her faithful protector's, were momentarily ascending to the ear of the good God above, there can be no question. Nor is it to be doubted for a moment but that some ministering angel aided the mother to unfasten the rope, and at the same time nerved the heart of poor Lear to endure the trying ordeal of her perilous situation. She declared that she had no fear.

After she had passed eighteen hours in the chest, the steamer arrived at the wharf in Philadelphia, and in due time the living freight was brought off the boat, and at first was delivered at a house in Barley street, occupied by particular friends of the mother. Subsequently chest and freight were removed to the residence of the writer, in whose family she remained several days under the protection and care of the Vigilance Committee.

Such hungering and thirsting for liberty, as was evinced by Lear Green, made the efforts of the most ardent friends, who were in the habit of aiding fugitives, seem feeble in the extreme. Of all the heroes in Canada, or out of it, who have purchased their liberty by downright bravery, through perils the most hazardous, none deserve more praise than Lear Green.

She remained for a time in this family, and was then forwarded to Elmira. In this place she was married to William Adams, who has been previously alluded to. They never went to Canada, but took up their permanent abode in Elmira. The brief space of about three years only was allotted her in which to enjoy freedom, as death came and terminated her career. About the time of this sad occurrence, her mother-in-law died in this city. The impressions made by both mother and daughter can never be effaced. The chest in which Lear escaped has been preserved by the writer as a rare trophy, and her photograph taken, while in the chest, is an excellent likeness of her and, at the same time, a fitting memorial.

ISAAC WILLIAMS,
HENRY BANKS,
AND KIT NICKLESS

*MONTHS IN A CAVE – SHOT BY
SLAVE-HUNTERS.*

Rarely were three travelers from the house of bondage received at the Philadelphia station whose narratives were more interesting than those of the above-named individuals. Before escaping they had encountered difficulties of the most trying nature. No better material for dramatic effect could be found than might have been gathered from the incidents of their lives and travels. But all that we can venture to introduce here is the brief account recorded at the time of their sojourn at the Philadelphia station when on their way to Canada in 1854. The three journeyed together. They had been slaves together in the same neighborhood. Two of them had shared the same den and cave in the woods, and had been shot, captured, and confined in the same prison; had broken out of prison and again escaped; consequently their hearts were thoroughly cemented in the hope of reaching freedom together.

Isaac was a stout-made young man, about twenty-six years of age, possessing a good degree of physical and mental ability. Indeed his intelligence forbade his submission to the requirements of Slavery, rendered him unhappy and led him to seek his freedom. He owed services to D. Fitchhugh up to within a short time before he escaped. Against Fitchhugh he made grave charges, said that he was a "hard, bad man." It is but fair to add that Isaac was similarly regarded by his master, so both were dissatisfied with each other. But the master had the advantage of Isaac, he could sell him. Isaac, however, could turn the table on his master, by running off. But the master moved quickly and sold Isaac to Dr. James, a negro trader. The trader designed making a good speculation out of his investment: Isaac determined that he should be disappointed;

indeed that he should lose every dollar that he paid for him. So while the doctor was planning where and how he could get the best price for him, Isaac was planning how and where he might safely get beyond his reach. The time for planning and acting with Isaac was, however, exceedingly short. He was daily expecting to be called upon to take his departure for the South. In this situation he made known his condition to a friend of his who was in a precisely similar situation; had lately been sold just as Isaac had to the same trader James. So no argument was needed to convince his friend and fellow-servant that if they meant to be free they would have to set off immediately.

That night Henry Banks and Isaac Williams started for the woods together, preferring to live among reptiles and wild animals, rather than be any longer at the disposal of Dr. James. For two weeks they successfully escaped their pursuers. The woods, however, were being hunted in every direction, and one day the pursuers came upon them, shot them both, and carried them to King George's Co. jail. The jail being an old building had weak places in it; but the prisoners concluded to make no attempt to break out while suffering badly from their wounds. So they remained one month in confinement. All the while their brave spirits under suffering grew more and more daring. Again they decided to strike for freedom, but where to go, save to the woods, they had not the slightest idea. Of course they had heard, as most slaves had, of cave life, and pretty well understood all the measures which had to be resorted to for security when entering upon so hazardous an undertaking. They concluded, however, that they could not make their condition any worse, let circumstances be what they might in this respect. Having discovered how they could break jail, they were not long in accomplishing their purpose, and were out and off to the woods again. This time they went far into the forest, and there they dug a cave, and with great pains had every thing so completely arranged as to conceal the spot entirely. In this den they stayed three months. Now and then they would manage to secure a pig. A friend also would occasionally serve them with a meal. Their sufferings at best were fearful; but great as they were, the thought of returning to Slavery never occurred to them, and the longer they stayed in the woods, the greater was their determination to be free. In the belief that their owner had about given them up they resolved to take the North Star for a pilot, and try in this way to reach free land.

Kit, an old friend in time of need, having proved true to them in their cave, was consulted. He fully appreciated their heroism, and determined that he would join them in the undertaking, as he was badly treated by his master, who was called General Washington, a common farmer, hard drinker, and brutal fighter, which Kit's poor back fully evinced by the marks it bore. Of course Isaac and Henry were only too willing to have him accompany them.

In leaving their respective homes they broke kindred ties of the tenderest nature. Isaac had a wife, Eliza, and three children, Isaac, Estella, and Ellen, all owned by Fitchhugh. Henry was only nineteen, single, but left parents, brothers, and sisters, all owned by different slave-holders. Kit had a wife, Matilda, and three children, Sarah Ann, Jane Frances, and Ellen, slaves.

"PETE MATTHEWS," ALIAS SAMUEL SPARROWS

"I MIGHT AS WELL BE IN THE PENITENTIARY"

Up to the age of thirty-five "Pete" had worn the yoke steadily, if not patiently under William S. Matthews, of Oak Hall, near Temperanceville, in the State of Virginia. Pete said that his "master was not a hard man," but the man to whom he "was hired, George Matthews, was a very cruel man." "I might as well be in the penitentiary as in his hands," was his declaration.

One day, a short while before Pete "took out," an ox broke into the truck patch, and helped himself to choice delicacies, to the full extent of his capacious stomach, making sad havoc with the vegetables generally. Peter's attention being directed to the ox, he turned him out, and gave him what he considered proper chastisement, according to the mischief he had done. At this liberty taken by Pete, the master became furious. "He got his gun and threatened to shoot him," "Open your mouth if you dare, and I will pat the whole load into you," said the enraged master. "He took out a large dirk-knife, and attempted to stab me, but I kept out of his way," said Pete. Nevertheless the violence of the master did not abate until he had beaten Pete over the head and body till he was weary, inflicting severe injuries. A great change was at once wrought in Pete's mind. He was now ready to adopt any plan that might hold out the least encouragement to escape. Having capital to the amount of four dollars only, he felt that he could not do much towards employing a conductor, but he had a good pair of legs, and a heart stout enough to whip two or three slave-catchers, with the help of a pistol. Happening to know a man who had a pistol for sale, he went to him and told him that he wished to purchase it. For one dollar the pistol became Pete's property. He had but three dollars left, but he was determined to make that amount answer his purposes under the circumstances. The last cruel beating maddened him almost to desperation, especially when he remembered how he had been compelled to work hard night and day, under Matthews. Then, too, Peter had a wife, whom his master prevented him from visiting; this was not among the least offences with which Pete charged his master. Fully bent on leaving, the following Sunday was fixed by him on which to commence his journey.

The time arrived and Pete bade farewell to Slavery, resolved to follow the North Star, with his pistol in hand ready for action. After traveling about two hundred miles from home he unexpectedly had an opportunity of using his pistol. To his astonishment he suddenly came face to face with a former master, whom he had not seen for a long time. Pete desired no friendly intercourse with him whatever; but he perceived that his old master recognized him and was bent upon stopping him. Pete held on to his pistol, but moved as fast as his wearied limbs would allow him, in an opposite direction. As he was running, Pete cautiously cast his eye over his shoulder, to see what had become of his old master, when to his amazement, he found that a regular chase was being made after him. Need of redoubling his pace was quite obvious. In this hour of peril, Pete's legs saved him.

After this signal leg-victory, Pete had more confidence in his "understandings," than he had in his old pistol, although he held on to it until he reached Philadelphia, where he left it in the possession of the Secretary of the Committee. Considering it worth saving simply as a relic of the Underground Rail Road, it was carefully laid aside. Pete was now christened

Samuel Sparrows. Mr. Sparrows had the rust of Slavery washed off as clean as possible and the Committee furnishing him with clean clothes, a ticket, and letters of introduction, started him on Canada-ward, looking quite respectable. And doubtless he felt even more so than he looked; free air had a powerful effect on such passengers as Samuel Sparrows.

The unpleasantness which grew out of the mischief done by the ox on George Matthews' farm took place the first of October, 1855. Pete may be described as a man of unmixed blood, well-made, and intelligent.

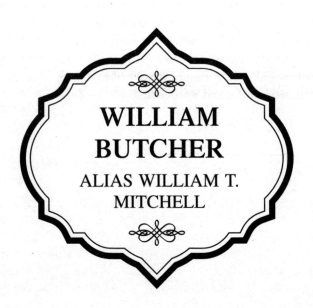

WILLIAM
BUTCHER
ALIAS WILLIAM T.
MITCHELL

"HE WAS ABUSEFUL."

This passenger reported himself from Massey's Cross-Roads, near Georgetown, Maryland. William gave as his reason for being found destitute, and under the necessity of asking aid, that a man by the name of William Boyer, who followed farming, had deprived him of his hard earnings, and also claimed him as his property; and withal that he had abused him for years, and recently had "threatened to sell" him. This threat made his yoke too intolerable to be borne.

He here began to think and plan for the future as he had never done before. Fortunately he was possessed with more than an average amount of mother wit, and he soon comprehended the requirements of the Underground Rail Road. He saw exactly that he must have resolution and self-dependence, very decided, in order to gain the victory over Boyer. In his hour of trial his wife, Phillis, and child, John Wesley, who were free, caused him much anxiety; but his reason taught him that it was his duty to throw off the yoke at all hazards, and he acted accordingly. Of course he left behind his wife and child. The interview which the Committee held with William was quite satisfactory, and he was duly aided and regularly despatched by the name of William T. Mitchell. He was about twenty-eight years of age, of medium size, and of quite a dark hue.

"WHITE ENOUGH TO PASS."

John Wesley Gibson represented himself to be not only the slave, but also the son of William Y. Day, of Taylor's Mount, Maryland. The faintest shade of colored blood was hardly discernible in this passenger. He relied wholly on his father's white blood to secure him freedom. Having resolved to serve no longer as a slave, he concluded to "hold up his head and put on airs." He reached Baltimore safely without being discovered or suspected of being on the Underground Rail Road, as far as he was aware of. Here he tried for the first time to pass for white; the attempt proved a success beyond his expectation. Indeed he could but wonder how it was that he had never before hit upon such an expedient to rid himself of his unhappy lot. Although a man of only twenty-eight years of age, he was foreman of his master's farm, but he was not particularly favored in any way on this account. His master and father endeavored to hold the reins very tightly upon him. Not even allowing him the privilege of visiting around on neighboring plantations. Perhaps the master thought the family likeness was rather too discernible. John believed that on this account all privileges were denied him, and he resolved to escape. His mother, Harriet, and sister, Frances, were named as near kin whom he had left behind. John was quite smart, and looked none the worse for having so much of his master's blood in his veins. The master was alone to blame for John's escape, as he passed on his (the master's) color.

ESCAPING WITH MASTER'S CARRIAGES AND HORSES

HARRIET SHEPHARD, AND HER FIVE CHILDREN, WITH FIVE OTHER PASSENGERS.

One morning about the first of November, in 1855, the sleepy, slave-holding neighborhood of Chestertown, Maryland, was doubtless deeply excited on learning that eleven head of slaves, four head of horses, and two carriages were missing. It is but reasonable to suppose that the first report must have produced a shock, scarcely less stunning than an earthquake. Abolitionists, emissaries, and incendiaries were farther below par than ever. It may be supposed that cursings and threatenings were breathed out by a deeply agitated community for days in succession.

Harriet Shephard, the mother of five children, for whom she felt of course a mother's love, could not bear the thought of having her offspring compelled to wear the miserable yoke of Slavery, as she had been compelled to do. By her own personal experience, Harriet could very well judge what their fate would be when reaching man and womanhood. She declared that she had never received "kind treatment." It was not on this account, however, that she was prompted to escape. She was actuated by a more disinterested motive than this. She was chiefly induced to make the bold effort to save her children from having to drag the chains of Slavery as she herself had done.

Anna Maria, Edwin, Eliza Jane, Mary Ann, and John Henry were the names of the children for whom she was willing to make any sacrifice. They were young; and unable to walk, and she was penniless, and unable to hire a conveyance, even if she had known any one who would have been willing to risk the law in taking them a night's journey. So there was no hope in these directions. Her rude intellect being considered, she was entitled to a great deal of credit for seizing the horses and carriages belonging to her master, as she did it for the liberation of her children.

Knowing others at the same time, who were wanting to visit Canada, she consulted with five of this class, males and females, and they mutually decided to travel together.

It is not likely that they knew much about the roads, nevertheless they reached Wilmington, Delaware, pretty direct, and ventured up into the heart of the town in carriages, looking as innocent as if they were going to a meeting to hear an old-fashioned Southern sermon – "Servants, obey your masters." Of course, the distinguished travelers were immediately reported to the noted Thomas Garrett, who was accustomed to transact the affairs of the Underground Rail Road in a cool masterly way. But, on this occasion, there was but little time for deliberation, but much need of haste to meet the emergency. He at once decided, that they must immediately be separated from the horses and carriages, and got out of Wilmington as quickly as possible. With the courage and skill, so characteristic of Garrett, the fugitives, under escort, were soon on their way to Kennett Square (a hot-bed of abolitionists and stock-holders of the Underground Rail Road), which place they reached safely. It so happened, that they reached Long Wood meeting-house in the evening, at which place a fair circle had convened. Being invited, they stayed awhile in the meeting, then, after remaining all night with one of the Kennett friends, they were brought to Downingtown early in the morning and thence, by daylight, within a short distance of Kimberton, and found succor with friend Lewis, at the old headquarters of the fugitives.

[A letter may be found from Miss G.A. Lewis, on page thirty-nine, throwing much light on this arrival.] After receiving friendly aid and advice while there, they were forwarded to the Committee in Philadelphia. Here further aid was afforded them, and as danger was quite obvious, they were completely divided and disguised, so that the Committee felt that they might safely be sent on to Canada in one of the regular trains considered most private.

Considering the condition of the slave mother and her children and friends, all concerned rejoiced, that they had had the courage to use their master's horses and vehicles as they did.

EIGHT AND A
HALF MONTHS
SECRETED

WASHINGTON SOMLOR,
ALIAS JAMES MOORE

But few could tell of having been eye-witnesses to outrages more revolting and disgraceful than Washington Somlor. He arrived per steamer *Pennsylvania* (secreted), directly from Norfolk, Virginia, in 1855. He was thirty-two years of age – a man of medium size and quite intelligent. A merchant by the name of Smith owned Washington.

Eight and a half months before escaping, Washington had been secreted in order to shun both master and auction-block. Smith believed in selling, flogging, cobbing, paddling, and all other kinds of torture, by which he could inflict punishment in order to make the slaves feel his power. He thus tyrannized over about twenty-five head.

Being naturally passionate, when in a brutal mood, he made his slaves suffer unmercifully. Said Washington, "On one occasion, about two months before I was secreted, he had five of the slaves (some of them women) tied across a barrel, lashed with the cow-hide and then cobbed – this was a common practice."

Such treatment was so inhuman and so incredible, that the Committee hesitated at first to give credence to the statement, and only yielded when facts and evidences were given which seemed incontestible.

The first effort to come away was made on the steamship *City of Richmond*. Within sixty miles of Philadelphia, in consequence of the ice obstruction in the river, the steamer had to go back. How sad Washington felt at thus having his hopes broken to pieces may be imagined but cannot be described. Great as was his danger, when the steamer returned to Norfolk, he was safely gotten off the boat and under the eye of officers walked away. Again he was secreted in his old doleful quarters, where he waited patiently for the Spring. It came. Again the opportunity for another trial was presented, and it was seized unhesitatingly. This time, his tried faith was rewarded with success. He came through safely to the Committee's satisfaction as well as his own. The recital of his sufferings and experience had a very inspiring effect on those who had the pleasure of seeing Wash. in Philadelphia.

Although closely secreted in Norfolk, he had, through friends, some little communication with the outside world. Among other items of information which came to his ears, was a report that his master was being pressed by his creditors, and had all his slaves advertised for sale. An item still more sad also reached his ear, to the effect that his wife had been sold away to North Carolina, and thus separated from her child, two years old. The child was given as a present to a niece of the master. While this is only a meagre portion of his interesting story, it was considered at the time sufficient to identify him should the occasion ever require it. We content ourselves, therefore, simply with giving what was recorded on the book. Wash. spent a short while in Philadelphia in order to recruit, after which, he went on North, where colored men were free.

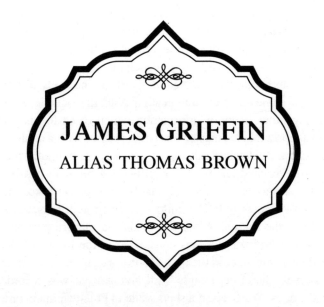

JAMES GRIFFIN

ALIAS THOMAS BROWN

*SLAVE-HOLDER IN MARYLAND WITH
THREE COLORED WIVES.*

James was a tiller of the soil under the yoke of Joshua Hitch, who lived on a farm about seventeen miles from Baltimore. James spoke rather favorably of him; indeed, it was through a direct act of kindness on the part of his master that he procured the opportunity to make good his escape. It appeared from his story, that his master's affairs had become particularly embarrassed, and the Sheriff was making frequent visits to his house. This sign was interpreted to mean that James, if not others, would have to be sold before long. The master was much puzzled to decide which way to turn. He owned but three other adult slaves besides James, and they were females. One of them was his chief housekeeper, and with them all his social relations were of such a nature as to lead James and others to think and say that they "were all his wives." Or to use James's own language, "he had three slave women; two were sisters, and he lived with them all as his wives; two of them he was very fond of," and desired to keep them from being sold if possible. The third, he concluded he could not save, she would have to be sold. In this dilemma, he was good enough to allow James a few days' holiday, for the purpose of finding him a good master. Expressing his satisfaction and gratification, James, armed with full authority from his master to select a choice specimen, started for Baltimore.

On reaching Baltimore, however, James carefully steered clear of all slave-holders, and shrewdly turned his attention to the matter of getting an Underground Rail Road ticket for Canada. After making as much inquiry as he felt was safe, he came to the conclusion to walk of nights for a long distance. He examined his feet and legs, found that they were in good order, and his faith and hope strong enough to remove a mountain. Besides several days still remained in which he was permitted to look for a new master, and these he decided could be profitably spent in making his way towards Canada. So off he started, at no doubt a very diligent pace, for at the end of the first night's journey, he had made much headway, but at the expense of his feet.

His faith was stronger than ever. So he rested next day in the woods, concealed, of course, and the next evening started with fresh courage and renewed perseverance. Finally, he reached Columbia, Pennsylvania, and there he had the happiness to learn, that the mountain which at first had tried his faith so severely, was removed, and friendly hands were reached out and a more speedy and comfortable mode of travel advised. He was directed to the Vigilance Committee in Philadelphia, from whom he received friendly aid, and all necessary information respecting Canada and how to get there.

James was thirty-one years of age, rather a fine-looking man, of a chestnut color, and quite intelligent. He had been a married man, but for two years before his escape, he had been a widower – that is, his wife had been sold away from him to North Carolina, and in that space of time he had received only three letters from her; he had given up all hope of ever seeing her again. He had two little boys living in Baltimore, whom he was obliged to leave. Their names were Edward and William. What became of them afterwards was never known at the Philadelphia station.

James's master was a man of about fifty years of age – who had never been lawfully married, yet had a number of children on his place who were of great concern to him in the midst of other pressing embarrassments. Of course, the Committee never learned how matters were settled after James left, but, in all probability, his wives, Nancy and Mary (sisters), and Lizzie, with all the children, had to be sold.

OWEN AND OTHO TAYLOR'S FLIGHT WITH HORSES

*THREE BROTHERS, TWO OF THEM
WITH WIVES AND CHILDREN.*

About the latter part of March, 1856, Owen Taylor and his wife, Mary Ann, and their little son, Edward, together with a brother and his wife and two children, and a third brother, Benjamin, arrived from near Clear Springs, nine miles from Hagerstown, Maryland. They all left their home, or rather escaped from the prison-house, on Easter Sunday, and came *via* Harrisburg, where they were assisted and directed to the Vigilance Committee in Philadelphia. A more interesting party had not reached the Committee for a long time.

The three brothers were intelligent, and heroic, and, in the resolve to obtain freedom, not only for themselves, but for their wives and children, desperately in earnest. They had counted well the cost of this struggle for liberty, and had fully made up their minds that if interfered with by slave-catchers, somebody would have to bite the dust. That they had pledged themselves never to surrender alive, was obvious. Their travel-worn appearance, their attachment for each other, the joy that the tokens of friendship afforded them, the description they gave of incidents on the road, made an impression not soon to be effaced.

In the presence of a group like this, Sumner's great and eloquent speech on the Barbarism of Slavery, seemed almost cold and dead, – the mute appeals of these little ones in their mother's arms – the unlettered language of these young mothers, striving to save their offspring from the doom of Slavery – the resolute and manly bearing of these brothers expressed in words full of love of liberty, and of the determination to resist Slavery to the death, in defence of their wives and children – this was Sumner's speech enacted before our eyes.

Owen was about thirty-one years of age, but had experienced a deal of trouble. He had been married twice, and both wives were believed to be living. The first one, with their little child, had been sold in the Baltimore market, about three years before, the mother was sent to Louisiana, the child to South Carolina. Father, mother, and child, parted with no hope of ever seeing each other again in this world. After Owen's wife was sent South, he sent her his likeness and a dress; the latter was received, and she was greatly delighted with it, but he never heard of her having received his likeness. He likewise wrote to her, but he was not sure that she received his letters. Finally, he came to the conclusion that as she was forever dead to him, he would do well to marry again. Accordingly he took to himself another partner, the one who now accompanied him on the Underground Rail Road.

Omitting other interesting incidents, a reference to his handiwork will suffice to show the ability of Owen. Owen was a born mechanic, and his master practically tested his skill in various ways; sometimes in the blacksmith shop – at other times as a wheelwright – again at making brushes and brooms, and at leisure times he would try his hand in all these crafts. This Jack-of-all-trades was, of course, very valuable to his master. Indeed his place was hard to fill.

Henry Fiery, a farmer, "about sixty-four years of age, a stout, crusty old fellow," was the owner of Owen and his two brothers. Besides slaves, the old man was in possession of a wife, whose name was Martha, and seven children, who were pretty well grown up. One of the sons owned Owen's wife and two children. Owen declared, that they had been worked hard, while few privileges had been allowed them. Clothing of the poorest texture was only sparingly furnished. Nothing like Sunday raiment was ever given them; for these comforts they were compelled to do over-work of nights. For a long time the idea of escape had been uppermost in the minds of this party. The first of January, past, was the time "solemnly" fixed upon to "took out," but for some reason or other (not found on the record book), their strategical minds did not see the way altogether clear, and they deferred starting until Easter Sunday.

On that memorable evening, the men boldly harnessed two of Mr. Fiery's steeds and placing their wives and children in the carriage, started off *via* Hagerstown, in a direct line for Chambersburg, Pennsylvania, at a rate that allowed no grass to grow under the horses' feet. In this manner they made good time, reached Chambersburg safely, and ventured up to a hotel where they put up their horses. Here they bade their faithful beasts good-bye and "took out" for Harrisburg by another mode of travel, the cars. On their arrival they naturally fell into the hands of the Committee, who hurried them off to Philadelphia, apprising the Committee there of their approach by a dispatch sent ahead. Probably they had scarcely reached Philadelphia ere the Fierys were in hot haste after them, as far as Harrisburg, if not farther.

It hardly need be hinted, that the community in which the Fierys lived was deeply agitated for days after, as indeed it was along the entire route to Chambersburg, in consequence of this bold and successful movement. The horses were easily captured at the hotel, where they were left, but, of course, they were mute as to what had become of their drivers. The furious Fierys probably got wind of the fact, that they had made their way to Harrisburg. At any rate they made very diligent search at this point. While here prosecuting his hunting operations, Fiery managed to open communication with at least one member of the Harrisburg Committee, to whom his grievances were made known, but derived little satisfaction.

After the experience of a few weeks, the pursuers came to the conclusion, that there was no likelihood of recovering them through these agencies, or through the Fugitive Slave Law. In their despair, therefore, they resorted to another "dodge." All at once they became "sort-o'-friendly" – indeed more than half disposed to emancipate. The member of the Committee in Harrisburg had, it is probable, frequently left room for their great delusion, if he did not even go so far as to feed their hopes with plausible suggestions, that some assistance might be afforded by which an amicable settlement might be made between masters and slaves.

The following extract, from the Committee's letter, relative to this matter, is open to this inference, and may serve to throw some light on the subject:

HARRISBURG,
April 28, '56.

Friend Still: – Your last came to hand in due season, and I am happy to hear of the safe arrival of those gents.

I have before me the Power of Attorney of Mr. John S.

Fiery, son of Mr. Henry Fiery, of Washington county, Md., the owner of those three men, two women and three children, who arrived in your town on the 24th or 25th of March. He graciously condescends to liberate the oldest in a year, and the remainder in proportional time, if they will come back; or to sell them their time for $1,300. He is sick of the job, and is ready to make any conditions. Now, if you personally can get word to them and get them to send him a letter, in my charge, informing him of their whereabouts and prospects, I think it will be the best answer I can make him. He will return here in a week or two, to know what can be done. He offers $500 to see them.

Or if you can send me word where they are, I will endeavor to write to them for his special satisfaction; or if you cannot do either, send me your latest information, for I intend to make him spend a few more dollars, and if possible get a little sicker of this bad job. Do try and send him a few bitter pills for his weak nerves and disturbed mind.

Yours in great haste,

Jos. C. Bustill.

A subsequent letter from Mr. Bustill contains, besides other interesting Underground Rail Road matter, an item relative to the feeling of disappointment experienced by Mr. Fiery on learning that his property was in Canada.

HARRISBURG,
May 26, '56.

Friend Still: – I embrace the opportunity presented by the visit of our friend, John F. Williams, to drop you a few lines in relation to our future operations.

The Lightning Train was put on the Road on last Monday, and as the traveling season has commenced and this is the Southern route for Niagara Falls, I have concluded not to send by way of Auburn, except in cases of great danger; but hereafter we will use the Lightning Train, which leaves here at 1-1/2 and arrives in your city at 5 o'clock in the morning, and I will telegraph about 5-1/2 o'clock in the afternoon, so it may reach you before you close. These four are the only ones that have come since my last. The woman has been here some time waiting for her child and her beau, which she expects here about the first of June. If possible, please keep a knowledge of her whereabouts, to enable me to inform him if he comes.

I have nothing more to send you, except that John Fiery has visited us again and much to his chagrin received the information of their being in Canada.

Yours as ever,

Jos. C. Bustill.

Whilst the Fierys were working like beavers to re-enslave these brave fugitives, the latter were daily drinking in more and more of the spirit of freedom and were busy with schemes for the deliverance of other near kin left behind under the galling yoke.

Several very interesting letters were received from Otho Taylor, relative to a raid he designed making expressly to effect the escape of his family. The two subjoined must suffice, (others, much longer, cannot now be produced, they have probably been loaned and not returned).

APRIL 15th, 1857.

SIR – We arrived here safely. Mr. Syrus and his lady is well situated. They have a place for the year round 15 dollars per month. We are all well and hope that you are all the same. Now I wish to know whether you would please to send me some money to go after those people. Send it here if you please.

Yours truly,

OTHO TAYLOR.

ST. CATHARINES,
Jan. 26, 1857.

MR. WM. STILL: – Dear Sir – I write at this time in behalf of Otho Taylor. He is very anxious to go and get his family at Clear Spring, Washington county, Md. He would like to know if the Society there would furnish him the means to go after them from Philadelphia, that you will be running no risk in doing this. If the Society can do this, he would not be absent from P. more than three days.

He is so anxious to get his family from slavery that he is willing to do almost anything to get them to Canada. You may possibly recollect him – he was at your place last August. I think he can be trusted. If you can do something for him, he has the means to take him to your place.

Please let me know immediately if you can do this.

Respectfully yours,

M.A.H. WILSON.

Such appeals came very frequently from Canada, causing much sadness, as but little encouragement could be held out to such projects. In the first place, the danger attendant upon such expeditions was so fearful, and in the second place, our funds were so inadequate for this kind of work, that, in most cases, such appeals had to be refused. Of course, there were those whose continual coming, like the poor widow in the Gospel, could not be denied.

CAPTAIN F. ARRIVES
WITH FOURTEEN
"PRIME ARTICLES"
ON BOARD

Thomas Garrett announced this in the following letter:

WILMINGTON, 3d mo.,
23d, 1856.

DEAR FRIEND, WILLIAM STILL: – Captain Fountain has arrived all safe, with the human cargo thee was inquiring for, a few days since. I had men waiting till 12 o'clock till the Captain arrived at his berth, ready to receive them; last night they then learned, that he had landed them at the Rocks, near the old Swedes church, in the care of our efficient Pilot, who is in the employ of my friend, John Hillis, and he has them now in charge. As soon as my breakfast is over, I will see Hillis and determine what is best to be done in their case. My own opinion is, we had better send them to Hook and there put them in the cars to-night and send a pilot to take them to thy house. As Marcus Hook is in Pennsylvania, the agent of the cars runs no risk of the fine of five hundred dollars our State imposes for assisting one of God's poor out of the State by steamboat or cars.

As ever thy friend,

THOS. GARRETT.

From the tenor of Thomas Garrett's letter, the Committee was prepared for a joyful reception, knowing that Captain F. was not in the habit of doing things by the halves – that he was not in the habit of bringing numbskulls; indeed he brought none but the bravest and most intelligent. Yet notwithstanding our knowledge of his practice in this respect, when he arrived we were surprised beyond measure. The women outnumbered the men. The two young mothers – with their interesting, hearty and fine-looking children representing in blood the two races about equally – presented a very impressive spectacle.

The men had the appearance of being active, smart, and well disposed, much above the generality of slaves; but, compared with those of the opposite sex, their claims for sympathy were very faint indeed. No one could possibly avoid the conclusion, that these mothers, with their handsome daughters, were valued on the Ledger of their owners at enormously high prices; that lustful traders and sensualists had already gloated over the thought of buying them in a few short years. Probably not one of those beautiful girls would have brought less than fifteen hundred or two thousand dollars at the age of fifteen. It was therefore a great satisfaction to think, that their mothers, who knew full well to what a fate such slave girls were destined, had labored so heroically to snatch them out of this danger ere the critical hour arrived.

Rebecca Jones was about twenty-eight years of age; mulatto, good-looking, considerably above medium size, very intelligent, and a true-born heroine.

The following reward, offered by the notorious negro-trader, Hall, proved that Rebecca and her children were not to be allowed to go free, if slave-hunters could be induced by a heavy pecuniary consideration to recapture them:

$300 REWARD is offered for the apprehension of negro woman, REBECCA JONES and her three children, and man

ISAIAH, belonging to W.W. Davidson, who have disappeared since the 20th inst. The above reward will be paid for the apprehension and delivery of the said Negroes to my Jail, by the attorney in fact of the owner, or the sum of $250 for the man alone, or $150 for the woman and three children alone.

WM. W. HALL, for the Attorney,
feb. 1.

Years before her escape, her mistress died in England; and as Rebecca had always understood, long before this event, that all the slaves were to be freed at the death of her mistress, she was not prepared to believe any other report. It turned out, however, as in thousands of other instances, that no will could be found, and, of course, the administrators retained the slave property, regardless of any verbal expressions respecting freeing, etc. Rebecca closely watched the course of the administrators, and in the meanwhile firmly resolved, that neither she nor her children should ever serve another master. Rather than submit, she declared that she would take the lives of her children and then her own. Notwithstanding her bold and decided stand, the report went out that she was to be sold, and that all the slaves were still to be held in bondage. Rebecca's sympathizers and friends advised her, as they thought for the best, to get a friend or gentleman to purchase her for herself. To this she replied: "Not three cents would I give, nor do I want any of my friends to buy me, not if they could get me for three cents." It would be of no use, she contended, as she was fully bent on dying, rather than remain a slave. The slave-holders evidently understood her, and were in no hurry about bringing her case to an issue – they rather gave her time to become calm. But Rebecca was inflexible.

Six years before her arrival, her husband had escaped, in company with the noted fugitive, "Shadrach." For a time after he fled, she frequently received letters from him, but for a long while he had ceased to write, and of late she had heard nothing from him.

In escaping stowed away in the boat, she suffered terribly, but faithfully endured to the end, and was only too happy when the agony was over. After resting and getting thoroughly refreshed in Philadelphia, she, with others, was forwarded to Boston, for her heart was there. Several letters were received from her, respecting her prospects, etc., from which it appears that she had gained some knowledge of her husband, although not of a satisfactory nature. At any rate she decided that she could not receive him back again. The following letter has reference to her prospects, going to California, her husband, etc.:

PARKER HOUSE, School street, Boston,
Oct. 18th, '56.

MY DEAR SIR: – I can hardly express the pleasure I feel at the receipt of your kind letter; but allow me to thank you for the same.

And now I will tell you my reasons for going to California. Mrs. Tarrol, a cousin of my husband, has sent for me. She says I can do much better there than in Boston. And as I have my children's welfare to look to, I have concluded to go. Of course I shall be just as likely to hear from home *there* as *here*. Please tell Mr. Bagnale I shall expect one letter from him before I leave here.

I should like to hear from my brothers and sisters once more, and let me hear every particular. You never can know how anxious I am to hear from them; do please impress this upon their minds.

I have written two letters to Dr. Lundy and never received an answer. I heard Mrs. Lundy was dead, and thought that might possibly be the reason he had not replied to me. Please tell the Doctor I should take it as a great favor if he would write me a few lines.

I suppose you think I am going to live with my husband again. Let me assure you 'tis no such thing. My mind is as firm as ever. And believe me, in going away from Boston, I am going away from him, for I have heard he is living somewhere near. He has been making inquiries about me, but that can make no difference in my feelings to him. I hope that yourself, wife and family are all quite well. Please remember me to them all. Do me the favor to give my love to all inquiring friends. I should be most happy to have any letters of introduction you may think me worthy of, and I trust I shall ever remain

Yours faithfully,

REBECCA JONES.

P.S. – I do not know if I shall go this Fall, or in the Spring. It will depend upon the letter I receive from California, but whichever it may be, I shall be happy to hear from you very soon.

Isaiah, who was a fellow-servant with Rebecca, and was included in the reward offered by Hall for Rebecca, etc., was a young man about twenty-three years of age, a mulatto, intelligent and of prepossessing manners. A purely ardent thirst for liberty prompted him to flee; although he declared that he had been treated very badly, and had even suffered severely from being shamefully "beaten." He had, however, been permitted to hire his time by the year, for which one hundred and twenty dollars were regularly demanded by his owner. Young as he was, he was a married man, with a wife and two children, to whom he was devoted. He had besides two brothers and two sisters for whom he felt a warm degree of brotherly affection; yet when the hour arrived for him to accept a chance for freedom at the apparent sacrifice of these dearest ties of kindred, he was found heroic enough for this painful ordeal, and to give up all for freedom.

Caroline Taylor, and her two little children, were also from Norfolk, and came by boat. Upon the whole, they were not less interesting than Rebecca Jones and her three little girls. Although Caroline was not in her person half so stately, nor gave such promise of heroism as Rebecca – for Caroline was rather small of stature – yet she was more refined, and quite as intelligent as Rebecca, and represented considerably more of the Anglo-Saxon blood. She was a mulatto, and her children were almost fair enough to pass for white – probably they were quadroons, hardly any one would have suspected that they had only one quarter of colored blood in their veins. For ten years Caroline had been in the habit of hiring her time at the rate of seventy-five dollars per year, with the exception of the last year, when her hire was raised to eighty-four dollars. So anxious was she to have her older girl (eleven years old) at home with her, that she also hired her time by the year, for which she was compelled to pay twenty-four dollars. As her younger child was not sufficiently grown to hire out for pay, she was permitted to have it at home with her on the conditions that she would feed, clothe and take good care of it, permitting no expense whatever to fall upon the master.

Judging from the appearance and manners of the children, their mother had, doubtless, been most faithful to them, for more handsome, well-behaved, intelligent and pleasing children could not easily be selected from either race or any station of life. The younger, Mary by name, nine years of age, attracted very great attention, by the deep interest she manifested in a poor fugitive (whom she had never seen before), at the Philadelphia station, confined to the bed and suffering excruciating pain from wounds he had received whilst escaping. Hours and hours together, during the two or three days of their sojourn, she spent of her own accord, by his bed-side, manifesting almost womanly sympathy in the most devoted and tender manner. She thus, doubtless, unconsciously imparted to the sufferer a great deal of comfort. Very many affecting incidents had come under the observation of the acting Committee, under various circumstances, but never before had they witnessed a sight more interesting, a scene more touching.

Caroline and her children were owned by Peter March, Esq., late of Norfolk, but at that time, he was living in New York, and was carrying on the iron business. He came into possession of them through his wife, who was the daughter of Caroline's former master, and almost the only heir left, in consequence of the terrible fever of the previous summer. Caroline was living under the daily fear of being sold; this, together with the task of supporting herself and two children, made her burden very grievous. Not a great while before her escape, her New York master had been on to Norfolk, expressly with a view of selling her, and asked two thousand dollars for her. This, however, he failed to get, and was still awaiting an offer.

These ill omens aroused Caroline to think more seriously over the condition of herself and children than she had ever done before, and in this state of mind she came to the conclusion, that she would strive to save herself and children by flight on the Underground Rail Road. She knew full well, that it was no faint-hearted struggle that was required of her, so she had nerved herself with the old martyr spirit to risk her all on her faith in God and Freedom, and was ready to take the consequences if she fell back into the hands of the enemy. This noble decision was the crowning act in the undertakings of thousands similarly situated. Through this faith she gained the liberty of herself and her children. Quite a number of the friends of the slave saw these interesting fugitives, and wept, and rejoiced with them.

Col. A. Cammings, in those days Publisher of the *Evening Bulletin*, for the first time, witnessed an Underground Rail Road arrival. Some time previous, in conversation with Mr. J.M. McKim, the Colonel had expressed views not altogether favorable to the Underground Rail Road; indeed he was rather inclined to apologize for slavery, if not to defend the Fugitive

Slave Law. While endeavoring somewhat tenaciously to maintain his ground, Mr. McKim opposed to him not only the now well established Anti-Slavery doctrines, but also offered as testimony Underground Rail Road facts – the results of personal knowledge from daily proofs of the heroic struggles, marvellous faith, and intense earnestness of the fugitives.

In all probability the Colonel did not feel prepared to deny wholly Mr. McKim's statement, yet, he desired to see "some" for himself. "Well," said Mr. McK., "you shall see some." So when this arrival came to hand, true to his promise, Mr. McK. called on the Colonel and invited him to accompany him to the Underground Rail Road station. He assured the Colonel that he did not want any money from him, but simply wanted to convince him of his error in the recent argument that they had held on the subject. Accordingly the Colonel accompanied him, and found that twenty-two passengers had been on hand within the past twenty-four hours, and at least sixteen or seventeen were then in his presence. It is needless to say, that such a sight admitted of no contradiction – no argument – no doubt. The facts were too self-evident. The Colonel could say but little, so complete was his amazement; but he voluntarily attested the thoroughness of his conversion by pulling out of his pocket and handing to Mr. McK. a twenty dollar gold piece to aid the passengers on to freedom.

In these hours of rest and joyful anticipation the necessities of both large and small were administered to according to their needs, before forwarding them still further. The time and attention required for so many left but little opportunity, however, for the Secretary to write their narratives. He had only evening leisure for the work. Ten or twelve of that party had to be sent off without having their stories recorded. Daniel Robertson was one of this number; his name is simply entered on the roll, and, but for letters received from him, after he passed on North, no further knowledge would have been obtained. In Petersburg, whence he escaped, he left his wife, for whose deliverance he felt bound to do everything that lay in his power, as the subjoined letters will attest:

HAVANA, Schuylkill Co., N.Y.
August 11, 1856.

MR. WM. STILL – Dear Sir: – I came from Virginia in March, and was at your office the last of March. My object in writing you, is to inquire what I can do, or what can be done to help my wife to escape from the same bondage that I was in. You will know by your books that I was from Petersburg, Va., and that is where my wife now is. I have received two or three letters from a lady in that place, and the last one says, that my wife's mistress is dead, and that she expects to be sold. I am very anxious to do what I can for her before it is too late, and beg of you to devise some means to get her away. Capt. the man that brought me away, knows the colored agent at Petersburg, and knows he will do all he can to forward my wife. The Capt. promised, that when I could raise one hundred dollars for him that he would deliver her in Philadelphia. Tell him that I can now raise the money, and will forward it to you at any day that he thinks that he can bring her. Please see the Captain and find when he will undertake it, and then let me know when to forward the money to you. I am at work for the Hon. Charles Cook, and can send the money any day. My wife's name is Harriet Robertson, and the agent at Petersburg knows her.

Please direct your answer, with all necessary directions, to N. Coryell, of this village, and he will see that all is right.

Very respectfully,

DANIEL ROBERTSON.

HAVANA,
Aug. 18, 1856.

MR. WM. STILL – Dear Sir: – Yours of the 18th, for D. Robertson, was duly received. In behalf of Daniel, I thank you kindly for the interest you manifest in him. The letters that have gone from him to his friends in Virginia, have been written by me, and sent in such a manner as we thought would best ensure safety. Yet I am well aware of the risk of writing, and have restrained him as far as possible, and the last one I wrote was to be the last, till an effort was made to reclaim his wife. Daniel is a faithful, likely man, and is well liked by all who know him. He is industrious and prudent, and is bending his whole energies toward the reclaiming his wife. He can forward to you the one hundred dollars at any day that it may be wanted, and if you can do anything to forward his interests it will be very gratefully received as an additional favor on your part. He asks for no money, but your kindly efforts, which he regards more highly than money.

Very respectfully, N. CORYELL.

The letters that have been written for him were dated "Niagara Falls, Canada West," and his friends think he is there – none of them know to the contrary – it is important that they never do know. N.C.

HAVANA,
Sept. 29, 1856.

MR. WM. STILL – Dear Sir: – I enclose herewith a draft on New York, payable to your order, for $100, to be paid on the delivery at Philadelphia of Daniel Robertson's wife.

You can readily see that it has been necessary for Daniel to work almost night and day to have laid up so large an amount of money, since the first of April, as this one hundred dollars. Daniel is industrious and prudent, and saves all of his earnings, above his most absolute wants. If the Captain is not successful in getting Daniel's wife, you, of course, will return the draft, without charge, as you said. I hope success will attend him, for Daniel deserves to be rewarded, if ever man did. Yours, &c.

N. CORYELL.

HAVANA,
Jan. 2, 1857.

DEAR SIR: – Your favor containing draft on N. York, for Daniel Robertson, came to hand on the 31st ult. Daniel begs to tender his acknowledgments for your kind interest manifested in his behalf, and says he hopes you will leave no measure untried which has any appearance of success, and that the money shall be forthcoming at a moment's notice. Daniel thinks that since Christmas, the chances for his wife's deliverance are fewer than before, for at that time he fears she was disposed of and possibly went South.

The paper sent me, with your well-written article, was received, and on reading it to Daniel, he knew some of the parties mentioned in it – he was much pleased to hear it read. Daniel spent New Year's in Elmira, about 18 miles from this place, and there he met two whom he was well acquainted with.

Yours, &c.,

N. CORYELL.

WM. STILL, Esq., Phila.

Such devotion to freedom, such untiring labor, such appeals as these letters contained awakened deep interest in the breasts of Daniel's new friends, which spoke volumes in favor of the Slave and against slave-holders. But, alas, nothing could be done to relieve the sorrowing mind of poor Daniel for the deliverance of his wife in chains. The Committee sympathized deeply with him, but could do no more. What other events followed, in Daniel's life as a fugitive, were never made known to the Committee.

Tom Page. At the time of his arrival, his name only was enrolled on the book. Yet he was not a passenger soon to be forgotten – he was but a mere boy, probably eighteen years of age; but a more apt, ready-witted, active, intelligent and self-reliant fellow is not often seen.

Judging from his smartness, under slavery, with no chances, it was easy to imagine how creditably he might with a white boy's chances have climbed the hill of art and science. Obviously he had intellect enough, if properly cultivated, to fill any station within the ordinary reach of intelligent American citizens. He could read and write remarkably well for a slave, and well did he understand his advantages in this particular; indeed if slave-holders had only been aware of the growing tendency of Tom's mind, they would have rejoiced at hearing of his departure for Canada; he was a most dangerous piece of property to be growing up amongst slaves.

After leaving the Committee and going North his uncaged mind felt the need of more education, and at the same time he was eager to make money, and do something in life. As he had no one to depend on, parents and relatives being left behind in Norfolk, he felt that he must rely upon himself, young as he was. He first took up his abode in Boston, or New Bedford, where most of the party with whom he escaped went, and where he had an aunt, and perhaps some other distant kin. There he worked and was a live young man indeed – among the foremost in ideas and notions about freedom, etc., as many letters from him bore evidence. After spending a year or more in Massachusetts, he had a desire to see how the fugitives were doing in Upper and Lower Canada, and if any better chances existed in these parts for men of his stamp.

Some of his letters, from different places, gave proof of real thought and close observation, but they were not generally saved, probably were loaned to be read by friendly eyes. Nevertheless the two subjoined will, in a measure, suffice to give some idea of his intelligence, etc.

BOSTON, Mass.,
Feb. 25th, 1857.

WILLIAM STILL, Esq.: – Dear Sir – I have not heard from you for some time. I take this opportunity of writing you a few lines to let you and all know that I am well at present and thank God for it. Dear Sir, I hear that the under ground railroad was in operation. I am glad to hear that. Give my best respects to your family and also to Dr. L., Mr. Warrick, Mr. Camp and familys, to Mr. Fisher, Mr. Taylor to all Friends names too numerous to mention. Please to let me know when the road arrived with another cargo. I want to come to see you all before long, if nothing happens and life lasts. Mrs. Gault requested me to learn of you if you ask Mr. Bagnal if he will see father and what he says about the children. Please to answer as soon as possible. No more at present from a friend,

THOMAS F. PAGE.

NIAGARA FALLS, N.Y.,
Oct. 6th, '58.

DEAR SIR: – I received your kind letter and I was very glad to hear from you and your family. This leaves me well, and I hope when this comes to hand it may find you the same. I have seen a large number of your U.G.R.R. friends in my travels through the Eastern as well as the Western States. Well there are a good many from my own city who I know – some I talk to on private matters and some I wont. Well around here there are so many – Tom, Dick, and Harry – that you do not know who your friend is. So it don't hurt any one to be careful. Well, somehow or another, I do not like Canada, or the Provinces. I have been to St. John, N.B., Lower Province, or Lower Canada, also St. Catharines, C.W., and all around the Canada side, and I do not like it at all. The people seem to be so queer – though I suppose if I had of went to Canada when I first came North to live, I might like it by this time. I was home when Aunt had her Ambrotype taken for you. She often speaks of your kindness to her. There are a number of your friends wishes you well. My little brother is going to school in Boston. The lady, Mrs. Hillard, that my Aunt lives with, thinks a good deal of him. He is very smart and I think, if he lives, he may be of some account. Do you ever see my old friend, Capt. Fountain? Please to give my love to him, and tell him to come to Boston, as there are a number of his friends that would like to see him. My best respects to all friends. I must now bring my short epistle to a close, by saying I remain your friend truly,

THOMAS F. PAGE.

While a portion of the party, on hand with him, came as passengers with Capt. P., another portion was brought by Capt.

B., both parties arriving within twelve hours of each other; and both had likewise been frozen up on the route for weeks with their respective live freight on board.

The sufferings for food, which they were called upon to endure, were beyond description. They happened to have plenty of salt fat pork, and perhaps beans, Indian meal and some potatoes for standing dishes; the more delicate necessaries did not probably last longer than the first or second week of their ice-bondage.

Without a doubt, one of these Captains left Norfolk about the twentieth of January, but did not reach Philadelphia till about the twentieth of March, having been frozen up, of course, during the greater part of that time. Men, women and children were alike sharers in the common struggle for freedom – were alike hungered, in prison, naked, and sick, but it was a fearful thing in those days for even women and children to whisper their sad lamentations in the city of Philadelphia, except to those friendly to the Underground Rail Road.

Doubtless, if these mothers, with their children and partners in tribulation, could have been seen as they arrived direct from the boats, many hearts would have melted, and many tears would have found their way down many cheeks. But at that time cotton was acknowledged to be King – the Fugitive Slave Law was supreme, and the notorious decision of Judge Taney, that "black men had no rights which white men were bound to respect," echoed the prejudices of the masses too clearly to have made it safe to reveal the fact of their arrival, or even the heart-rending condition of these Fugitives.

Nevertheless, they were not turned away empty, though at

a peril they were fed, aided, and comforted, and sent away well clothed. Indeed, so bountifully were the women and children supplied, that as they were being conveyed to the Camden and Amboy station, they looked more like a pleasuring party than like fugitives. Some of the good friends of the slave sent clothing, and likewise cheered them with their presence.

WILLIAM AND
ELLEN CRAFT

FEMALE SLAVE IN MALE ATTIRE,
FLEEING AS A PLANTER, WITH HER
HUSBAND AS HER BODY SERVANT.

A quarter of a century ago, William and Ellen Craft were slaves in the State of Georgia. With them, as with thousands of others, the desire to be free was very strong. For this jewel they were willing to make any sacrifice, or to endure any amount of suffering. In this state of mind they commenced planning. After thinking of various ways that might be tried, it occurred to William and Ellen, that one might act the part of master and the other the part of servant.

Ellen being fair enough to pass for white, of necessity would have to be transformed into a young planter for the time being. All that was needed, however, to make this important change was that she should be dressed elegantly in a fashionable suit of male attire, and have her hair cut in the style usually worn by young planters. Her profusion of dark hair offered a fine opportunity for the change. So far this plan looked very tempting. But it occurred to them that Ellen was beardless. After some mature reflection, they came to the conclusion that this difficulty could be very readily obviated by having the face muffled up as though the young planter was suffering badly with the face or toothache; thus they got rid of this trouble. Straightway, upon further reflection, several other very serious difficulties stared them in the face. For instance, in traveling, they knew that they would be under the necessity of stopping repeatedly at hotels, and that the custom of registering would have to be conformed to, unless some very good excuse could be given for not doing so.

Here they again thought much over matters, and wisely concluded that the young man had better assume the attitude of a gentleman very much indisposed. He must have his right arm placed carefully in a sling; that would be a sufficient excuse for not registering, etc. Then he must be a little lame, with a nice cane in the left hand; he must have large green spectacles over his eyes, and withal he must be very hard of hearing and dependent on his faithful servant (as was no uncommon thing with slave-holders), to look after all his wants.

William was just the man to act this part. To begin with, he was very "likely-looking;" smart, active and exceedingly attentive to his young master – indeed he was almost eyes, ears, hands and feet for him. William knew that this would please the slave-holders. The young planter would have nothing to do but hold himself subject to his ailments and put on a bold air of superiority; he was not to deign to notice anybody. If, while traveling, gentlemen, either politely or rudely, should venture to scrape acquaintance with the young planter, in his deafness he was to remain mute; the servant was to explain. In every instance when this occurred, as it actually did, the servant was fully equal to the emergency – none dreaming of the disguises in which the Underground Rail Road passengers were traveling.

They stopped at a first-class hotel in Charleston, where the young planter and his body servant were treated, as the house was wont to treat the chivalry. They stopped also at a similar hotel in Richmond, and with like results.

They knew that they must pass through Baltimore, but they did not know the obstacles that they would have to surmount in the Monumental City. They proceeded to the depot in the usual manner, and the servant asked for tickets for his master and self. Of course the master could have a ticket, but "bonds will have to be entered before you can get a ticket," said the ticket master. "It is the rule of this office to require bonds for all negroes applying for tickets to go North, and none but gentlemen of well-known responsibility will be taken," further explained the ticket master.

The servant replied, that he knew "nothing about that" – that he was "simply traveling with his young master to take care of him – he being in a very delicate state of health, so much so, that fears were entertained that he might not be able to hold out to reach Philadelphia, where he was hastening for medical treatment," and ended his reply by saying, "my master can't be detained." Without further parley, the ticket master very obligingly waived the old "rule," and furnished the requisite tickets. The mountain being thus removed, the young planter and his faithful servant were safely in the cars for the city of Brotherly Love.

Scarcely had they arrived on free soil when the rheumatism departed – the right arm was unslung – the toothache was gone – the beardless face was unmuffled – the deaf heard and spoke – the blind saw – and the lame leaped as an hart, and in the presence of a few astonished friends of the slave, the facts of this unparalleled Underground Rail Road feat were fully established by the most unquestionable evidence.

The constant strain and pressure on Ellen's nerves, however, had tried her severely, so much so, that for days afterwards, she was physically very much prostrated, although joy and gladness beamed from her eyes, which bespoke inexpressible delight within.

Never can the writer forget the impression made by their arrival. Even now, after a lapse of nearly a quarter of a century, it is easy to picture them in a private room, surrounded by a few friends – Ellen in her fine suit of black, with her cloak and high-heeled boots, looking, in every respect, like a young gentleman; in an hour after having dropped her male attire, and assumed the habiliments of her sex, the feminine only was visible in every line and feature of her structure.

Her husband, William, was thoroughly colored, but was a man of marked natural abilities, of good manners, and full of pluck, and possessed of perceptive faculties very large.

It was necessary, however, in those days, that they should seek a permanent residence, where their freedom would be more secure than in Philadelphia; therefore they were advised to go to headquarters, directly to Boston. There they would be safe, it was supposed, as it had then been about a genera-tion since a fugitive had been taken back from the old Bay State, and through the incessant labors of William Lloyd Garrison, the great pioneer, and his faithful coadjutors, it was conceded that another fugitive slave case could never be toler-ated on the free soil of Massachusetts. So to Boston they went.

On arriving, the warm hearts of abolitionists welcomed them heartily, and greeted and cheered them without let or hindrance. They did not pretend to keep their coming a secret, or hide it under a bushel; the story of their escape was heralded broadcast over the country – North and South, and indeed over the civi-lized world. For two years or more, not the slightest fear was entertained that they were not just as safe in Boston as if they had gone to Canada. But the day the Fugitive Bill passed, even the bravest abolitionist began to fear that a fugitive slave was no longer safe anywhere under the stars and stripes, North or South, and that William and Ellen Craft were liable to be captured at any moment by Georgia slave hunters. Many abolitionists counselled resistance to the death at all hazards. Instead of running to Canada, fugitives generally armed themselves and thus said, "Give me liberty or give me death."

William and Ellen Craft believed that it was their duty, as citizens of Massachusetts, to observe a more legal and civilized mode of conforming to the marriage rite than had been permitted them in slavery, and as Theodore Parker had shown himself a very warm friend of their's, they agreed to have their wedding over again according to the laws of a free State. After performing the ceremony, the renowned and fearless advocate of equal rights (Theodore Parker) presented William with a revolver and a dirk-knife, counselling him to use them manfully in defence of his wife and himself, if ever an attempt should be made by his owners or anybody else to re-enslave them.

But, notwithstanding all the published declarations made by abolitionists and fugitives, to the effect, that slave-holders and slave-catchers in visiting Massachusetts in pursuit of their runaway property, would be met by just such weapons as Theodore Parker presented William with, to the surprise of all Boston, the owners of William and Ellen actually had the effrontery to attempt their recapture under the Fugitive Slave Law. How it was done, and the results, taken from the *Old Liberator* (William Lloyd Garrison's organ), we copy as follows:

From the *Liberator,*
Nov. 1, 1850.

SLAVE-HUNTERS IN BOSTON.

Our city, for a week past, has been thrown into a state of intense excitement by the appearance of two prowling villains, named Hughes and Knight, from Macon, Georgia, for the purpose of seizing William and Ellen Craft, under the infernal Fugitive Slave Bill, and carrying them back to the hell of Slavery. Since the day of '76, there has not been such a popular demonstration on the side of human freedom in this region. The humane and patriotic contagion has infected all classes. Scarcely any other subject has been talked about in the streets, or in the social circle. On Thursday, of last week, warrants for the arrest of William and Ellen were issued by Judge Levi Woodbury, but no officer has yet been found ready or bold enough to serve them. In the meantime, the Vigilance Committee, appointed at the Faneuil Hall meeting, has not been idle. Their number has been increased to upwards of a hundred "good men and true," including some thirty or forty members of the bar; and they have been in constant session, devising every legal method to baffle the pursuing bloodhounds, and relieve the city of their hateful presence. On Saturday placards were posted up in all directions, announcing the arrival of these slave-hunters, and describing their persons. On the same day, Hughes and Knight were arrested on the charge of slander against William Craft. The Chronotype says, the damages being laid at $10,000; bail was demanded in the same sum, and was promptly furnished. By whom? is the question. An immense crowd was assembled in front of the Sheriff's office, while the bail matter was being arranged. The reporters were not admitted. It was only known that Watson Freeman, Esq., who once declared his readiness to hang any number of negroes remarkably cheap, came in, saying that the arrest was a shame, all a humbug, the trick of the damned abolitionists, and proclaimed his readiness to stand bail. John H. Pearson was also sent for, and came – the same John H. Pearson, merchant and Southern packet agent, who immortalized himself by sending back, on the 10th of September, 1846, in the bark *Niagara*, a poor fugitive slave, who came secreted in the brig *Ottoman*, from New Orleans – being himself judge, jury and executioner, to consign a fellow-being to a life of bondage – in obedience to the law of a slave State, and in violation of the law of his own. This same John H. Pearson, not contented with his previous infamy, was on hand. There is a story that the slave-hunters have been his table-guests also, and whether he bailed them or not, we don't know. What we know is, that soon after Pearson came out from the back room, where he and Knight and the Sheriff had been closeted, the Sheriff said that Knight was bailed – he would not say by whom. Knight being looked after, was not to be found. He had slipped out through a back door, and thus cheated the crowd of the pleasure of greeting him – possibly with that rough and ready affection which Barclay's brewers bestowed upon Haynau. The escape was very fortunate every way. Hughes and Knight have since been twice arrested and put under bonds of $10,000 (making $30,000 in all), charged with a conspiracy to kidnap and abduct William Craft, a peaceable citizen of Massachusetts, etc. Bail was entered by Hamilton Willis, of Willis & Co., 25 State street, and Patrick Riley, U.S. Deputy Marshal.

The following (says the Chronotype), is a *verbatim et literatim* copy of the letter sent by Knight to Craft, to entice him to the U.S. Hotel, in order to kidnap him. It shows, that the school-master owes Knight more "service and labor" than it is possible for Craft to:

BOSTON,
Oct. 22, 1850, 11 Oclk P.M.

Wm. Craft – Sir – I have to leave so Eirley in the moring that I cold not call according to promis, so if you want me to carry a letter home with me, you must bring it to the United States Hotel to morrow and leave it in box 44, or come your self to morro eavening after tea and bring it. let me no if you come your self by sending a note to box 44 U.S. Hotel so that I may know whether to wate after tea or not by the Bearer. If your wife wants to see me you cold bring her with you if you come your self.

JOHN KNIGHT.

P.S. I shall leave for home eirley a Thursday moring. J.K.

Index